JUVENILE JUSTICE

Juvenile Justice

Debating the issues

Edited by Fay Gale, Ngaire Naffine
and Joy Wundersitz

ALLEN & UNWIN

First published 1993
Allen & Unwin Pty Ltd
9 Atchison Street, St Leonards, NSW 2065 Australia

National Library of Australia
Cataloguing-in-Publication entry:

Juvenile justice: debating the issues.

Bibliography
ISBN 1 86373 405 8

1. Juvenile justice, Administration of—Australia. I. Gale, Fay, 1932–
II. Naffine, Ngaire. III. Wundersitz, Joy.

364.36

Typeset by the Publications Unit, The University of Western Australia
Printed by Chong Moh Offset Printing Pte Ltd, Singapore

Contents

Tables

Figures

Contributors

Conveners

Fay Gale
Vice-Chancellor, University of Western Australia

Ngaire Naffine
Faculty of Law, University of Adelaide

Joy Wundersitz
Department for Family and Community Services, Adelaide

Contributors

Christine Alder
Department of Criminology, University of Melbourne

Michael Barry
South Australian Public Libraries Support Centre, Adelaide

Rod Blackmore
Senior Children's Magistrate, Bidura Children's Court, New South Wales

Linda Hancock
School of Social Sciences, Deakin University

Michael Hogan
Public Interest Advocacy Centre, Sydney, New South Wales

Kathy Laster
Department of Legal Studies, La Trobe University

Garth Luke
Community Aid Abroad, New South Wales

Ken Polk
Department of Criminology, University of Melbourne

John Pratt
Institute of Criminology, Victoria University of Wellington, New Zealand

John Seymour
Faculty of Law, Australian National University

Compiler of workshop transcripts

Lynn Atkinson
Australian Institute of Criminology

Discussants

David Alcock
Legal Services Commission, South Australia

John Braithwaite
Philosophy and Law Division, Research School of Social Sciences, Australian National University

Kay Bussey
School of Behavioural Sciences, Macquarie University, New South Wales

Judy Cashmore
School of Behavioural Sciences, Macquarie University, New South Wales

James Hackler
Department of Sociology, University of Alberta, Canada

Jeanette Lawrence
Department of Psychology, University of Melbourne

Ian O'Connor
Department of Social Work, University of Queensland

Michael O'Connor
Department of Sociology, University of New England, New South Wales

Fred Wojtasik
South Australian Police Department

Biographical Notes

The Editors

Fay Gale is Vice-Chancellor of The University of Western Australia. She has published numerous articles and several books on Aboriginal issues, heritage management and juvenile justice. She is an Officer of the Order of Australia, a Fellow of the Australian Academy of Social Sciences and a Commissioner of the Australian Heritage Commission.

Ngaire Naffine is a Lecturer in Law at the University of Adelaide. Her main research interests are in criminal law, criminology and feminist legal theory. She is the author of *Female crime: the construction of women in criminology* (1987) and *Law and the sexes: explorations in feminist jurisprudence* (1990).

Joy Wundersitz is Principal Researcher in juvenile justice in the South Australian Department for Family and Community Services. Prior to that, she was a Research Associate in the Department of Geography, University of Adelaide. She has published numerous articles on Aboriginal youth and juvenile justice, and is co-author of the book *Aboriginal youth and the criminal justice system: the injustice of justice* (1990).

The Contributors

David Alcock is now with the Australian Legal Services Commission. Prior to this appointment, he was Barrister/Solicitor with the Aboriginal Legal Rights Movement and spent many years practising in the children's court in South Australia, where he represented Aboriginal youths appearing in that jurisdiction.

Christine Alder is a Senior Lecturer in the Department of Criminology at the University of Melbourne. She is also a member of the Youth Parole Board in Victoria and the Children and Family Services Council. Her principal areas of teaching and research are juvenile justice and issues concerning young women. Her more recent publications have dealt with homeless youth as victims of violence, drug use among young offenders and the policing of young people.

Lynn Atkinson has taught in Aboriginal schools in the Northern Territory and Western Australia, and has been involved in education programmes for detained youth in Western Australia. She has been involved in programmes and research to improve Aboriginal/police relations in Western Australia, and has undertaken a study of Aboriginal women and imprisonment in Western Australia. She is now Senior Research Officer at the Australian Institute of Criminology.

Michael Barry is currently Manager of the South Australian Public Libraries Support Centre. Before taking up this appointment he was Manager of Young Offender Programs in the Department of Family and Community Services, overseeing juvenile justice policy and operations in South Australia. Prior to that, he was supervisor of the main children's detention facility in that state.

Rod Blackmore is Senior Children's Magistrate of the children's court in New South Wales. He has been a magistrate since 1970, specialising in the children's court since 1977, a member of the Juvenile Justice Advisory Council (NSW) since 1978, and in other capacities has been a consultant to the government on associated issues over many years. He is the author of *The children's court and community welfare in New South Wales* (1989), as well as numerous papers and articles concerned with juvenile justice.

Michael Hogan is Director of the Public Interest Advocacy Centre in Sydney. He was previously Convenor of the Youth Justice Coalition (NSW) and co-authored *Kids in justice: a blue-print for the 90s*. Prior to this he was a Research Consultant with the Australian Law Reform Commission and co-author of its Report, *Sentencing young offenders*. He is the co-author of a monograph on deaths involving state agencies, *Death in the hands of the state*, and has written numerous papers on issues concerning juvenile justice and child welfare.

Linda Hancock is a Senior Lecturer in Policy Studies at the School of Social Sciences at Deakin University. She was a Law Reform Commissioner on the Law Reform Commission, Victoria, from 1984–1988 and a Presiding member of the Social Security Appeals Tribunal from 1989–90. Her current research projects include a study of young people in prostitution, funded by the Criminology Research Council and the Victorian Law Foundation.

Kathy Laster is a lawyer and historian. She was Research and Executive Officer of the Victorian Child Welfare Practice and Legislation Review. Currently, she lectures in Criminology and Law in the Department of Legal Studies at La Trobe University.

Garth Luke has extensive experience of the practice of juvenile justice in New South Wales. As a project officer in the Department of Family and Youth Services, NSW, he coordinated juvenile justice evaluation in New South Wales in the mid-1980s. He was also principal researcher with the Judicial Commission of New South Wales and co-authored *Sentencing juvenile offenders and the Sentencing Act, 1989 (NSW)*.

Ken Polk is Associate Professor in the Department of Criminology, University of Melbourne. He has published extensively on youth unemployment, schooling and delinquency and juvenile offending. In the United States he evaluated various delinquency prevention programs and diversionary procedures.

John Pratt is a Senior Lecturer at the Institute of Criminology, Victoria University of Wellington, New Zealand. He is an international expert on the philosophy of juvenile justice. He has researched and written extensively on juvenile justice, indigenous justice systems and the history and sociology of punishment. His latest book is *Punishment in a perfect society: the New Zealand penal system 1840–1939*. He is now undertaking research on the history of dangerousness.

John Seymour is Reader in Law at the Australian National University, Commissioner in Charge of the Australian Law Reform Commission's inquiry into child welfare in the Australian Capital Territory, and responsible for the Commission's report *Child Welfare* (1981—Report No.18). He has published extensively on Australian juvenile justice. His books include *Juvenile justice in South Australia*, 1983, and *Dealing with young offenders*, 1988.

Acknowledgments

The research which brought together the editors of this volume was made possible by a grant from the Australian Research Council. The workshop on which these papers are based, and which generated material for the discussion sections of this book, was sponsored by the Academy of the Social Sciences in Australia, under the guidance of the Executive Director, Professor J. D. B. Miller. The assistance of Elizabeth Spoor and Shirley Marsh in finalising the manuscript is greatly appreciated.

Introduction

FAY GALE

Juvenile justice remains a central concern in Australian society in the 1990s. For many years it has attracted substantial public and government attention, which, in its turn, has prompted considerable changes to legislation, court procedures, policing matters and welfare intervention.

Because these changes have often not been supported by systematic research, it seemed timely to bring together experts in the area of juvenile justice in Australia. This book is the outcome of a workshop at which academics, lawyers, police, magistrates and social workers were asked to discuss the major issues of youth offending. All participants had studied different aspects of the problem of dealing with young offenders in a just, humane and effective manner. All sought solutions which might lead to the rehabilitation of the young people concerned, while at the same time providing more effective protection to the victims of juvenile crime.

There is enormous ambivalence in the adult population as to how young offenders should be dealt with. To what extent should society be punitive or benign? Are young offenders to be given their 'just deserts', or re-educated? Many of the underlying causes of juvenile alienation in our society are poorly understood, and many of the reactions to it are counter-productive. 'Law and order' for juveniles is a emotive issue and, especially at election time, can become highly political.

Whilst much of the public debate about youth offending and the media coverage of particular incidents can be alarmist and depressing, the papers in this volume give some cause for optimism. Braithwaite, who was a participant in the workshop, argues elsewhere in this volume that a theoretical revolution in criminology might help replace the current pessimism that 'nothing works in reducing crime' with an optimistic vision.

This book is a collection of essays and discussions by a cross-section of specialists in various fields of juvenile justice. Whilst it began with an intensive workshop much follow-up research and debate has led to the final production of this volume. The first two chapters provide background material necessary for an informed discussion on juvenile justice. In the area of public debate on youth crime, it is often claimed that facts make for poor argument, and it is certainly true that often the public appears to be more concerned with its own views and emotional responses than with a more scholarly response to youth crime. Nevertheless, contributors to this volume are concerned about the social and legal realities of juvenile justice, and the background data provide a necessary starting point.

Ngaire Naffine's description of the philosophy of juvenile justice sets the scene for the discussion on changing attitudes to juvenile offending. Her chapter also summarises the key legislative issues in various states in Australia, and illustrates the considerable diversity from one jurisdiction to another in the timing of legislative change and in the processes selected for dealing with young people. Naffine shows the variety of approaches to youth justice and highlights many of the conflicts which invariably result from such a contentious and volatile issue.

The second chapter deals with the statistics of juvenile offending. Here Joy Wundersitz outlines the magnitude of the problem and how it varies over time and from state to state. It is clear that there are substantial differences from one jurisdiction to another in the relative numbers of juveniles processed by the criminal justice system, as well as marked variations in the ways in which they are processed. These locational differences reflect variations in social and judicial attitudes, and offer an important starting point for the debate.

The workshop itself was organised around four major themes: philosophical perspectives, policing, informal processing, and the courts. It is these themes which provide the structure for this book. Each section of the workshop entailed the delivery of formal papers followed by group discussion. In addition, small discussion groups tried to highlight the principal issues and identify the major problems.

The first theme to be dealt with was the philosophy of juvenile justice. Theories underpinning legislation have undergone major shifts: from a 'justice model', to a 'welfare model', and back to a 'justice model'. We have also seen varying blends or combinations of the two. Are young people primarily to be punished, or are they to be redeemed? Are young people to be treated as adults according to an adversarial system of justice, or are they to be regarded as children needing to be cared for, re-educated and rehabilitated through a social welfare system?

John Pratt argues that welfare and justice are incompatible philosophies. The attempt in recent times to merge the two has, in his view, led to a great deal of internal friction, heated public debate, and much expense. Pratt highlights this conflict by comparing the pure welfare model currently operating in Scotland, with the mixed welfare–justice approaches which predominate in England and Wales and in the various Australian jurisdictions.

The theme is then taken up by John Seymour who has written extensively on Australian juvenile justice. By placing the present philosophical conflict in an historic setting, he helps to explain the confused logic of much of the youth offending legislation across Australia. He also shows the dangers of drawing too heavily on overseas debates.

The third chapter in this section, by Kathy Laster, looks at how the adult world perceives the child. She asks if the child is someone to be punished or saved? Are children entirely responsible for their actions, or is it society or the parents who are responsible? Why are juveniles viewed differently from adults in the whole process of justice? Where do these conflicting views lead us in terms of the reform agenda for juvenile justice? These are important questions that highlight the tensions in the changing philosophy on juveniles, and our society's ambivalence towards children.

There follows a chapter which summarises the key philosophical issues raised in workshop discussions. It considers how far we have come and where we have gone wrong. What theory should underpin juvenile justice in the future? These discussions highlight the confusion in the arguments which dichotomise welfare versus justice legislation, and identify the complexities of current issues and the varying theoretical perspectives.

The next section deals with police—the 'gatekeepers' of the criminal justice system. Police attitudes to youth and the way police use their considerable powers of discretion are central to any debate about juvenile justice. Police are ill-equipped to use their discretion in positive and preventative ways when faced with groups of young people on the streets, nor are they well qualified to deal with the various possible forms of diversion other than cautioning.

Christine Alder highlights the use of violence by police and the way in which children perceive that violence. Her chapter is based on her study of 'street kids' in Melbourne, and addresses a host of questions. Is punishment at street level essential, or is it creating greater problems than it solves? Should children be dealt with more summarily than adults? Does their punishment need to be more immediate? In this context, what is the role of police violence and what are the frustrations for police in terms of the expectations placed on them by society? Why do so many young people see their often abusive treatment by police as an expected and acceptable form of adult behaviour? Alder suggests that police violence is perceived to be normal because often the young people who come to the attention of the law have grown up accustomed to violence and abuse by adults. As a result of such experiences, they see police violence as an inevitable part of the 'game'. Alder explores the consequences of a violent youth being treated violently by the adults who set the role models.

Linda Hancock's chapter explores further the problem of police violence and discriminatory processing. Most states now have some form of police cautioning or use panels as a means of diverting youths from courts. These are used selectively by police with the result that certain groups of young people, such as Aborigines, are more likely to be referred direct to court than to be given the option of discussion. Hancock also considers the unequal and therefore unjust use of arrest and detention by police, but her major concern is that of police accountability. In particular, she examines the implications of the considerable discretionary powers available to police. She highlights the difficulty of achieving police accountability in a system that depends largely on the discretion of individual police officers. She also examines the conflicting roles of police in dealing with young people who have no alternative but to use public spaces for all social activity even though the public expects police to keep these spaces 'clean' and 'safe'.

The ensuing discussion deals with important, but often neglected, issues of juvenile justice associated with the police. In particular it considers the crucial role of police as the first point of contact with the child. Participants in the workshop highlighted the poor training received by police for the demanding position they are asked to play in society. Not only are they frequently ill-equipped, but often police in the streets are only a little older than the youths whom they are required to manage. The expectations placed on these young, inexperienced and largely untrained 'upholders of the law' by our society are unrealistic. Why are these problems so seldom recognised? Why is the use of violence by police so often rationalised not only by the police themselves, but also by society and even by the young offenders themselves? What can young people do when they receive inappropriate treatment, and how should they be dealt with? All the evidence suggests that violence begets violence and the problems merely escalate. Yet many members of the public and even some professional participants in the administration of juvenile justice appear to condone it.

The third theme of the book is informal justice. During the 1960s, it became clear that formal courtroom justice had not brought about a reduction in youth offending. The search for alternatives began. In this section Ken Polk summarises the differing philosophies that emerged during the 1960s and 1970s, as various alternatives to formal court processing were introduced. He describes the progressive history of these approaches in terms of a shift from enthusiasm, to reform, to dismay. From the introduction of a children's court in the late nineteenth century, through the growth of informal mechanisms, we have witnessed the expansion of coercive state control over young people. Polk argues that many diversionary mechanisms have led to greater manipulation and control of young people, without achieving the stated goals of reform. Polk is critical of society's failure to provide educational and economic solutions for many young people. He is also critical of the contemporary state for failing to give priority to policies of positive, inclusive development for young people.

Michael Barry uses the South Australian system to illustrate both the negative and positive aspects of informal justice. Like Polk, he highlights the problems of net-widening (that is, increasing the numbers of young people brought to the official notice of the State for very minor criminal actions that may reflect nothing more than the exuberance of youth). The provision of children's panels has drawn more young people into the justice system. He suggests, however, that these increases are offset by a reduction in the number of youth going the route of formal courts and detention. Barry also stresses the need to develop diversionary systems that cater, in culturally and socially appropriate ways, for those for whom they are intended and who most need them.

Much has been said about diversionary techniques and their effectiveness. The media often portray them as soft options. Yet the evidence suggests that, in the long run, they may be the most effective means of rehabilitation. Discussants considered a range of questions associated with diversion. What are effective screening measures? How can we ensure that an increase in diversionary mechanisms does not lead to net-widening? How can we be sure that these measures are, indeed, diverting youths away from formal court processing and are not merely drawing more children into a system from which they may find it difficult to escape? Is diversion simply another form of welfare intervention which may deprive young people of the opportunity to achieve proper representation and formal due process? How can confidentiality be maintained to ensure that a minor offence, leading to a warning or counselling, does not lock young people into the justice system and endanger their future by applying an 'offender' label which they will carry for the rest of their lives?

The children's court—the end point of juvenile justice—formed the final topic of debate. Informal processing seeks to keep young people out of the courts which are not only expensive, but also largely ineffective in rehabilitating youths who have already offended frequently or seriously. Indeed, children's courts may well represent the slippery face of the final slide into a life of crime. The three chapters in this section examine the performance of the court in different ways.

All three authors have practised in New South Wales: Blackmore as a senior children's magistrate, Hogan as an academic lawyer and Luke as a social worker. As such they provide quite different perspectives on the recent history of juvenile legislation and its administration in that state.

Rod Blackmore discusses the processes of reform drawing on his experience. He clearly defines the major goals and procedures which he believes children's courts should aim for. However, he warns against prescriptive legislation which diminishes flexibility of sentencing and undermines the very rehabilitative justice it seeks to achieve. He outlines the major influences of the children's court, including the local politicians and community pressures as well as the international forces. He also comments on the problems of achieving a balance between the extreme 'law and order' lobby and the 'dewy-eyed social workers'.

To Michael Hogan, the effect of new legislative changes in the juvenile area has been to move children's courts closer to the model of adult courts. As with Blackmore he also draws on his practical and research experiences in criminal justice in New South Wales. He identifies a veritable cocktail of motives and philosophies leading to the changes in that state. He also suggests that, despite all the rhetoric of reform, much has, in fact, remained unchanged. His chapter illustrates some of the many and varied opinions about the effectiveness of the children's court and argues strongly for its retention in spite of its current weaknesses.

Garth Luke reiterates earlier claims that juvenile justice in Australia is a mixture of welfare and justice ideologies and that the reality is much more complex than the dichotomising of these two models would suggest. The complexities and contradictions are clearly presented in Luke's case study of New South Wales. He is able to demonstrate that the swing to a more justice-oriented approach did not substantially increase the levels of punishment; in fact it seemed to reduce the use of incarceration. Moreover the greater use of diversionary mechanisms did not have the net-widening effect observed in other jurisdictions.

The complexities of the issues are well illustrated in these three chapters. By focusing on the one state, jurisdictional differences in legislation and administration are not allowed to confuse the arguments.

The final chapter in this book centres on the processes and outcomes of the children's court. Participants in the discussion which provides the material for the summary presented in this chapter agreed that courts must always be seen as the last resort of a society that has not allowed its children to grow up in a peaceful and respectful environment. Courts are an essential part of the juvenile justice system, but their role needs careful analysis. What form should they take? How should they act? How can courts be made more effective? Should children's courts differ from adult courts, and if so, how? What type of personnel should be involved in the children's court and how should they be trained? What should the sentencing process involve? Many questions were asked about the whole experience of young people in the court process and various recommendations for change were canvassed.

In general terms, this book concludes that many of the changes seen in recent years have been ineffectual and, indeed, may even have worsened the plight of some young offenders. And yet valuable insights have been gained. We are now beginning to learn from our own past experiences and from those of others and to use those insights to develop more appropriate programmes for reform. Important issues still need to be tackled, however. How do we establish preventative rather than punitive reforms? Can we achieve true justice in a way that society can understand and accept, so that communities can be more involved in the rehabilitation of young people? Young people are a major resource in our community. We cannot afford to alienate them at such an early period in their lives.

More radical and imaginative reforms are needed if we are to assist young people who are socially and economically marginalised. They need opportunities to develop their skills and initiative and absorb their energies in ways that are more constructive than the contests some presently engage in against middle-class society in general and against the police in particular. It will be evident in reading this book that there are some important differences of opinion amongst experts on the topic. In the end however, it must be realised, as all contributors to this volume agreed, that the justice system alone, and certainly the courts, cannot be expected to deal with the social and economic inequalities that contribute both to the juvenile offending itself, and to the inequitable treatment of society's young offenders.

Part I

An overview: theories and figures

1 Philosophies of juvenile justice

NGAIRE NAFFINE

Philosophical debate about the purpose of juvenile justice is often couched in the language of conceptual 'models'. These provide a type of intellectual shorthand to describe a general approach to justice which encompasses a number of related ideas. Two particular models feature consistently in the literature on criminal justice for children: one is the 'welfare' model, the other is the 'justice' model. Both these models function at a number of levels. Each contains an interpretation of the human being or of human nature; a political theory which casts the state in a particular role; and a notion of the purpose of the law and its reform (Friedmann, 1967: chapter 6; Evans, 1979; Hirst, 1986: chapter 2).

It is usual to find the welfare and the justice model presented as antinomies for the purposes of discussion about law reform (Friedmann, 1967: chapter 6; O'Hagan, 1984:5). It is said that they describe life in diametrically opposing ways and may indeed represent mutually exclusive approaches to juvenile justice. As a consequence, there is a tendency for analysts of justice to endorse one approach while rejecting the other. Law reformers, too, tend to demonstrate a high degree of polarisation. One finds therefore that the history of legislative change in this area is a history of dramatic swings in ideology, as first one theory and then the other receives official endorsement (Parsloe, 1978; Bortner, 1982; Asquith, 1983; Farrington, 1984; Debele, 1987; Morris and Giller, 1987; Harris and Webb, 1987).

The models

The welfare model of justice finds its intellectual roots in communitarianism and socialism. Its model of humanity is therefore of beings intimately connected with the particular community in which they live. That community both shapes their desires and needs, and also satisfies them. Individuals are therefore to be understood in terms of their social context and their particular circumstances (MacIntyre, 1981; Sandel, 1982).

2

In the welfare model, people are thought to derive their humanity not from any transcendent qualities which are essential to all human beings— that is, qualities which are universal in the sense that they survive across time and place. Instead our humanity derives from our particular context, and so to understand the person one must look to the circumstances in which one finds the person. In this view, people both constitute and are constituted by their social place in the world. Their values and their priorities are shaped by their social and historical circumstances (Wolff, 1976; Fisk, 1980; MacIntyre, 1981; Hirst, 1986).

By contrast, the justice model finds its home in traditional liberal theory— the political philosophy which underpins modern justice in the Anglo– American tradition. In the liberal analysis of society, human beings are viewed as self-determining agents whose principal concern is to secure the maximum degree of liberty for themselves. In this model, people are thought to be free, rational and responsible agents. They determine their circumstances rather than their circumstances determining them. Indeed the notion of citizenship, in the liberal view, derives from what is believed to be the essential rationality of human beings. People have a right to participate in public life because they have the ability to reason and thus to decide what is in their own interests (Sandel, 1982; Naffine, 1990).

In the welfare model, the purpose of the state is to secure the general needs of the community. The interests of the group or the community are thought to come before the needs or rights of the individual. The state therefore plays a more interventionist role in the identification and implementation of social policies. It may be more benevolent (provide more social services) and more controlling (place legal constraints on the behaviour of citizens) (Campbell, 1983).

The justice model, by contrast, gives priority to the liberty and agency of its individual citizens. It therefore accords a minimal role to the state whose purpose is to ensure that citizens do not infringe the liberty of each other. In the justice model, the state is agnostic about the social good. It does not set out to achieve particular social policies which are thought to be beneficial to its citizens, for this would be an infringement of personal liberties. It would impinge on personal decisions about how to pursue one's life (Nino, 1989).

Law, in the welfare view, has a legitimate role to play in securing the social good. In the context of the criminal justice system, the welfare model accords considerable power to the court and its representatives to decide what is beneficial for those individuals who come before it. The emphasis is less on the liberties and rights of those who appear in the courts than on their perceived needs and interests and on the needs and interests of the community (Campbell, 1983).

The decisions of the welfare-oriented court are therefore less a response to the individual culpability of the defendant as it relates to a particular set of antisocial actions than to the perceived needs of the defendant as they are manifested by criminal-wrongdoing. Crime is a sign of personal pathology rather than social irresponsibility. The principal concern therefore is not how far the individual has intentionally infringed the rights of others and the appropriate degree of punishment to match that degree of wrong. Rather, the welfare court is more likely to treat the antisocial action as a cry for help, not as a deliberate and culpable action. It follows that the culpability of the behaviour does not set the limits of punishment. Instead the order of the court is deemed to be a cure, not a punishment, and the extent of the cure depends on the particular needs of the defendant (Kamenka and Tay, 1986).

By contrast, in the justice model, the task of the criminal court is to determine whether there has been individual culpability on the part of individual citizens who are deemed to be responsible for their actions. The court must decide whether there has been a deliberately antisocial act on the part of a rational citizen. If so, the task of the court is to find a fitting punishment for this antisocial action, one which will serve notionally to correct the imbalance of freedoms caused by the infringement by one citizen of the rights of another (Kamenka and Tay, 1986).

In this account of criminal justice, the court as state representative is thought to pose a substantial threat to the freedoms of the defendant as citizen. It must therefore be hampered by a range of procedural formalities designed to ensure that the individual citizen is not too vulnerable to the state. Consequently, individual defendants are believed to have an essential right to defend themselves against the accusations of the state, armed with a range of legal devices. These are designed to enhance the defendant's position in relation to the state only to the point that the state and the defendant are roughly equal antagonists (Packer, 1964).

Indeed, so important is the liberty of the individual in the justice model that defendants are provided with an armoury of legal assumptions, presumptions and rules designed positively to favour them against the actions of the state. Thus, the state is itself held accountable for the incursions into the freedoms of the citizen represented by the legal process. It must therefore demonstrate that due process of law has been followed (McBarnet, 1981:chapter 1; Hammond, 1989:4).

The welfare and the justice models are ideal types in the Weberian sense (Weber, 1971) which means that they do not exist in a pure form. Instead, legal systems tend to draw from both models. Some systems may therefore be characterised by the priority they accord to the welfare model, others by their commitment to the justice model. Yet, in both instances one will find the countervailing influence of the other model (Kamenka and Tay, 1986).

In the adult sphere of Anglo–American criminal justice, a modified justice model prevails. Defendants are deemed, in the main, to be responsible and rational agents who should be called to account if they threaten or injure the freedoms of others. If found guilty by due process of law, they will be punished according to their degree of culpability. The justice model may be said to be modified in the sense that there are available various criminal defences which recognise that adults are not always fully in control of their actions. For example the defence of provocation which is available to the person charged with murder recognises that people can kill in the heat of passion. At the point of sentencing, there is also some amelioration of the justice model in that courts will take into account social, economic and cultural constraints on actions in a way that they do not tend to do when determining criminal responsibility (Naffine, 1990:66).

In the juvenile sphere of criminal justice, as we will see, there have been various attempts to soften the harshness of the justice model by incorporating ideas from the welfare approach. The intention here is to consider the degree to which welfare has been mixed with justice and whether this admixture has achieved the desired results.

Putting the models to work: some historical trends

Criminal justice for Australian children has undergone significant changes, both in its theory and in its practice. Early in the nineteenth century, Australian children were treated much the same as adults. In other words, a justice model largely prevailed, so that children were held to be responsible for their criminal actions: they were processed by conventional criminal courts and punished according to the perceived extent of their wrongdoing (Freiberg, Fox and Hogan, 1988).

From the middle of the nineteenth century, there were moves around the country to mitigate the harsh effects of this equality of treatment. Several methods were adopted. Penalties for children were reduced, young people were housed in separate penal institutions and summary justice was introduced in the juvenile sphere for all but the most serious offences. The idea of this last change was to provide quicker justice for children through the vehicle of modified magistrates' courts. In 1890, South Australia administratively established the first Australian court specifically for children. Most of the other Australian states were to follow suit shortly thereafter. New South Wales passed legislation setting up a children's court in 1905, Victoria in 1906, Queensland and Western Australia in 1907 (Seymour, 1985, 1988: 27; Freiberg, Fox and Hogan, 1988).

For much of this century, the rhetoric of children's justice has drawn heavily from the welfare model. With the establishment of separate courts for children, the assumption seems to have been that children were in fact being offered a new, distinctive and welfare-oriented style of justice—that new courts meant a different, more compassionate style of justice. And yet the observable changes were not as substantial as the rhetoric seemed to suggest (Seymour, 1985).

True, a welfare approach was reflected in the efforts of court officials to create a more informal court atmosphere, in the closure of courts to the public, in the greater prominence accorded to welfare workers in the courtroom, in the departure from the tariff principle in sentencing and in the availability of indeterminate sentences for children, designed to secure sufficient time for the proper implementation of rehabilitation programs. It was also reflected in the greater powers of the court to intervene in the lives of children whose behaviour may not have been criminal but was nevertheless considered morally reprehensible. That is, the jurisdiction of the children's court was extended to include a power to punish children who were deemed to be uncontrollable (Seymour, 1985,1988).

But in other ways children's justice remained faithful to the justice model. Indeed given their location within the system of summary courts of justice, the impact of the welfare approach to children was necessarily limited. Within the summary system of justice, Australian courts for children were to remain essentially magistrates' courts which largely operated on adversarial principles according to the standard rules of evidence and procedure (Seymour, 1988). This is in clear contrast with the American model of children's justice which, until recently, dispensed altogether with the notion of a specific criminal charge and focused instead on whether children should be deemed delinquent in view of their social background (Bortner, 1982). And yet one can still discern, among the protagonists of Australian children's justice (among its welfare workers, its court officials and its members of the bench), a strong commitment to a welfare model which often took the form of an interesting blend of compassion and moral censure followed by positive intervention.

If we look at some contemporary documents from the peak of the welfare period in South Australia, the complex meaning of 'welfare' to the protagonists of children's justice becomes more apparent. They illustrate what has been described in the literature as the welfare ideology of 'childsaving' (Platt, 1977). In 1960, for example, the official commentary from the state's Welfare Department on the number of girls brought before the court for the offence of uncontrollability referred to the fact that 'most of those charged were girls who had acquired habits of immorality and freely admitted sexual intercourse with a number of youths'. In 1961, the Department's *Annual Report* was concerned that most of the girls charged with uncontrollability 'were involved sexually with numerous youths and men'. In the following year the *Annual Report* was even more reproving: 'The girls [who came to official notice] were permitted to choose their own companions who were unknown to their parents, and no restrictions were placed on their evening and leisure activities' (Department for Community Welfare, 1961).

It was not until the mid 1960s and the birth of the civil rights movement in the United States that such attitudes were challenged and the welfare model subjected to careful scrutiny. American critics of the approach challenged the rhetoric of the childsavers which conceived of the children's court as a benign and protective institution seeking to rehabilitate offenders. They argued instead that the legal process was in fact highly punitive and stigmatising; that it was more injurious than curative (Andrews and Cohn, 1974, 1977). As a consequence, a series of American Supreme Court decisions in the late 1960s and early 1970s gave official recognition to the need to safeguard children against the excesses of the children's court, and to guarantee due process of law (Asquith, 1983:5; Debele, 1987).

In the 1970s, Australia was to feel the effects of these new concerns about the rights of young offenders. Much influenced by American debates about the denial of due process to children, law reformers in most states began to express dissatisfaction with the welfare or treatment philosophy believed to characterise Australian children's courts. With their American counterparts, they now argued that benign intervention designed to help and rehabilitate children could no longer be justified as the court's primary *raison d'etre* (Freiberg, Fox and Hogan, 1988).

'Back to justice' was the invocation of the new school of juvenile justice reformers (Cohen, 1985). What was needed, they said, was a more traditional form of justice in which the state was once again limited in its powers in relation to young offenders and less euphemistic about its purpose. Punishment should be seen to be just that, not treatment. Accordingly, children should be afforded full due process of law and if found guilty of a crime, should be punished neither more nor less than was warranted. Indeterminate sentences in particular came under attack, because they were considered to be excessively intrusive on the life of the child (Seymour, 1988; Freiberg, Fox and Hogan, 1988). Nor did they ensure that treatment programs would work.

In the various reports on children's justice commissioned around the country over the past fifteen years or so, one finds repeated expressions of concern about the perceived abuse of children by the more discretionary aspects of children's justice—an abuse which, it was said, would not be tolerated in the adult jurisdiction. What was needed, according to the law reformers, was a greater focus on the crime, not the child, and more effective constraints on the powers of the court (see for example, Mohr, 1977).

If we remind ourselves that Australian children's courts had always functioned as modified conventional courts of law—that their departure from conventional principles and procedures of justice was not substantial when compared with their American counterparts—some of this rhetoric now seems overstated. As Seymour (1988) has observed, there are concerns about the justice of one system (that is the American system, which had largely abandoned the adversarial model of justice with its associated procedural protections) being imported into quite another system (the Australian one which had retained many of the features of conventional adversarial justice). Little account was taken of the differences between the two systems and the consequent need to modify the (American) rhetoric of reform to suit local (Australian) conditions. And yet in other ways there was legitimate cause for concern about the due process of Australian juvenile justice. In particular, there was good reason to question the considerable powers vested in courts to deal with children they deemed to come within the vague charge of uncontrollable.

Current Australian laws

The reform push of the 1970s led to the passage of new juvenile laws in most of the Australian states and territories. In different ways, the new laws reflect the increased philosophical commitment to the idea of formal justice for children: that children should be accorded both greater rights and responsibilities. Implicit in this legislation is the idea that children should have the legal rights of adults (to be dealt with according to formal procedures which control the powers of the state) but that they should also now be required to shoulder more of the responsibilities associated with adult status (that is, they should be punished for their criminal actions) (Freiberg, Fox and Hogan, 1988; Seymour, 1988).

In what follows, the intention is to consider three Australian jurisdictions in which one can discern a clear shift of children's justice away from a commitment to welfare and towards justice. These are the states of South Australia, New South Wales and Victoria. The chapter will consider some of the rhetoric of justice which supported these changes as well as the specific nature of the legislative endeavours to translate the rhetoric into practice. It will also comment on the success of the new laws in bringing justice to children.

With the enactment of the *Children's Protection and Young Offenders Act* 1979, South Australia was the first of the three states to pass new justice-oriented laws dealing with young offenders. New South Wales followed suit in 1987 with the passage of four new pieces of legislation which were proclaimed in January of 1988. That legislation governing proceedings in relation to young offenders is appropriately entitled the *Children (Criminal Proceedings) Act* 1987. In 1989 Victoria enacted the *Children and Young Persons Act* , though it would seem that not all elements of the new law have yet been implemented.

In all three jurisdictions, the superseded legislation shared several features which gave it a welfare flavour. In each state uncontrollability was treated as an offence in children for which the offender could be charged, arrested and detained. The offensive behaviour over which the court had jurisdiction was therefore greater in the juvenile sphere than in the adult sphere. In each state, no clear distinction was drawn between the hearing of cases for offending children and cases for the neglected. In both categories, children were thought to be in need of care and so appeared before the same court according to similar procedures. Thus there was a fusion of the civil and criminal jurisdiction. A further common feature of these laws was the availability of indeterminate sentencing. This was to allow sufficient time for the relevant welfare personnel to reform and rehabilitate the delinquent child.

There was, however, one important distinction between the treatment of criminal children in South Australia and its sister states. In South Australia, less serious offenders were dealt with by aid panels rather than by a court, an option which strengthened the welfare dimension of children's justice in this state. Children sent to an aid panel could not be punished, only warned or admonished and their appearance could not be entered on their record (Nichols, 1985). In New South Wales and Victoria, all children, other than those cautioned by the police, were sent to court.

In most other respects, the treatment of offending children in the three states under review was much the same as the treatment of adults. The courts were run along adversarial lines according to the usual rules of evidence and procedure, although there was an endeavour to generate a more informal atmosphere. The 'welfare' model was thus significantly diluted by the application of conventional justice procedures and concerns such that a person walking into a children's court for the first time could well confuse it with an adult magistrate's court.

In each of the states, the virtues of the justice model were vaunted by those who pressed for change. One of the fullest expositions of the benefits of this style of justice for children is contained in the Report of the Royal Commission conducted by Justice Mohr (1977) which provided the intellectual base for the current South Australian legislation. Here we find clear evidence of disenchantment with the welfare model and a new faith in the value of a more traditional style of justice for children.

Commissioner Mohr (1977:7–8)) stated his commitment to formal justice in the strongest terms, indeed spoke of his 'one overriding determination' to make available the justice approach to young offenders.

> I took as a starting point the basic factor that I was dealing with a system of criminal justice, albeit a specialised one . . . I was determined that . . . there was to be no erosion of the fundamental rights of accused persons nor indeed of convicted persons under the guise of 'helping the child'.

Thus he took it to be axiomatic 'that no child shall be found guilty of a crime by means which would not, and do not apply, in the adult world'. A child, he said, 'because of youth and immaturity needs more protection from the processes of the criminal law rather than less than that offered to an adult. A child needs to be protected at all stages from unfair and arbitrary treatment.' Commissioner Mohr thereby invoked the traditional justice model of liberal theory. He employed a concept of rights which he took to be fundamental to the person. He stressed the need to protect those rights from the incursions of the state and so emphasised the concept of a constrained, predictable and limited state.

In different ways, the current juvenile justice legislation of South Australia, New South Wales and Victoria each reflect this traditional set of justice concerns. In terms of their chronology, we can also observe a strengthening commitment to the 'justice' model over time—from the mid 1970s to the late 1980s. With growing conviction, the idea is endorsed of the constrained state, and the need to protect the liberties of child defendants who are now viewed more as agents than objects—individuals who should participate in and play a determining role in the case against them.

South Australia

The South Australian legislation reflects an ongoing commitment to the value of the welfare model as well as a new commitment to formal justice.

This mixed philosophy may be traced directly to the Mohr Report (Mohr, 1977). While expressing a firm belief in the benefits of formal justice, Commissioner Mohr offered recommendations which reflected a combination of the two approaches. On the one hand, he favoured the retention of the welfare-orientated aid panels which secured a more informal style of justice for less serious offenders. On the other hand he recommended a clear separation of the criminal and civil jurisdictions, the elimination of the charge of uncontrollability and the introduction of determinate sentencing. All of these recommendations were to become law.

Those parts of the *Children's Protection and Young Offenders Act* 1979 which indicate the principles to be followed by those administering the Act also reveal that South Australia now has a philosophical commitment to both welfare and justice. These two elements are stated clearly in the preamble of the Act which announces that this is 'An Act to provide for the protection, care and rehabilitation of children [and] to provide for the welfare of the community'. Section 7 then lays down the factors to be considered when dealing with a child. Some of these have a justice bent, while others are pure welfare. It states that:

> In any proceedings under this Act, any court, panel or other body or person, in the exercise of power in relation to the child the subject of the proceedings, must seek to secure for the child such care, correction, control or guidance as will best lead to the proper development of the child's personality and to the child's development into a responsible and useful member of the community and, in so doing, shall consider the following factors:
>
> (a) the need to preserve and strengthen the relationship between the child and parents and other members of the family;
>
> (b) the desirability of leaving the child within the child's own home;
>
> (c) the desirability of allowing the education or employment of the child to continue without interruption;
>
> (ca) the child's ethnic or racial background and the need to guard against damage to the child's sense of cultural identity;
>
> (d) where appropriate, the need to ensure that the child is aware of their responsibility to bear the consequences of any action against the law; and
>
> (da) where the child is being dealt with as an adult for an offence, the deterrent effect that any sentence under consideration may have on the child or other persons;
>
> (e) where appropriate, the need to protect the community, or any person, from the violent or other wrongful acts of the child.

Under s.91(1) of the South Australian Act, the court is placed under an obligation to explain proceedings to the child and 'satisfy itself that the child . . . understands the nature of those proceedings'. Where a child is not represented by counsel, the burden on the court is greater still. In these circumstances the court

(a) must explain to the child in simple language the nature of the allegations against, or concerning, the child and the legal implications of those allegations; and
(b) must, where the child has been charged with an offence, explain to the child in simple language the elements of the offence that must be established by the prosecution (s.91(2)(a) and (b)).

Children are also to be advised in writing of their rights to legal representation and how to obtain it (s.91(4)). Moreover, where the court is of the opinion that a child needs representation, it may make provision for such representation (s.90). These provisions are clearly intended to increase the participation and comprehension of children brought before the court, intentions which are clearly consistent with the voluntarism implicit in the justice model.

New South Wales

The New South Wales laws represent an even clearer philosophical move towards justice considerations, although some welfare components are retained. It has therefore been described as 'a partial justice model' (Freiberg, Fox and Hogan, 1988:9). Section 6 of the *Children's (Criminal Proceedings) Act 1987 (C. (C.P.) Act)* sets down the principles which the children's court must follow. Here there is an explicit reference to the need to secure for children the same legal rights as adults (s.6(a)) as well as a statement to the effect that they should also be responsible for their criminal actions (s.6(b)). The rights and responsibilities of the justice model are thereby endorsed. As in South Australia, the New South Wales Act also now effects a complete separation of hearings for criminal and civil matters in relation to children. The children's court, in its criminal jurisdiction, hears only criminal matters.

In other respects, traditional welfare concerns are endorsed by the current laws in the same manner as the South Australian legislation. Section 6(b) states that the court should endeavour to allow the education and employment of children to continue (s.6(c)), and to allow them to remain at home (s.6(d)). In addition, the penalties imposed on children should not be greater than those imposed on adults (s.6(e)).

The New South Wales legislation goes further than the South Australian Act in placing specific constraints on the agents of the law. Several sections of the *C. (C.P.) Act* impose restrictions on the police in their dealings with children. Section 8 of the Act places limits on the situations in which children can be arrested. It states that unless the offence is a specified one, or there are grounds for believing the child will be violent or is unlikely to appear in court, the matter should proceed by way of summons or citations. Section 9 requires expedition when the child is in custody.

Section 13 of the *C. (C.P.) Act* governs the admissibility of statements made to the police. In general, it requires the presence of a responsible third party when children are being questioned by the police. Under s.13(b), however, the court has the discretion to admit evidence obtained, notwithstanding the absence of a third party.

The New South Wales legislation also places constraints on the sentencing official. Indeed, here we find a clear departure from the general sentencing principle adopted in children's courts, that the person presiding may impose any of the nominated penalties for any offence. Under the New South Wales legislation there is a clear commitment to the justice model in that it restricts the sentencing discretion of magistrates.

Section 33 of the Act lays down a scale of penalties and then requires the court to consider whether a less serious penalty than that proposed is not more appropriate. Section 33(1) sets out the range of penalties available to the court which are listed in an ascending order of seriousness. Section 33(2) then states that 'The children's court shall not deal with a person under a paragraph of subsection (1) unless it is satisfied that it would be wholly inappropriate to deal with the person under a preceding paragraph of that subsection'. Section 35 also obliges the court to give a reason for its sentence and to indicate why a lesser sentence is inappropriate. Thus the legislation places a burden on the judicial officer to explain why they elected a penalty when it is more than the available minimum.

An effort to ensure that children participate in, and comprehend, proceedings is to be found in s.12 of the *C. (C.P.) Act* which requires the court to explain proceedings to children. A practice direction issued by the senior children's magistrate, however, has stated that a lawyer's assurance is sufficient to establish that the child understands the proceedings.

Victoria

The *Children and Young Persons Act* 1989 deals with the treatment of welfare and criminal matters related to children in Victoria. The principles to be followed by the court are laid down specifically in relation to sentencing. Again these reflect a mixed set of concerns. In common with its sister states, the Act recognises the traditional welfare concerns of the importance of home and education. Equally, it stresses the justice issues of the child's responsibility to the community. According to s.139(1):

> In determining which sentence to impose on a child, the court must, as far as practicable, have regard to—
>
> (a) the need to strengthen and preserve the relationship between the child and the child's family; and
> (b) the desirability of allowing the child to live at home; and
> (c) the desirability of allowing the education, training or employment of the child to continue without interruption or disturbance; and

(d) the need to minimise the stigma to the child resulting from a court determination; and

(e) the suitability of the sentence to the child; and

(f) if appropriate, the need to ensure that the child is aware that he or she must bear a responsibility for any action by him or her against the law; and

(g) if appropriate, the need to protect the community, or any person, from the violent or other wrongful acts of the child.

There are extensive provisions governing the procedures to be adopted in court, the general thrust of which is towards a greater involvement of children in proceedings, their greater comprehension of the case and their greater say over what happens to them. Under s.18(1)

As far as practicable the court must in any proceeding

(a) take steps to ensure that the proceeding is comprehensible to
   (i) the child; and
   (ii) the child's parents; and
   (iii) all other parties who have a direct interest in the proceedings; and

(b) seek to satisfy itself that the child understands the nature and implications of the proceeding and of any other order made in the proceeding; and

(c) allow the ... child to participate fully in the proceeding; and

(d) consider any wishes expressed by the child; and

(e) respect the cultural identity and needs of
   (i) the child; and
   (ii) the child's parents and other members of the child's family; and

(f) minimise the stigma to the child and their family.

Section 23 extends even further the duties of the court to ensure that the child appreciates the nature of the proceedings. Under s.23(1) 'If the court makes an order, it must explain the meaning and effect of the order as plainly and simply as possible and in a way in which it considers the child, the child's parents and the other parties to the proceeding will understand'. A Children's Liaison Office is also established by the Act whose purpose includes the provision of information and advice about the court to children, families and the community (s.36).

The importance of legal representation is also recognised by the Victorian Act. Thus s.20(1) states that 'If at any stage—(b) in a proceeding in the Criminal Division a child is not legally represented; ... the Court may adjourn the hearing of the proceeding to enable the child or the child's parents ... to obtain legal representation'. Under certain circumstances legal representation is compulsory, for example where the prosecution intends to oppose an application for bail (s.21(2)(a)) or where the charge entails an offence punishable, in the case of an adult, by imprisonment (s.21(2)(c)).

Consistent with the move towards the greater accountability of children implicit in the justice model is s.19 which states that proceedings are to be conducted in open court. (In fact, Victorian children's courts were opened to the public as early as 1973 under the *Children's Court Act*.) The court, however, is granted the authority, upon application, to make proceedings closed in certain prescribed circumstances.

The Victorian Act imposes a constraint on sentencing similar to that imposed by the New South Wales legislation. That is to say, it lays down a scale of penalties and then requires the court to consider whether a less serious penalty than that proposed is not more appropriate. The sentencing hierarchy is created by s.138 according to which 'The court must not impose a sentence referred to in any of the paragraphs of s.137(1) unless it is satisfied that it is not appropriate to impose a sentence referred to in any preceding paragraph of that section.' In the other Australian states, the person presiding over the court has the discretion to impose any one of a range of penalties, though the seriousness of the offence is usually a guiding consideration.

Some reflections on the new laws

The current laws governing the treatment of young offenders in each of the three states considered here share a commitment to the idea that children are, to a large extent, rational and responsible agents who require protection from the interventions of the court. The prevailing notion is that the position of children before the court can be improved by securing for them the conventional range of legal rights available to adults and ensuring that they have access to full due process of law. Thus each piece of legislation may be seen to derive its philosophical base from classical justice theory.

The current laws also represent at least a partial rejection of the welfare model which informed many aspects of the superseded laws. Under the previous legislation, the emphasis was on the vulnerability of children and their need for the benign intervention of the court. The cost of this approach was believed by many to be an excessive degree of control over the lives of children. Discretion and arbitrariness characterised many aspects of the welfare-oriented system of justice and children had little say over the process. By contrast, the new justice-oriented laws endeavour to invest the child with volition and a greater measure of control.

The model of the human being which now guides the legal process is more closely attuned to liberal theory. It is the notion of independent, rational, legal actors who are informed of their rights against the state and duly assert them. We may now consider whether this justice model is in fact working and, indeed, whether it can work for children. Though the present intention is not to attempt a detailed appraisal of the new laws, we may nevertheless make some preliminary observations about their effectiveness.

Perhaps the most obvious point one can make from the outset is that the return of children's justice to a style which has always prevailed in the adult sphere of summary justice is unlikely to cause a dramatic improvement in the position of children. The simple reason is that adult defendants in magistrates' courts do not appear themselves to derive much benefit from the panoply of legal rights afforded them. So why should children?

In theory, the adult defendant has the benefit of the presumption of innocence, the right to put the prosecution to the test, a favourable burden of proof and the right to legal representation. But as a matter of practice, few defendants seize these rights. Instead the vast majority plead guilty (and are expected to do so) and are processed by the courts in a matter of minutes.

The reasons for this capitulation have been well researched and documented elsewhere (Bottoms and McClean, 1976; McBarnet, 1981). This research suggests that adult defendants appear to display few of the characteristics of the person anticipated by liberal theory: that is, a sense of self-determination and an ability to participate effectively in the legal process (Naffine, 1990: chapter 6). Instead, the typical adult brought before the court experiences a sense of incomprehension and impotence, and commonly feels a desire simply to get the matter over with as quickly as possible (Feeley, 1979).

Children are in an even weaker position than adults for the very reason that they are children. Even more than adult defendants, children brought before the courts may be characterised by their powerlessness. They may generally be described as poorly educated, inarticulate and ignorant of the legal process. Indeed on almost every social indicator, child defendants can be characterised by their disadvantage. Confronted with a legal system which appears hostile and alien, which speaks in a different and technical language, children do not stand up for themselves (Gale, Bailey-Harris and Wundersitz, 1990).

Emphasising the legality of children's justice may only exacerbate this problem. It is unlikely to equip children as legal combatants. Indeed it may well serve only to strengthen the role of the lawyer in the children's court and so entrench even further the role of the child defendant as an amateur in the legal process (Naffine and Wundersitz, 1990). In short, it is possible that children will make even less use of their legal rights than adults.

Some basic statistics from the children's court suggests that this is, in fact, the case. Both before and after the new laws, the large majority of children pleaded guilty. The largest group of children therefore did not, and still do not, avail themselves of their rights to challenge the state and have the prosecution prove its case (Wundersitz, Naffine and Gale, 1991; Wundersitz and Naffine, 1991).

Observations conducted by the author of the operation of the central children's courts in South Australia and New South Wales also confirm that under the new laws children still tend not to assert their rights. Typically, cases are processed quickly by way of a guilty plea, with the assistance of a lawyer who speaks entirely for the child. In fact in New South Wales, children are not even required to give their own plea. There are many reasons for this emphasis on speed and efficiency, the constraints of time and heavy caseloads being the more obvious ones. This is not to say that reforms such as that contained within s.13 of the New South Wales Act, which requires the presence of a third party at the police interview of a child, have not been beneficial. Interviews conducted by the author with lawyers and police prosecutors in New South Wales indicate that this section does indeed function as a significant control on police discretion, and is of assistance to the child at the time of the interview and subsequently in court.

This suggests that reforms which seek to protect the interests of children by placing constraints on the agents of the law in their dealings with children may be more effective than reforms which depend on children asserting their rights (to put the prosecution to the test, to ask questions in court, to participate positively in the legal process). That is, in the case of children it may be more useful to think in terms of protecting their interests by controlling the behaviour of others, by placing obligations on those others, than by seeking to enhance the self-determination of child defendants so that they can function as active combatants in the manner anticipated by the justice model.

It is perhaps surprising that Australian law reformers appear to have had such confidence in the idea of formal justice for children. Had they looked at the actual operation of adult courts which were providing the model, they would have seen that the quick case via the guilty plea was the norm. Mimicking adult justice therefore seems an odd solution to the perceived deficiencies of children's justice. For even with the protections afforded to them by the rule of law and its associated procedural formalities, adult defendants demonstrate little fight. Quickly, they cave in to their accusers. So why should the same set of legal armoury have the effect of turning children into free-willing litigants?

Also, had the law reformers looked at the actual operation of children's courts they would have seen that in many ways they were already very similar to adult courts, adopting an adversarial style, with formal charges, the requirement that the defendant plead to a charge and most children electing to plead guilty. To seek to improve the fairness of children's courts by modelling them on the adult system was therefore only to secure more of the same for child defendants, rather than introducing an entirely new concept into children's justice.

It would seem that the tendency has been for law reform to take place in an empirical vacuum. Theory is often advanced without reference to the legal practice. Law reformers tend not to take note of such basic facts as the high rate of guilty pleas which characterises both adult and children's justice. While the talk persists of the need to strengthen the rights of children in an adversary system, justice proceeds by way of admissions and little real challenge. Theories are invoked with little reference to the actual context in which they are to be used and so without substantiation (Naffine, Wundersitz and Gale, 1990).

Again this may not be surprising if we take note of the circumstances in which law reform takes place. It is often in ignorance of local conditions and in the thrall of theories imported from other places (Farrington, 1984:90, Seymour, 1988). Also the timing, the speed and the content of legal change tend to depend on a range of political factors, which can accelerate or retard the legislative process and also the language of reform. Conceptual clarity, intellectual rigour and empirical verification therefore do not necessarily characterise the law reform process.

To return to our original philosophical models, we may now reflect on the uneasy relationship which pertains between the theory and practice of juvenile justice and the problems it generates for legal change. A brief look at some specific Australian juvenile justice laws and practices has revealed that often the theory fails to inform the practice and the practice fails to inform theory. The effect is that the theories persist and are recycled according to the philosophical or political concerns of any given historical moment.

The current view is that the justice model is now in the ascendancy. Both the law and its practice are now supposed to reflect a more formal style of justice for children, one which more closely approximates the approach to adults and so is intended to accord more effective legal rights to children. It is timely to consider whether this is indeed so.

Postscript

Since this paper was written, concern among reformers about the need to involve victims in the juvenile justice process has become more pronounced. Growing dissatisfaction with the two traditional approaches to juvenile justice (those of 'welfare' and 'justice') has led reformers to consider the merits of a third approach which might be dubbed 'restorative justice' (Galaway and Hudson, 1990:1). Here the purpose is to bring together victims, offenders and their families in order to arrive at a mutual solution and so restore the balance of peace and harmony between the parties. This is a model which, in many ways, builds upon principles of traditional village justice.

It is this approach which underpins the new juvenile justice legislation of New Zealand (the *Children, Young Persons and Their Families Act*, 1989). The focus here is on the Family Group Conference: a meeting of the offender, the victim, their families, and other persons selected by the key parties, at which (in theory) the parties themselves negotiate a solution (which usually involves offender reparation to the victim). It is therefore an attempt to restore the conflict to the main protagonists, with the agents of the State relegated to the role of mediators. The New Zealand legislation is now attracting considerable attention in Australia and may represent a new direction for legal reform.

2 Some statistics on youth offending: an inter-jurisdictional comparison

JOY WUNDERSITZ

The 1980s witnessed a great deal of activity in the youth arena, with most states in Australia embarking on major overhauls of their juvenile justice legislation. But despite the significant changes embodied in these new Acts, public concern about what is perceived to be an escalation in youth crime has not been assuaged and the calls for tougher penalties have become more strident.

Media headlines such as 'Juvenile Crime Out of Control' (Adelaide *Advertiser*, 13.8.1991) have become commonplace and in response, a plethora of Parliamentary enquiries have been launched. Thus, the Western Australian Select Committee into Youth Affairs, the Queensland Parliamentary Criminal Justice Committee, the South Australian Select Committee on the Juvenile Justice System and the New South Wales Standing Committee on Social Issues have all been directed to investigate juvenile justice issues. The most extreme response to public expressions of concern however, has come from Western Australia where Parliament reacted to a number of public demonstrations calling for a 'crackdown' on young offenders by passing the *Crime (Serious and Repeat Offenders) Sentencing Act, 1992*. This requires mandatory gaol sentences for young repeat violent offenders.

Yet, despite this frenzy of activity, few attempts have been made to determine whether community fears about escalating juvenile crime are realistic. Have the levels of offending by young people risen to the point where they are 'out of control', as is claimed, or is public perception being moulded by a relatively few, but highly publicised incidents? In South Australia, for example, public outrage has been generated by several occurrences of vandalism on public transport (all given considerable exposure in the media). Similarly, in Western Australia, much of the impetus for the tough 'law and order' regime which is now in place has come from the well publicised high speed car chases between police and youths driving stolen vehicles. But are these incidents indicative of an across-the-board increase in juvenile offending?

The aim of this chapter is to examine trends in officially recorded youth crime in an attempt to identify whether criminal behaviour amongst young people has escalated. Also, by comparing offending statistics across the different Australian jurisdictions, it seeks to determine whether, and to what extent, the situation varies from one state to another.

Some methodological problems

This chapter presents and compares, for each Australian state,[1] information relating to the total number of young people processed by the juvenile justice system, either by way of a police caution, panel hearing or court appearance. It also assesses the nature of the charges involved, the methods of processing and the outcomes recorded. (The data sources are outlined in Appendix 1.)

It should be noted at the outset, however, that any such state-by-state comparison of juvenile crime statistics is fraught with difficulties not only because of variations in the philosophy and practice of juvenile justice from one jurisdiction to another, but also because there is no uniform national data collection system. The compilation of statistics on youth offending remains a state responsibility. In South Australia and New South Wales, where specialised government bureaux exist to compile and publish crime data, comprehensive information is readily accessible. But in other states, information must be gleaned from a variety of sources—in particular, from the annual reports of the different agencies involved in the administration of juvenile justice. Because of this fragmentation, the type and range of data available vary not only across jurisdictions, but also within jurisdictions over time, as responsibility for offending statistics is transferred from one government department to another. Thus even the task of assessing long-term trends in youth offending within the one state may prove difficult.

Moreover, official crime statistics, such as those used here, are a product not only of young people's offending behaviour, but also of the way in which the justice system itself operates. To be counted in these statistics, a youth must be officially processed either by way of a formal caution, a panel appearance or a children's court hearing. Before such processing can occur, a number of actions must take place. First, the incident must be reported to police or otherwise brought to their notice. The police then face the task of identifying and 'catching' a suspect. This is easier for some offences than for others.[2] Finally, even when a suspect has been identified, the police may, for various reasons, choose not to proceed with the matter. Variations in responses at any of these levels may lead to changes in the numbers of youths selected for formal processing by the justice system, even when actual levels of offending behaviour in the community remain constant.

To illustrate, an increase in the number of apprehensions may result, not from increased levels of crime, but from an increased allocation of police resources which enable police to apprehend more suspects. Alternatively, an upswing in one type of offence may reflect a concentrated police 'blitz' on that type of behaviour (e.g. drink driving or graffiti), or an increased willingness by the public to report the offence (e.g. child abuse). Other factors also have to be considered. Juveniles, for example, tend to be more visible than adults and come under closer scrutiny. They may therefore be easier to apprehend. This applies particularly to certain subgroups of youths such as Aborigines, who may in consequence be differentially 'targeted' for official processing.

Nevertheless, although official crime statistics do not provide a completely accurate measure of real levels of juvenile offending, it could be argued that if youth crime really is 'out of control', then this would be mirrored by a definite upswing in the number of youths being officially processed by the system. In other words, there should at least be some coincidence between offending patterns and official crime statistics.

Trends in recorded juvenile offending: total intervention rates

Overall, only a very small proportion of young people become involved with the formal juvenile justice system in Australia. To illustrate, in 1988–89 (which represents the last year for which information was available for all six states), only 40.8 cases per 1000 youth population were processed by the juvenile justice system either by way of a formal police caution, a panel hearing or a court appearance: that is, of the total juvenile population in these jurisdictions, only 4.1 per cent were targeted for some form of official intervention. More recent figures, based on 1990–91 data drawn from five states, indicate a slight reduction in this figure to 38.5 per 1000.

Nevertheless, there are some significant variations between the states as illustrated in Table 2.1.

Table 2.1 Rate of official intervention per 1000 youth population

State	Rate	Year
WA	64.1	1990–91
SA	54.7	1990–91
Qld	39.5	1990–91
Tas.	35.7	1990
Vic.	30.5	1988–89
NSW	27.0	1990–91

Note: In Victoria 1988–89 represents the most recent year for which police cautioning data are available.

As shown, Western Australia recorded the highest intervention rate of the six states, while South Australia recorded the second highest intervention rate. At the other end of the scale was New South Wales. This means that the jurisdiction which has the largest youth population also has the smallest rate of official intervention by the juvenile justice system.

Longitudinal trends

What then, are the longitudinal trends in recorded youth offending and more importantly, have they escalated in recent years? Figure 2.1 graphs the total rates of intervention per 1000 youth population for each Australian jurisdiction from 1979–80 onwards.

Figure 2.1 Total number of matters processed: rates per 1000 youth population

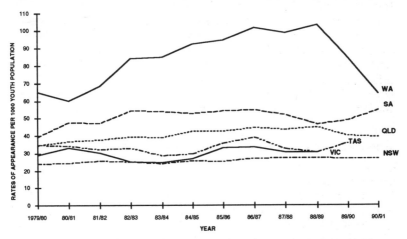

Not only does Western Australia have the highest intervention rate of the six jurisdictions, but in terms of longitudinal trends, it is totally out of step with the other states. As shown, it is the only jurisdiction which recorded a persistently strong increase during the 1980s and it is the only one which, according to the figures, experienced a substantial decrease during the last two years.

At the beginning of the decade (1980–81) the rate of official intervention in Western Australia was 60.3 per 1000 youth population. By 1984–85 it had increased to 92.3 per 1000 youth population and to 103.4 in 1988–89. As a result, the gap between this state and the other jurisdictions became progressively wider. In 1980–81 for example, the Western Australian intervention rate was only 1.3 times greater than the South Australian rate of 47.6. By 1988–89, however, it had risen to 2.2 times that of the South Australian rate which by this stage, had actually declined slightly to 46.6. As a second point of comparison, in 1980–81, youth offending rates in Western Australia were 2.5 times greater than those recorded in New South Wales. By 1988–89 they were 3.8 times greater.

However, a dramatic reversal to this upward trend occurred in the final year of the decade, when the rate of official interventions dropped substantially from 103.5 to 84.6 per 1000. A further decrease, to 64.1 per 1000 was evident in 1990–91. This reversal seems to have been the result of a combination of factors which came into play at this time. For one thing, 1989–90 marked the first year of operation of the *Children's Court Act* 1989 (WA) which brought significant changes to the way in which young offenders were processed. In particular, the establishment of a reconstituted children's court, headed by a judge of district court status, resulted in greater efficiency, consistency and accountability which, it has been suggested, had some impact on police processing. Some six months later, the State Government Advisory Committee on Young Offenders was set up to facilitate stronger inter-agency cooperation and consultation. This Committee, it is claimed, has provided the impetus for the establishment or extension of a number of crime prevention strategies and treatment options which were designed not only to reduce the overall levels of juvenile offending, but to provide alternative responses to any offending detected by police. To some extent then, the observed decrease in official intervention rates may be real; i.e. it may actually be the case that fewer youths are now being processed by the juvenile justice system in Western Australia than was previously the case.

However, there is, in the Western Australian data, another confounding factor which must be taken into account: namely, changes in data recording procedures. With the inception of the new Act, responsibility for the administration of the children's court was transferred to the Crown Law Department, which also took over the task of publishing the court statistics. This transfer, it seems, coincided with a 'cleanup' of the data system to eliminate an overcounting problem which had become increasingly evident during the latter part of the decade. Consequently, in their Annual Report for 1989–90, the Crown Law Department clearly stipulated that their court appearance figures (which they described as 'refined') did not correspond with those published in previous years by the Department for Community Services. To some extent then, the marked decrease in official interventions for 1989–90 may simply be due to more accurate data processing. If this is the case, then the very high levels of intervention recorded during the latter part of the 1980s may be artificially inflated. In other words, data recording errors may have given the impression that the Western Australian juvenile justice system was processing far more young people than was actually the case.

What then of the other states? In direct contrast to the situation in Western Australian, New South Wales not only recorded the lowest intervention rates throughout the 1980s, but moreover, these rates remained extremely stable during this twelve year period, increasing only marginally from 24.2 per 1000 in 1979–80 to 27.1 per 1000 in 1986–87, before dropping back slightly to 27.0 in 1989–90. And again in contrast to Western Australia, the major legislative changes which came into effect in New South Wales in 1987 had no apparent impact whatsoever on processing levels.

Queensland experienced a slight but steady increase from 1979–80 to 1988–89, followed by a decrease in 1989–90 and again in 1990–91. As a result, at the end of the decade, on a per capita basis, the number of youths being processed in that state either by way of an official police caution or a court appearance was the lowest recorded for some six years.

In Victoria and Tasmania, official intervention rates showed some fluctuations during the 1980s. But again, there is no evidence of any substantial increase over this period. In Victoria, rates actually declined during the first half of the decade, from 33.3 in 1980–81 to 27.1 per 1000 in 1984–85. This was followed by an upward shift in 1985–86. However, during the last two years for which data were available, rates again fell. Consequently, the figure of 30.5 per 1000 youth population recorded in 1988–89 was actually lower than that recorded some seven years earlier in 1980–81.

Like Victoria, Tasmania also experienced a noticeable decline in official intervention rates in the early and mid 1980s, with the rate recorded in 1985 (29.7) being well below that of 1980 (34.9 per 1000 youth population). Figures continued to fluctuate during the second half of the decade, with the rate recorded in 1990 being the same as that in 1986 (namely 35.7 per 1000).

Even in South Australia, the state with the second highest rate of intervention, the situation during the 1980s remained relatively stable. While the introduction of screening panels in July 1979 had some net-widening effect,[3] by 1982–83 this had peaked and during the next six years, total appearances by young people before aid panels and the children's court first stabilised and then decreased. Hence, although figures increased slightly in 1989–90 and again in 1990–91, the rates of appearance recorded at the end of the decade were still considerably lower than during the early 1980s.

Overall then, with the exception of Western Australia, there is no evidence from any of the jurisdictions of a massive blow-out in official intervention rates. In turn, this must cast some doubts on media claims that juvenile crime is 'out of control'. Nor does Western Australia support the claim, in that, although it experienced a major escalation in recorded intervention rates during the 1980s, this trend has been dramatically reversed in the last two years, with the rate recorded in 1990–91 being lower than that recorded some ten years earlier. Moreover, it is interesting to note that this downturn preceded the introduction of the new 'law and order' sentencing legislation in that state.

Informal mechanisms for the processing of young offenders

Over recent decades, there has been a strong shift towards the adoption of informal mechanisms for the treatment of young Australian offenders. These mechanisms have generally been characterised as diversionary procedures, designed to channel first or minor offenders away from formal prosecution in the children's court. However, the nature of these informal options varies from one jurisdiction to another. During the period under discussion, (i.e. 1979–80 to 1990–91) a system of formal police cautioning operated in Queensland, Victoria and New South Wales.[4] By contrast, Western Australia and South Australia had in place a system of children's panels, consisting of a police officer and a social worker whose primary task was to warn and counsel the child.

Figure 2.2 details, over a twelve year period, that proportion of all youths brought to official notice who were dealt with via these informal processing mechanisms; that is, either by way of a police caution or a panel appearance. Several interesting points emerge. Firstly, Victoria and Queensland, which have had a system of formal police cautioning in operation since the early

Figure 2.2 Proportion of matters dealt with informally

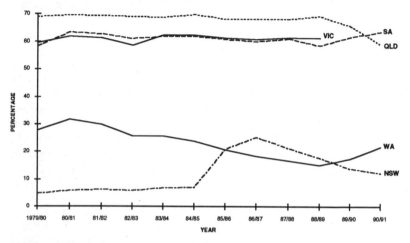

1960s, make extensive use of this diversionary option. From 1979–80 to 1989–90, on average some 68.5 per cent of juveniles apprehended each year in Queensland were dealt with by way of a police caution rather than being channelled into the court system. The figure for Victoria was almost as high: over the same period, an average of 61.4 per cent of all apprehended youths were cautioned while conversely, only 38.6 per cent were sent to court.

By contrast, in New South Wales, where formal police cautions are a far more recent innovation and where government support has been less forthcoming, proportionately few youths are dealt with in this way. In the first half of the 1980s, on average only 6.1 per cent of youths were cautioned, while the remaining 93.9 per cent went to court. With the introduction of new cautioning procedures in September 1985, the use of police diversion increased substantially, reaching 21.0 per cent in 1985–86. But this increase was not sustained, and by 1990–91 the proportion had dropped back to 12.2 per cent.

Figure 2.2 also reveals a clear difference between South Australia and Western Australia—the only two states to have opted for a system of children's panels. The proportion of youths selected for processing by aid panels in South Australia is comparable to the proportion of youths cautioned in Victoria. From 1979–80 to 1990–91, on average 61.2 per cent of youths in South Australia were dealt with informally without recourse to the children's court. This compares very closely with the figure of 61.4 per cent recorded for cautions in Victoria. Aid panels in South Australia therefore seem to fulfil a similar function (at least in terms of the numbers with which they deal) to that of the more established police cautioning schemes. This is not the case, however, in Western Australia where children's (suspended proceedings) panels service a relatively small and, perhaps more significantly, a declining proportion of young offenders. In that state, the high point of panel operations occurred in 1980–81 when they processed 31.6 per cent of all young offenders. By 1988–89, this figure had been halved to 15.1 per cent.

Panels thus occupy a very different place in the South Australian jurisdiction compared with Western Australia. A partial explanation lies in the different referral procedures operating in the two states. In South Australia, decisions as to whether a case should go to an aid panel or a children's court are made by screening panels, each of which comprises a police officer and a social worker. These mechanisms have operated since July 1979 and their referral decisions are totally discretionary. In other words, all youths (irrespective of age, prior record, offending behaviour etc.) are technically eligible for an aid panel hearing if the screening personnel consider it appropriate. By contrast, no such independent screening body exists in Western Australia. Instead, the eligibility of a young person for a panel hearing is predetermined by rigid criteria. These include the individual's age, the nature of the offence and prior record, together with a willingness and ability to pay restitution to the victim.

Recognition that the panel system in Western Australia has, in fact, failed to divert sufficient numbers of cases from the children's court has prompted that state to introduce a formal police cautioning system. *The Child Welfare Amendment Act No. 2*, which was passed in December 1990 and came into effect on 1 August 1991, provides the statutory base for this cautioning program, giving police the option to administer either an oral or a written caution. It is too early, however, to assess its impact on juvenile justice processing in this state.

Court appearance rates

In view of the significant variations from one state to another in the proportion of interventions dealt with informally by the juvenile justice system, it is useful at this point to examine and compare the role of the children's court across the six jurisdictions.

Figure 2.3 depicts longitudinal trends in the rate of children's court appearances only. Western Australia is, once again, out of step with all other states. Its very high rate of official intervention, combined with the fact that only a very small percentage of such interventions are dealt with informally by way of children's (suspended proceedings) panels, meant that by 1988–89, its children's court was, at least according to the official statistics, actually processing a higher number of cases than the New South Wales children's court (17 487 compared to 15 553). And this is despite the fact that the size of the juvenile population in New South Wales was 3.5 times that of Western Australia. Even with the dramatic decrease recorded during the last two years,

Figure 2.3 Court appearance rates

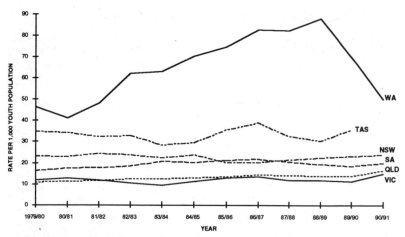

it still processes more matters than children's courts in South Australia, Victoria, Tasmania and Queensland.

What then, of these other states? A comparison between children's court appearance rates (as depicted in Figure 2.3) and total intervention rates (see Figure 2.1) reveals some important shifts in the relative positioning of these other jurisdictions—shifts which are directly attributable to the degree to which informal processing mechanisms are utilised. To illustrate, South Australia and Queensland recorded the second and third highest rates of official intervention respectively. But because some 60 to 70 per cent of all such interventions were dealt with informally, the actual rate of appearance before the children's court in these two states was comparatively low— lower, in fact, than in Tasmania and New South Wales where police cautions are used so infrequently.

The state with the lowest court appearance rates is Victoria. Not only does this state have a relatively low rate of intervention to start with, but some 60 per cent of juvenile matters are dealt with outside of the formal court setting by way of a police caution. As a result, in 1990–91, Victoria's court appearance rate was only 14.8 per 1000 youth, compared with a rate of 50.1 in Western Australia and 23.7 per 1000 in New South Wales—the state with the most comparably sized youth population.

Demographic characteristics of processed young offenders

Information on the demographic characteristics of young people processed by the juvenile justice system in each state is difficult to obtain. In fact, the only such variable which is available across all jurisdictions is that of gender. For factors such as ethnicity, employment status and family background, the data presented in the ensuing discussion have been derived almost exclusively from the South Australian jurisdiction.

Gender

It is well established that the majority of young offenders processed by juvenile justice systems are males. This is illustrated in Table 2.2 which provides a gender breakdown of all official interventions, whether by way of a police caution, panel hearing or court appearance. (For each state, the most recent year of data available has been used.)

Table 2.2 Gender of youths subjected to official intervention

	WA %	Vic. %	NSW %	Tas. %	SA %
Males	80.9	83.7	84.5	71.5	81.3
Females	19.1	16.3	15.5	28.5	18.7
Total	100.0	100.0	100.0	100.0	100.0
	n=20 587	n=14 092	n=17 223	n=1661	n=8689

Notes:
1. NSW = 1989–90: WA = 1988–89: Tas. = 1990: Vic. = 1987–88: SA = 1990–91.
2. Queensland was omitted because no gender breakdown was available for cautions. However, for the 4364 offence-related children's court appearances in 1988–89, 87.5 per cent involved males.

Males clearly predominate in all jurisdictions, irrespective of whether the system involves a children's court only (as is effectively the case in Tasmania), a court and cautioning system (New South Wales and Victoria), or a panel and court (Western Australia and South Australia). It has been hypothesised that, because they offer a 'softer' option for the treatment of young offenders, informal mechanisms tend to bring more females into the system (Alder, 1984; Alder and Polk, 1982). On this basis, one would expect that in those states where a formal cautioning or panel system processes a substantial proportion of all cases, there would be a higher percentage of females in the youth offending population compared with those states where only a children's court exists. Yet this is obviously not the case: Tasmania, which had no effective informal mechanism operating, recorded the highest percentage of females of the five jurisdictions listed.

While the existence of an effective cautioning or panel system may not result in more females being brought into the system in the first place, it is nevertheless true that once in the system, females are more likely than males to be 'diverted' to these informal processing mechanisms. This is illustrated in Table 2.3, which shows the proportion of each gender who were dealt with informally. In South Australia, where aid panels process over one half of all cases proceeded with by police, some 79.8 per cent of females were directed to these informal hearings, compared with a lower figure of 59.8 per cent for males. Even in Western Australia, where the diversionary panel system is substantially underutilised, 24.6 per cent of

females were dealt with in this way compared with only 12.8 per cent of
males.

**Table 2.3 Proportion of all male and female cases dealt with informally by way
of a police caution or a panel hearing**

	WA %	SA %	NSW %	Vic. %
Males	12.8	59.8	13.8	58.2
Females	24.6	79.8	20.8	77.7

Note:
Vic. = 1987–88: SA = 1990–91: WA = 1988–89: NSW = 1989–90

One must be cautious, however, in interpreting this finding in terms of
discrimination against males or conversely, chivalrous treatment of females.
An analysis of South Australian data (Wundersitz, Naffine and Gale, 1988)
demonstrates that females are more likely than males to possess those
characteristics which meet the specific criteria for an informal hearing; that
is, they are charged with fewer, less serious offences and are less likely
than males to have a prior offending record.

Employment status

Information on the employment status of offending youth is available only for
South Australia and so cannot be generalised to other states. Though limited,
the data highlight the very high levels of unemployment amongst young
people brought into contact with the juvenile justice system. Of the 8225
appearances finalised by both panels and the children's court in that state in
1990–91 and for which information on employment status was available, the
majority (59.1 per cent) were students. This is only to be expected, given the
age range of the jurisdiction. What is significant, however, is the relatively
high proportion who were unemployed (27.3 per cent) compared with those
who had at least some form of employment (13.6 per cent).

A more accurate insight into unemployment levels is obtained if analysis
is limited only to those 3365 young offenders who had left school and who
were therefore technically part of the workforce at the time of their
appearance. Of these youth, two thirds (66.7 per cent) were unemployed,
while only one third had some form of either part- or full-time work.

Family status

The significant feature of Table 2.4, which details the living arrangements of
those youths dealt with by both panels and the children's court in South
Australia, is the high proportion who belong to what could be classified as
non-normative family structures. Overall, some 34.0 per cent came from
single-parent families, 7.9 per cent were living either in foster homes or with

relatives, while 4.7 per cent were living independently. Only one half (51.8 per cent) lived in two-parent families and, according to the definition used, one of these two parents could be either a de facto partner or a step-parent.

Table 2.4 **Family status of youths selected for formal intervention, South Australia, 1990–91**

Family Status	n	%
Two-parent family	3933	51.8
One-parent family	2584	34.0
Foster parents/relatives	604	7.9
Independent	355	4.7
Other	124	1.6
Total	7600	100.0

(Unknown = 1088)

Racial identity

The over-representation of Aborigines in the adult criminal justice system has been well-documented (Eggleston, 1976; Martin and Newby, 1984; Cunneen and Robb, 1987; Report of the Royal Commission into Aboriginal Deaths in Custody, 1991). The situation for juveniles is no different (Gale, Bailey-Harris and Wundersitz, 1990), with young Aborigines experiencing a disproportionately high degree of contact with the judicial system.

In South Australia, although Aborigines account for only approximately 1.7 per cent of all young people in that state, in 1990–91 they constituted 9.5 per cent of all finalised panel and court appearances. Thus, on a per capita

Figure 2.4 **Aborigines as a percentage of all finalised children's aid panel and court appearances**

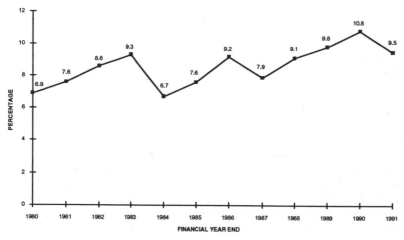

basis, their rate of representation in the system was 5.6 times greater than expected. And their position has not improved over the last decade. As Figure 2.4 shows, in 1989–90, Aborigines accounted for a greater per centage of all appearances than was the case some ten years earlier in 1979–80.

Nor is the situation much better in other states, as indicated by children's court data from Western Australia. In 1988–89, 21.9 per cent of the 17 844 children's court appearances in that state involved Aborigines. Yet this group comprised only 4 per cent of the state's youth population. Thus the rate of Aboriginal representation before the court was 5.5 times greater than expected.

Type of offence

Another public perception which has received widespread media attention in recent times is that juveniles are becoming more violent. Again however, an assessment of official crime statistics does not support this argument. Although an inter-jurisdictional comparison of the types of offences with which young people are charged is problematic,[5] nevertheless, as Table 2.5 shows, some broad similarities do emerge. Most notably, in all six jurisdictions examined, property theft dominates the charge profile of young offenders processed by the system. In South Australia, Victoria and New South Wales, this offence grouping accounts for over 50 per cent of all major charges dealt with, while in Tasmania and Western Australia, the proportion is in the mid 40s. Moreover, of the individual property offences listed, it is the generally less serious category of 'other theft' (consisting of larceny and shoplifting) which dominates. Thus in South Australia, in 1990–91, 'other theft' accounted for 31.5 per cent of all major charges finalised by panels and the children's court, whereas the more serious property crime of break and enter made up only 14.0 per cent. A similar pattern is evident in Victoria and New South Wales where 'other theft' constituted 42.6 per cent and 21.2 per cent of all major charges finalised respectively, compared with 15.4 per cent and 14.0 per cent for break and enter counts. Interestingly, vehicle theft, which has received so much media coverage in recent months, particularly in South Australia and Western Australia, featured in a relatively small proportion of all matters finalised. In South Australia, this offence represented only 8.7 per cent of all major charges dealt with, while in Victoria and New South Wales (the only other jurisdictions where figures for this offence are detailed separately) it made up only 7.2 per cent and 10.2 per cent of all major charges respectively.

In contrast to the dominant position occupied by property offences in the criminal profile of young people, offences against the person occur relatively infrequently. They accounted for only 2.0 per cent of all major charges in Victoria, 4.5 per cent in Tasmania and 7.9 per cent in South Australia. They were most prevalent in New South Wales, accounting for 14.8 per cent of all major charges dealt with by way of cautions and the children's court in 1989–90.

Table 2.5 Type of offences involved in official interventions: cautions, panels, courts

Offence	SA (1990–91) %	Vic. (1988–89) %	NSW (1989–90) %	Tas. (1990) %	WA (1988–89) %
Against person	7.9	2.0	14.8	4.5	3.3
Against property	57.2	65.6	53.2	46.5	45.0
Fraud	1.3	0.8	2.6	0.5	2.0
Break and enter	14.0	15.4	14.0	*18.3	**43.0
Vehicle theft	8.7	7.2	10.2	—	—
Other theft	31.5	42.6	21.2	25.8	—
Unlawful possession	1.7	—	5.2	1.9	—
Damage property	9.4	6.1	7.7	3.4	5.4
Driving/traffic	2.2	7.6	3.0	1.4	21.8
Drug	8.2	1.2	3.8	0.8	3.7
Against good order	11.2	10.6	8.1	33.4	13.4
Other	4.0	6.5	9.4	10.1	7.4
Total	100.0	100.0	100.0	100.0	100.0
	n=8688	n=13 695	n=18 445	n=1661	n=34 530

Note:
For SA, Vic., NSW and Tas., the most serious offence finalised per case is detailed. For WA, all finalised offences are listed. Queensland was omitted because no offence data were provided for cautioned matters.

* Break and enter, and vehicle theft combined
** Break and enter, vehicle theft, other theft, receive/unlawful possession combined

Children's court outcomes

Because the overwhelming majority of matters dealt with informally by way of a police caution or panel hearing result in nothing more than a simple warning and counselling, only the outcomes handed down by the children's court will be considered here. Moreover, wherever possible, analysis is limited to outcomes imposed for the most serious charge per appearance, rather than to all counts dealt with.[6]

In New South Wales, almost one quarter of all major charges (26.8 per cent) were either dismissed with a caution or were proven, but attracted no penalty. In other words, these charges received the least serious outcomes of those available to the court. At the other end of the scale, only 7.3 per cent resulted in committal to an institution while 0.1 per cent involved imprisonment. Recognisances and probations in combination accounted for the majority of outcomes (39.6 per cent), while fines were imposed in 17.4 per cent of cases.

In Western Australia, fines constituted the most frequently imposed penalty (34.2 per cent), followed by dismissals (21.3 per cent). Again, only a very small proportion of cases (3.6 per cent) resulted in a detention order.

Fines were also the most frequently imposed sentence in South Australia where they accounted for 35.5 per cent of all major charge outcomes. These were closely followed by discharge without penalty (34.4 per cent). Good behaviour bonds (with or without conditions attached to them) accounted for a further 24.8 per cent. Again, the number of detention orders was relatively low (2.3 per cent) although there were an additional 2.6 per cent of detention orders which were suspended.

In Queensland, the number of admonished–discharged outcomes was extremely high (50.5 per cent). Of the remainder, most youths were either placed under supervision (19.1 per cent) or committed to care (18.8 per cent). None was imprisoned.

This high rate of discharge is particularly interesting, given that, on average, only about 30 to 35 per cent of young offenders in Queensland are brought before the children's court in the first place. In fact, of the 12 679 youths officially dealt with by the juvenile justice system in 1989–90, 82.9 per cent received either a police caution or had the charges totally withdrawn or dismissed by the children's court. The number of matters which received an actual penalty was thus relatively small (see Table 2.6).

Table 2.6 Outcomes for all youth interventions in Queensland, 1989–90

Outcomes		n	%
Cautions		8305	65.5
Children's court:	Not proven: discharged/withdrawn	119	0.9
	Proven: admonished/discharged	2089	16.5
	Proven: other outcome	2054	16.2
Referred to higher court		109	0.9
Total		12679	100.0

Of the six states analysed, Victoria is the only one which did not have a large proportion of its children's court matters dismissed. In fact, in 1990 only 3.1 per cent of major charges were dismissed without conviction. The penalty most frequently imposed was that of a 'good behaviour bond adjourned' (31.0 per cent) and 'good behaviour-recognisance' (18.2 per cent). Fines accounted for a further 24.0 per cent of all major charge outcomes, while detention orders accounted for only 3.8 per cent.

The only data on children's court outcomes available for Tasmania relate specifically to the southern portion of the state. However, these were judged to be fairly representative of the whole. As in South Australia, the outcome most frequently imposed was admonish and discharge, accounting for 34.4 per cent of all offences proven. Of the other penalties, the one most often imposed was that of probation (30.3 per cent). Fines were used rather sparingly (9.2 per cent) while the number of major charges which attracted a sentence of imprisonment was extremely low (0.2 per cent).

Number of youths in juvenile corrective institutions

One clear finding to emerge from the preceding discussion is the very small proportion of custodial orders. But given the substantial differences from one jurisdiction to another in the absolute number of cases processed by the court, these outcomes provide little insight into the number of youths held in each state's juvenile corrective institutions at any one time.

Figures presented in Table 2.7 detail, for each of the six states, the numbers of juveniles ten to seventeen years of age in juvenile corrective institutions who, at 30 June 1991, were actually serving a sentence of detention.[7] Rates per 1000 population are also presented.

Table 2.7 Persons aged 10–17 years in juvenile corrective institutions serving detention orders, June 1991

	NSW	Vic	Qld	WA	SA	Tas
Number	210	41	50	68	21	2
Rate per 1000 youth	31.0	8.1	13.7	34.3	13.2	3.6

Source: Australian Institute of Criminology: Persons in Juvenile Corrective Institutions, June 1991, no. 55

Once again, Western Australia had the highest rate of detention of the six states listed—namely, 34.3 per 1000 youth population. It was closely followed by New South Wales, with a rate of 31.0 per 1000 youth. These two figures are considerably higher than those of the other states. As shown, both Queensland and South Australia had a detention rate of only 13.7 and 13.2 per 1000 youth population while Tasmania recorded the lowest rate of 3.6 per 1000 population.

Nevertheless, it should be stressed that, even in Western Australia and New South Wales, the actual numbers involved were relatively small in comparison with the total youth population in those states. In New South Wales for example, on 30 June 1991, only 210 youths ten to seventeen years of age were serving detention orders out of a total population of some 676 462 young people. By comparison, in South Australia, only 21 young people out of a total population of 158 795 were serving a sentence of detention, and only two out of 56 144 in Tasmania.

These very low numbers are not unexpected given that relatively few youths ever come into contact with the justice system in the first place and that, of those who do, only a very small proportion are ever given a custodial order by the court.

Conclusion

Despite the difficulties of comparing juvenile justice processing across state jurisdictions, this analysis found little empirical evidence to substantiate various media claims that juvenile crime is 'out of control'. Overall, only a very small proportion of young people ever come into contact with the official justice system. Moreover, in five of the six states examined, the rate of official intervention either remained constant during the 1980s or showed only a slight increase.

The one exception is Western Australia. This state, in fact, fares poorly on a number of measures. It has by far the highest rate of processing of the six states examined. It is the only state in which processing rates escalated dramatically during the 1980s. Its diversionary panel system has been clearly underutilised, which means that most young people are dealt with by the children's court and thus leave the system with a criminal record. And finally, it has the highest juvenile detention rate of the six states. Yet even in this state, figures for 1989–90 and 1990–91 show a substantial decrease in appearance rates. Although there is some debate about the cause of this decline, it does indicate that the situation in Western Australia is improving, despite media claims to the contrary.

Another finding to emerge from this inter-jurisdictional comparison, which tends to run counter to prevailing community perceptions, is that juveniles are not heavily involved in very serious offending. In the main, they are more likely to be charged with offences against property and, in particular, larceny and shoplifting. By contrast, offences against the person, which are regarded as more serious, account for only a small proportion of all major charges.

While information on the background characteristics of young offenders is generally lacking, the available data suggest that they are more likely to be drawn from the disadvantaged or marginalised sections of the community: they are more likely to be black, to be unemployed and to come from non-normative family situations. Inevitably the reasons for this are complex. While it may be true that Aboriginal and unemployed youth commit more offences, there is also evidence that the justice system itself discriminates against such individuals. Gale, Bailey-Harris and Wundersitz (1990) for example, found that factors such as unemployment influenced the decisions taken at each level of the system, and this applied irrespective of the nature or circumstances of the offence or the young person's prior offending record. They therefore concluded that the over-representation of Aboriginal and unemployed youth in the system was, at least in part, a product of class bias.

Another point worthy of comment is the high number of children's court matters which resulted in a warning or a dismissal compared with the extremely small proportion finalised by way of detention. Such results have tended to fuel public claims that the courts are too lenient on young offenders. Alternatively, they may indicate that the nature of offending by most young people is not serious enough to warrant more punitive dispositions. But perhaps the most important fact to emerge from this attempt at an inter-jurisdictional comparison is the absence of a national data base which would make such comparisons more accurate and comprehensive. The difficulties encountered in this exercise were more numerous than originally anticipated and constitute a strong argument for a standardised system of data recording and publication.

Notes

1 The ACT and the NT have been omitted because of the difficulty of obtaining accurate data on the numbers of youth processed by the justice system.

2 In South Australia, for example, in 1990–91 the 'clear-up' rate for homicide was 98.1 per cent compared with only 7.1 per cent for break–enter (Annual Report of the South Australian Police Department, 1990–91).

3 One of the main criticisms levelled against informal processing mechanisms is that they widened the net of social control. In other words, rather than dealing with young offenders who would otherwise have been processed through the courts, they brought into the official justice system those children who would previously have remained outside of it (Seymour, 1988: 233).

4 In Tasmania, although a formal police cautioning system for juveniles is sanctioned in Police Standing Orders (109.6), cautions are, it seems, used extremely infrequently—so infrequently, in fact, that the Tasmanian Department of Community Services, as part of its proposals for reform in that state, has called for the establishment of a 'police warning or cautioning system . . . as a front line in the juvenile justice system' (Dept of Community Services, 1991:24). Because Tasmania lacks a viable diversionary system, it has been omitted from the following discussion.

5 To illustrate, there is considerable variation from one state to another in how offences are defined and categorised. There arc also inconsistencies in the type of data presented. In South Australia, Victoria, New South Wales and Western Australia, information on the offence is provided for all matters, irrespective of whether they are resolved informally by way of a police caution or panel hearing or are dealt with formally by the children's court. By contrast, in Queensland and Tasmania, only those offences finalised by the children's court are presented, with no information being provided on offences committed by youths selected for a police caution. The absence of cautioning data is not a problem for Tasmania because of the extremely small number of cases dealt with in this manner. However, it constitutes a major shortcoming in relation to Queensland, where almost 70 per cent of young offenders are cautioned each year. For this reason, Queensland has been omitted from the ensuing analysis.

Even for those states where comprehensive data for both cautions, panels and courts are available, different units of measurement are used. In South Australia, Victoria and New South Wales, the data relate only to the most serious charge finalised at a given hearing, whereas for Western Australia, all offences dealt with are detailed, not just the most serious per case. Moreover, there is some interstate variation in how the major charge is defined.

6 This is an important distinction given that in states such as South Australia, usually only the major charge attracts an actual penalty while the other offences dealt with at the same hearing are dismissed without penalty or conviction. This means that if analysis is based on the outcomes recorded for each charge, then the number of dismissals would be exaggeratedly high.

Even if analysis is restricted to the major charge outcome, variations from one state to another in the range of sentencing options available to the children's court, combined with differences in data recording systems, still make it difficult to compare court penalties across jurisdictions. For this reason, no attempt has been made to integrate the data into a single table. It should also be noted that major charge outcomes were not available for Tasmania as a whole. Instead the only up-to-date statistics which could be obtained for that jurisdiction covered southern Tasmania only and related to the outcomes imposed for all offences dealt with, not just the major charge. Hence, it is not directly comparable with the other states.

7 Youths who were on remand awaiting finalisation of their court cases have not been included; nor have youths aged over seventeen years old being held in these centres.

Part II

Philosophical perspectives

3 Welfare and justice: incompatible philosophies

JOHN PRATT

Imagine a meeting between two people whose business temporarily brings them together. The exact location of the meeting is not important—it is just somewhere transitory, a neutral venue such as a club, an airport departure lounge or a hotel conference room—a place where people on such business matters come and go. The business meeting on this occasion is something of an enforced encounter, and neither party is really looking forward to it. They represent different interests in the matter, but must work out a resolution to it before they are thankfully allowed to go their separate ways. But why the antipathy between the two? First, they look completely different and the differences make them uneasy in each other's company. One is somewhat older than the other and dresses in a rather conservative but elegant fashion, and has the poise and confidence that is acquired through involvement in a profession that carries high status. The younger person is dressed altogether more casually: if male, he is wearing a sports jacket and corduroy trousers, sports a beard and an earring, and is zealous and earnest rather than assured and confident. In addition to their very different social and professional backgrounds, there is another problem. They have great difficulty in understanding each other, since they speak a different language from each other. Some words and concepts may sound familiar, but communication is made with the greatest difficulty. Indeed, they could be talking about two completely different matters.

Let it be understood that these two characters are stereotypes. They represent a lawyer and a social worker, and the setting which brings them together is a juvenile court which the legislative history of jurisdictions such as England and Wales has decreed must incorporate them both as well as the different perspectives they represent in discharging its business. The social worker is the representative of a tradition which decrees that the court must act in 'the best interests of the child' (s.1. *Children and Young Persons Act* 1933 [Eng.])—and should therefore make whatever order is

38

appropriate to serve those interests when coming to a decision in each particular case. The lawyer's presence necessitates that the business of the court be conducted in a strictly juridical way. Once guilt has been established, a sanction must be imposed which fits the lawyer's typical expectations of justice. There should be consistency in sentencing, the sanction should be appropriate to the offence rather than the offender and should be as low as possible on the available tariff scale of punishment.

The subsequent confusion and lack of understanding given the differing concepts, histories, training, traditions and languages that each of these key representatives (social worker and lawyer) brings with them should be of no surprise to us, as has been periodically illustrated in the development of juvenile justice systems in Australia, England and Wales. The criticisms by magistrates of the English *Children and Young Persons Act* 1969 were not simply that the legislation did not seem to be working very effectively and was not sufficiently punitive; it had also let social workers into the juvenile courts (replacing the more traditional probation officers). The social workers did not know how things worked; they themselves looked 'different'. Here, then, as in any other contest when two people are brought together from different backgrounds and speaking different languages, confusion is likely to arise and their concerns can appear to be mutually incompatible.

Clearly such divisions and antipathies are not typical of all juvenile justice jurisdictions. No doubt in some there are different traditions which allow social workers and lawyers to work much more effectively together. And it might be thought that much more forceful differences exist between say, police and social workers. Nonetheless, I have used the particular example to try to show how two crucial parties in the administration of juvenile justice are frequently forced to work together in this setting, as a result of the legislative history of a jurisdiction like that of England and Wales.

The end product of this history has been an amalgam of these two different traditions that the social worker and the lawyer in my example represent—what is known as the welfare model on the one hand and the justice model on the other—concepts discussed earlier by Naffine. Thus in this Anglo–Welsh system we find the format of the 'individualised juvenile court'. Its main features are the retention of the basic procedure and approach of the criminal court, but with the court sittings made private, and with an injection into the court proceedings of a more individualised approach to, and concern for, each young person appearing there. This is evident in both the general attitude of the court to children and their parents, and in the kinds of sanctions available to it (Bottoms, 1984). However, as I will attempt to demonstrate by reference to developments in this system over the course of the last two decades, the problem resulting from this amalgamation seems to reflect an inherent and inevitable tension between the combined welfare and justice goals of juvenile justice. The two, I will argue, simply cannot work coherently together. Naffine has discussed these two theoretical approaches mainly in the Australian context. To develop my argument, I will look at developments in the Scottish juvenile justice system and compare them with the juvenile jurisdictions in England and Wales.

In Scotland there seems to be as complete a commitment to a welfare model of juvenile justice as it is possible to find. And this seems to have successfully avoided the range of problems that have occurred in England. These two jurisdictions are exemplars of what, I would argue, is the fundamental incompatibility of welfare and justice models.

The welfare model

From the late nineteenth century until the 1960s, there had, in effect, been only one way forward for juvenile justice policy in the western world—at least as far as penal reformers were concerned. They were committed to what we now recognise as the welfare model.

The initial aim of welfare reformers was simply to separate child offenders from their adult counterparts to ensure that they would not be contaminated, and become even more inclined to criminality. Thus the late 19th century saw the development of juvenile reformatories in Britain, initially as the result of the pioneering work of Mary Carpenter. This shift in thinking was mirrored in the United States with the growth of the 'childsaving' movement (Platt, 1969)—the work of mainly middle-class (often women) reformers, again determined to 'save' child offenders from being contaminated by their adult counterparts and, more generally, by the vices of urban life (hence the building of reformatories out in the countryside away from such influences).

From these initiatives, aimed at providing separate *institutions* for juveniles, the next stage in the reform program was the provision of separate *systems* of justice for juveniles—based on a recognition that juvenile offenders were 'different' from adults, and should have a special status in law. Again, there was fear of contamination if they were not separated from adults. Indeed, in the early years of the twentieth century, when the pressure for juvenile justice reform was building (particularly in the United States), some extraordinary claims were made about the shift in the form of justice that was being advocated. One writer described the juvenile court movement as 'toiling to prepare for the building of the Kingdom of childhood on earth'. Another writer, himself a juvenile court judge, declared the newly constituted juvenile court to be 'the best plan for the conservation of human life and happiness ever conceived by civilised man' (see Parsloe, 1978: 59).

The *Children Act* 1908 established a separate juvenile justice system in England and Wales: sittings were to be in private and a specific system of penalties for juveniles was introduced. Subsequent developments and further reforms have produced the 'individualised juvenile court' format denoted earlier. This is not to say that there was a straightforward unilinear path towards such policy development. In the 1920s, for example, attempts to take the juvenile justice system further along a welfare trajectory by abolishing corporal punishment and raising the age of criminal responsibility were rejected (see Bailey, 1987).

The welfare model in England and Wales reached its highwater mark with the introduction of the *Children and Young Persons Act* 1969. The Act had a number of goals. It was directed towards phasing out existing punitive sanctions in the juvenile justice system such as detention, attendance centres and borstal training, as well as disposing of cases prior to court, where possible, through consultation between social services and the police. Dealing with cases informally would, it was argued, avoid the stigma of court appearances and the subjection of mainly working-class juvenile offenders to the scrutiny of unsympathetic middle-class magistrates. But at the same time—and importantly for the purposes of the welfare model this form of disposition would not only take children away from courts but allow for early intervention by appropriate experts in child care. Indeed, prior to the Act, there was criticism that the police caution per se meant that:

> the police are in this way taking the place of the professional experts who assess the child's needs . . . and of the trained social case workers who help him . . . They are not trained to recognise or to deal with the cases where deep emotional disturbance is present . . . the only tool they have is the threat of a court charge (Cavenagh, 1957:203).

This concern led to a provision in the 1969 Act prescribing pre-court consultation and liaison between police and social work agencies to prevent prosecution and to provide appropriate treatment and assistance. The Act also determined that the court would be a place of investigation and enquiry, trying to find a course of action which would resolve the problem thought to have led to a child's offending. To this end social workers (the child-care experts) would replace probation officers in the court, and would prepare reports for court. Sanctions would allow for full investigation into a child's background, would be non-punitive and quasi-indeterminate in nature and fitted to a child's needs rather than determined in advance by court order. This led to plans for the establishment of observation and assessment centres and intermediate treatment programs. The latter sanction was designed for delinquents and children at risk, a kind of midway stage between long-term residential provision and remaining at home.

The same hyperbole which was associated with the earlier juvenile justice reforms accompanied the introduction of the 1969 Act. For example, Boss (1967:91) in describing the reforms that were subsequently introduced in the 1969 legislation in England and Wales, observed that: 'the whole purpose . . . is to concentrate on treatment needs, and therefore what is done for a child is done in the interests of his welfare'. Then there is the remarkable claim made by Joan Cooper (1970:16) about the intermediate treatment sanction:

> A program of group activities to absorb aggressive feelings, to use up the abundant physical energy, and to enable adolescents to test their strength and abilities in acceptable but exciting and sometimes a dangerous way—for adolescents want to live dangerously before the inertia of middle age overwhelms them— will only be creative if it embraces a variety of young people who have the same needs but too few ways of expressing them without too much discomfort for the rest of us. But "muscular" groups alone offer a restricted program if we do not also provide in these situations for the artistic, musical and rhythmic talent of the young; above all for their yearning to learn more about man and his place in society and the universe.

More generally, the shift away from the procedures of adult criminal justice was most notable in the generic referrals to the juvenile justice system, so that it could accommodate both dangerous children and children in danger (Donzelot, 1979)—young offenders on the one hand and lost, abandoned, neglected or abused children on the other. Furthermore, such matters as the relaxing of formal procedures, the growing importance of social workers, and dispositions of an indeterminate nature (which were designed to 'meet the needs' of individual children) made for a very different approach and a very different language of justice from the adult court. As Boss (1967) indicates above, so great was the faith in the welfare model that its advocates assumed that justice would result without the need for procedural safeguards.

The justice model

By the 1970s the welfare model was beginning to seem increasingly ineffective, given the apparent growth of juvenile delinquency (at least as indicated by rising crime statistics) in most western countries. Indeed, in England, the 1969 Act was, in large part, held to be responsible for this growth because, as right-wing politicians claimed, it seemed to condone rather than punish juvenile crime (see Taylor, Lacey and Bracken, 1980). The welfare model also seemed expensive. Those involved in the planning of treatment-type institutions for young offenders established under the auspices of the welfare model often seemed oblivious to the costs of their programs (which, incidentally, achieved unsatisfactory results in terms of preventing further crime amongst their recipients).

It was in response to such criticisms that an alternative juvenile justice discourse—justice itself—began to emerge. Its characteristics are contrasted with those of the welfare model in Table 3.1.

Table 3.1 Models of juvenile justice

Parameter	Welfare	Justice
Characteristics	Informality	Due process
	Generic referrals	Offending
	Individualised sentencing	Least restrictive intervention
	Indeterminate sentencing	Determinate sentences
Key personnel	Child-care experts	Lawyers
Key agency	Social work	Law
Tasks	Diagnosis	Punishment
Understanding of client behaviour	Pathological	Individual responsibility
Purpose of intervention	Provide treatment	Sanction behaviour
Objectives	Respond to individual needs	Respect individual rights

In many respects, the justice model represented an inversion of the welfare model. It stipulated that the process of juvenile justice should be reorganised. This would mean the abandonment of the 'closed, informal and non-adversarial proceedings in the juvenile courts' (Morris 1978), and its replacement by due process, right to counsel, and visible and accountable decision-making (Morris et al. 1980). In effect, such ideas necessitated a return to what has been referred to as a *Gesellschaft* legal process. This style of justice

> emphasises formal procedure, impartiality, adjudicative justice, precise legal provisions and definitions and the rationality and predictability of legal administration. It distinguishes sharply between law and administration, between the public and the private, the legal and the moral, between the civil obligation and the criminal offence (Kamenka and Tay, 1975:137).

After adjudication of guilt, the court should then impose punishment. This would get 'rid of individualized (i.e. discriminatory) penalties, indefinite periods of control and wide discretion' (Morris and McIsaac, 1978:155). Here was a reform movement, then, which resurrected long-discarded ideas of classical penology, such as the moral obligation to inflict punishment and the right to receive it, the need for certainty in punishment, and approximation of punishment to the degree of harm done.

For the justice movement, there was a necessity to impose punishment. This would constitute retribution, but in a precise and restricted form. It would entail the least restrictive intervention, minimum programs rather than maximum, and community-based rather than custodial sentences. Moreover, such punishment was to be worked out in accordance with penological mathematics.

There was thus no scope for open-ended and indefinite social work intervention. At the same time, the specificity of the offence (rather than a generic set of problems) was to determine the form and mode of administration of punishment.

Amalgamating welfare and justice

Given their differing histories, it is hardly surprising that there is an inherent
tension between the two models of justice. Developments in the Anglo-
Welsh jurisdiction from the 1960s through to the 1980s illustrate that any
attempt to integrate them—to marry what are thought to be the best features
of both—not only highlights these tensions but may lead to an immeasurably
worse hybrid model.

The problems of combining the two began in England and Wales with
the *Children and Young Persons Act* 1969. It paved the way for the
introduction of social workers, indeterminate care orders and the like.
However, the framework of the formal criminal justice system was retained.
Existing punitive sanctions, such as detention centres were retained, as was
the adversarial setting of the juvenile court. This meant that social workers
were compelled to have a dialogue with lawyers and members of the
judiciary about their clients. Given the different languages of justice they
speak (the one whose etymology seemed to be derived from 'needs', the
other from 'rights'), it should hardly be surprising that there was little
mutual understanding between them.

Then in 1982, and partly as a response to the burgeoning criticisms of
welfare ideas and practices (see e.g. Thorpe et al., 1980), the *Criminal
Justice Act* 1982 attempted to incorporate further elements of the justice
model into the juvenile justice system. For example, in an attempt to legislate
for the principles of least intervention, the autonomy of the judiciary and
its power to impose custodial sentences was considerably restricted under
s.1(4). Custodial sentences could not be imposed unless non-custodial
penalties had already been tried with the particular offender or the
seriousness of the offence merited such a disposition. Furthermore, any
notion of the 'therapeutic community' associated with the Borstal training
sentence was abolished and replaced with the determinate sentence of 'youth
custody' (s.6). Also, in accordance with a stronger justice approach, the
Act was accompanied by further resources for the development of
alternative-to-custody programs and diversion for court schemes—both
initiatives being justified by the principle of least restrictive intervention.

Indeed, the popularity of diversion has led, in some parts of England
and Wales, to the development of a separate tariff system outside of the
court, and the development of penalties which are designed to minimise
the reaction to offending and also to take note of different kinds and
quantities of delinquent behaviour. To meet these demands in one area, for
example, a five-tier framework has been developed: 'no further action;
instant warning caution; warning by police sergeant; inspector's warning;
official caution' (Devon and Cornwall Constabulary, 1984). Thus the practice
of diversion in the justice model framework has lost all of its rehabilitative
overtones. However, the development of court diversion programs in the
1980s has had the perverse effect of undermining the power and authority
of the judiciary. It has also considerably enhanced the discretionary power

of social workers. This can be seen in the development of the precourt cautioning sector, where various organisations have become involved in the establishment of multiagency tribunals and juvenile bureaux. Take the following example:

> [the bureau] employs full time a social worker, probation officer, youth worker, teacher and police officer, and is administered by a management team consisting of local managers of the represented agencies . . . Team members . . . undertake the consultation process involving all the parent agencies and possibly some others as well, for example, the education welfare service and child guidance clinic (Northampton Juvenile Liaison Bureau, 1982:2).

A large majority of juvenile offenders are now diverted from court and cautioned: 86 per cent of males aged ten to thirteen in 1988, 60 per cent of males aged fourteen to sixteen in the same year (Home Office Statistics, 1989). Meanwhile, some of the tribunals that dispense justice in this way have become more court-like in form and have developed their own 'tariff' and range of sanctions:

> in straightforward cases, a file is closed when confirmation of the disposal is received from the police. When there is some further involvement this may range from supervising an apology, administering voluntary agreements to pay compensation, organising reparation, referring cases to other agencies, getting youngsters involved in community activities or undertaking to visit a family periodically for a length of time to monitor a child's progress (Northampton Juvenile Liaison Bureau, 1985:25).

In effect, administrative, rather than judicial, decision-making has become the most predominant form of justice dispensation.

The discretion of social workers in the administration of juvenile justice has also increased with the development of alternatives to custody projects. This has meant that the concept of intermediate treatment has changed markedly since Cooper's lyrical consideration of its possibilities (1970). These originally took the form of outward-bound type projects, then changed to more focused forms of group work in the late 1970s. In the last decade the main thrust of intermediate treatment has been towards providing facilities for diverting young offenders from custody (see Pratt, 1987). In these respects, the innovatory and discretionary powers of social workers have actually increased because the statutory vagueness of the sanction has remained largely unchanged since the 1969 Act. Program content is likely to be dependent on whatever they think is appropriate, depending on their own interests and local resources. This has led to considerable variation in the dispensation of punishment (which again seems to be in contradiction to justice model principles of uniformity and consistency).

In different parts of the country, an intermediate treatment condition in a supervision order (intended to function as an alternative to custody) may take such forms as community service or 'tracking' (consistent checking by the 'tracker' on the offender, whether by phone or visits to home, school or workplace) or derivatives of tracking (such as 'intensive befriending', which seem to involve 'shadowing' the offender as closely as possible) or a 'wagon train' adventure elsewhere (a kind of camping tour through the more remote parts of the British Isles). One project, known as 'linking', even involves the offender bringing a 'guest' home:

> in one scheme the linker lived with the family every weekend for a month and was responsible for the linkee from Friday at 4.30 p.m. until Monday at 8.30 p.m. The linkee in question had been involved in the commission of offences during the weekend period for some considerable time and this input over a relatively short period is effective and gives time for other less intensive alternatives to be worked out between the linkee, their family and the linker and caseholder (Thorpe, 1983: 2).

Additionally, in many projects, it seems that social workers have chosen to award themselves powers to deal with their clients' non-compliance rather than sending cases back to court for judicial punishment. For example,

> Minor breaches or problems will be dealt with by counselling and/or restriction of privileges etc. If these should continue, or when serious violations occur, the young person will be recalled to the residential unit and a conference held, in order to discuss reasons for the action, and to outline new objectives as necessary, with return to the community in mind. (Coventry PACE, n.d.: 3).

There would seem to be no doubt that some of these initiatives have been successful in restricting custodial sentencing. In England and Wales it declined from 7400 young offenders aged fourteen to sixteen in 1978 to 3200 in 1988, although custodial sentences as a percentage of court dispositions remained static at 13 per cent (Home Office Statistics, 1989). But this success should not be overstated. Other factors such as demographic change (Pratt, 1984) are also likely to have played a significant part in bringing about this reduction. Indeed, it remains a matter of conjecture as to whether, by simply restricting the sentencing power of the judiciary, some of this decline would have taken place anyway, without the vast and diverse range of projects now representing themselves as alternatives to custody.

What also seems inevitable is that some projects have led to net-widening: that is, more young people have been brought into the juvenile justice system because police have chosen to caution them rather than deal with them informally as they might have done if the diversion programs had not existed. They may also have encouraged an 'up-tariffing'; that is, giving alternative-to-custody dispositions to those juvenile offenders who might otherwise have received a less severe penalty such as a fine or discharge.

However, the empirical evidence for such contentions remains slight (see e.g. Ditchfield, 1976 on the effects of cautioning).

These developments raise other contentious issues. First, the wide-ranging differences in the form that intermediate treatment might take seems contrary to justice model principles (by which rhetoric such initiatives are usually justified). It also seems contrary to principles of natural justice by virtue of the fact that the form such punishment takes is likely to depend on its geographical location. Second, the commitment to justice model policies has increased (or at least extended into new areas) the discretionary power of social workers. That this now takes place under the guise of a different model of juvenile justice does not make it any less contentious than it was during the heyday of the welfare model and the attempt to redirect the Anglo-Welsh system along its lines.

Even if we cast the most favourable light on the effects of policy development in the 1980s, we must ponder the question of whether these ends justify the means to achieve them. For example, was there no other way of saving some juvenile offenders from custody other than by developing coercive and intrusive community-based sanctions which might have a much wider use?

One model system of justice

At this stage I want to stress that my main criticism of the effects of amalgamating two models of juvenile justice within the Anglo-Welsh jurisdiction relates to the way in which it has lent itself to intensified forms of control in the community while maintaining penal institutions, and enhancing the discretionary power of social workers. Indeed the very language of social workers has been modified in the course of this amalgamation to become a form of 'social control talk' (Cohen, 1985). The lesson to be learned is that if we wish to avoid such unwelcome developments, then we must recognise the incompatibility of the two concepts and the mutation produced by their amalgamation. Indeed, developments in 'one system' jurisdictions suggest that it is possible to avoid these unworkable tensions and unwanted effects. I will go on to suggest that a 'one system' jurisdiction may result in a style of justice which satisfies all parties concerned. In contrast to the history of partial accommodation and adaptation that lies behind current developments in England and Wales, full commitment to a welfare model in Scotland has produced very different results and has not engendered any significant pressure for change. The fact that the Scottish welfare model survived intact despite the right-wing social policy programs of successive Thatcher governments in Britain in the 1980s is, itself, a testament to its local popularity.

Advocacy of the welfare model, in the light of the foregoing criticisms, might seem strange, if not blatantly contradictory. I believe, though, that a case can be made for this position. But first let us consider the Scottish welfare model in some detail. Since the introduction of *The Social Work (Scotland) Act* 1968, the juvenile justice system has been well described by Stewart and Tutt (1987:21):

> Children who were deemed to be in need of compulsory measures of care were referred to a lay hearing as opposed to a court. The reasons why a child might be deemed to be in need of compulsory measures of care included allegations that a child was beyond the control of his parents, that he failed to attend school regularly without reasonable excuse, or that lack of parental care was likely to cause the child unnecessary suffering or seriously impair his health or development that he himself had been offended against. No distinction was made between those children who were referred on an allegation that an offence had been committed by the child, and the other grounds. Whatever the grounds, the welfare principle of whatever was in the best interests of an individual child was to be the sole criterion for decision making.

For offenders under the age of sixteen, disputed cases go to the Sheriff's court for adjudication. Other cases go to the lay hearings—or children's hearings as they are known—for disposition and treatment. These hearings are administered by lay people (usually with a social work or education background), and the only orders available are (i) no further action, (ii) supervision, or (iii) a residential order. Prior to this, each case will have been screened by the 'Reporter' (a lawyer with a social work background) and will only be sent on to a hearing if it is thought that compulsory intervention is necessary. In 1985, there were 25 100 offence referrals to the Reporter who subsequently sent on 9900 to the hearings (Stewart and Tutt 1987:25). Cases may also be referred back to the police or social work departments.

In 1983, a review of the 1968 Act rejected an attempt to put the children's hearings on a more judicial footing and to confer on the panel the power to impose fines and conditional discharges. It appears, then, that the large majority of cases are dealt with informally or that no action is taken. In their sample of 301 hearings (dealing mainly with offenders), Martin et al. (1981:97) found that 94 cases were discharged, supervision orders were made in 171 and a form of residential supervision was ordered in 36. Stewart and Tutt (1987:25), however, show a somewhat different pattern of outcomes: 6000 cases were discharged, 6400 led to supervision and 2000 entailed a residential order. The statistics, though, are somewhat ambiguous since they include outcomes of offence and non-offence cases. Importantly, no alternative to custody domain has been introduced to this system, perhaps because of lack of need, or perhaps because the system itself does not allow the space for it. If residential orders are only made in a child's best interests, as it is claimed, there is no point in trying to prevent them.

As to the administration of justice itself, then certainly some procedural slackness has been observed in the conduct of the hearings. In some cases information might be kept from families, or they might not be told of their right to appeal against the decision (Martin et al., 1981). At the same time, the dialogue that takes place therein tends to be commonsensical rather than being overlaid with treatment and rehabilitative mystique. Martin et al., (1981:138) comment that:

> panel members focused on a number of obvious areas of enquiry that are usually included in the reports, such as attendance record and behaviour at school and behaviour at home and in the community. They seemed to look for formal and informal responsibilities of children and parents in respect of these areas of life and sometimes to offer suggestions about ways of approaching these that might be more constructive. *A good deal of the dialogue did not appear to reflect any systematic searching for the specific etiology of the child's behaviour . . . What panel members strikingly did not do in the language of hearings was echo the terminology and thought processes of any professional group. The imperviousness of panel members to social work or any other professional language and ideology is manifest in our study of the dialogue of the hearings* (my emphasis).

The hearings also seem to produce large numbers of satisfied customers: 'in general parental response to the hearing was extremely favourable in certain key respects. In terms of perceived informality and ease of communication, the majority of parents spoke very positively of their experiences. Most parents also felt that they had understood everything that had happened' (Martin et al., 1981:233). Again, this stands in contrast to the consumer views of the Anglo-Welsh system of the same period. Parker et al. (1981) highlight the perception of the lack of fairness and the lack of understanding experienced by the consumers of that system.

In short, the Scottish system seems to have developed without the punitive aspects of the Anglo-Welsh model, and without the trappings and rhetoric of welfare that were so discredited in the 1970s. Interestingly, Asquith (1983) illustrates that the members of the children's panels 'think' about juvenile justice in a very different way from magistrates sitting in the Anglo-Welsh juvenile courts. This is partly because of their training and partly because of the structure of the system of justice itself. He suggests that systems of justice structure the 'frames of relevance' through which its participants come to understand the problem of delinquency. The Scottish welfare setting means that 'the frames of relevance espoused by the panel members were predominantly concerned with the social, environmental and personal characteristics of the children' (Asquith, 1983:210). This stands in contrast to the juvenile court magistrates in England and Wales whose frames of relevance are preoccupied with intention, guilt and punishment. Thus 'more concerned with welfare considerations, panel members will interpret information and reports about offenders generally in terms of the need for care rather than in terms of what he has done' (Asquith, 1983:212).

At the same time, it seems clear from the research of Martin et al. (1981) that the panel members do not allow their concerns for the welfare of children to become clouded by social work rhetoric. Furthermore, the emphasis on the welfare of children is a qualitatively different objective from that of the 'linkers' and 'trackers' in the Anglo-Welsh model whose purpose is to prevent custodial sentences. It is in the name of this latter objective that the innovative and controversial alternatives to custody have been developed.

In other words, Scotland seems to have overcome the problems of the welfare model by adopting a minimalist approach to juvenile delinquency. This is also the case in the Scandinavian countries which have developed a pure-welfare model. In Norway and Denmark it was observed that:

> [juvenile institutions] have been largely abolished, with no community-based replacements and there also seems to be a general consensus in the welfare boards: delinquency has only a very low profile and intervention is kept to a minimum. Accordingly, there is very little space for the development of a community corrections/ community control industry. As such, 'welfare' discourse and practice would seem to have produced very different results indeed from 'justice' counterparts (Pratt, 1985:47).

What of the previous criticisms of the welfare model? In the Scottish context, a number of replies come to mind. First, the criticisms themselves may have been exaggerated, based on anecdote rather than empirical data. Second, the Scottish panel members—the people who make the decisions— are not actually social workers themselves, and are thus not blindly uncritical of benevolent sounding social work rhetoric. Third, although there is still an element of social work discretion within the Scottish model, it seems in practice to be much more limited (e.g. in terms of inflicting penalties, devising new community-based sanctions and so on) than in the Anglo-Welsh system. Fourth, many of the problems in the latter system seem to have been facilitated by the attempted amalgamation of the welfare and justice principles. The pure welfare model in Scotland seems to have avoided these difficulties and produced a qualitatively different justice system. Here there is no penal institution designed specifically to be very unpleasant such as the English short, sharp shock detention centre. It is therefore unnecessary to construct alternative community-based sentences. And in contrast to Scotland, the Anglo-Welsh system, with its language of guilt and responsibility and the presence of police and lawyers, seems to have maximised the problem of delinquency and the level of reaction to it, as we can see in the development of coercive programs of control in the community, which have come to take their place *alongside* (rather than replacing) very punitive institutions.

If in Scotland there seems to be general satisfaction with the existing system, I know of no such satisfaction in those countries where there has been a commitment to the justice model. Perhaps this is because the justice model itself has never, to my knowledge, been fully operationalised but has, in effect, been cobbled with some longstanding ideas about the importance of the welfare of children who appear before the juvenile court. And yet new problems have emerged from the commitment to the justice model. Attempts to introduce diversion schemes have led to net-widening and the extension and enhancement of social control through attempts to introduce alternatives to custody programs. Sarri (1983:70), herself a leading advocate of diversion, rather apologetically states that 'the majority of those who have studied diversion state that about 70 per cent of all youth referred for diversion could just as well be "warned and released" '. Thus, one continuously confronts the conclusion that diversion has first and foremost resulted in an expansion of the juvenile justice system. It appears that systems of justice that are committed to the welfare model do not lend themselves to such developments. Their structure and conceptual parameters do not allow for such initiatives and their resulting problems.

The contrast between the Scottish and Anglo-Welsh systems of juvenile justice would seem to bear out the claim that there is an inherent tension between welfare and justice models. The results of this tension are manifest in the format and framework of the Anglo-Welsh system which moved away from the adult process of justice towards a welfare model and then tried to reintroduce elements of the justice model. It is in such a setting that we are likely to see those awkward, unsatisfactory meetings that I described at the beginning of this chapter. Indeed, in England, the common language has become that of 'social control talk'. North of the border, the wholesale commitment to welfare has produced a very different picture partly, it would seem, because everyone speaks the same language of justice. These developments contain important lessons for Australian juvenile justice which is also trying to amalgamate the incompatible concepts of welfare and justice. Perhaps Australia should reconsider the possibilities of the welfare model on its own.

4 Australia's juvenile justice systems: a comment

JOHN SEYMOUR

I would like to use John Pratt's chapter as the foundation on which to build a plea for a recognition of the special features of Australia's eight juvenile justice systems. There is a need for a close examination of the distinctive history and characteristics of these systems. It follows that we must ask questions about the relevance of overseas experience. It is my view, for example, that the American decision of *In re Gault*[1] has little direct relevance to Australia, although the ideology which it embodied has been extraordinarily influential here. Somehow, that decision and the academic writings which preceded it crystallised Australian doubts about methods of handling young offenders. These doubts give the impression of having been imported, rather than growing out of a careful appraisal of observed deficiencies in our children's courts. I would, therefore, like to see a moratorium on references to *Gault* and on references to that distinctively American product, 'due process'.

First, I must make one or two points relating to significant differences between United States and Australian procedures. Australia's children's courts are modified criminal courts. They are, in the main, presided over by non-specialist, legally trained magistrates (or, in some states, judges). The normal method of bringing young offenders before these courts is by way of specific charges. These facts mark off our courts from the juvenile courts of the United States. In the United States the juvenile court movement was built on the idea of special courts, presided over by special judges (who were not necessarily legally trained) and on a new procedure—the

---

[1] *In Re Gault* (1967), 387 US 1 involved the case of a 15-year-old Arizona youth who was convicted and sentenced to detention for the remainder of his minority for an obscene phonecall. On appeal, the American Supreme Court declared that due process had not been followed. The Court held that Gault was entitled to notice of charges, to legal counsel, to confront his accusers and to the privilege against self incrimination.

52

delinquency petition. The significance of this procedure must be emphasised. It was designed to put in issue the child's background; the court was required to decide, not whether children had committed specific acts, but whether they were a certain sort of child—a 'delinquent'.

It was this procedure which was the source of the problems identified by the Supreme Court of the United States in *Gault*. Whatever the deficiencies in our children's courts (and they are many), they are not the same as those revealed in that decision. *Gault* represented an assault on the foundations of the American juvenile courts. It is because our courts are built on different foundations that we must question the relevance to Australia of the majority opinion. Yet, as I have noted, *Gault* did have reverberations here. What must be recognised is that, whereas it is true to say that in the United States there has been a significant change in direction in juvenile court policy, in this country we are witnessing a change only of emphasis. And there is nothing particularly dramatic about this change. The history of children's courts in Australia is the history of such minor changes (Seymour, 1988:chs. 1–3). Given that the children's courts are modified criminal courts, they have always exhibited some elements of the justice model. They have also always exhibited some elements of the welfare model. The pendulum swings, first one way (are we showing sufficient understanding of our young offenders?) and then the other (are we being too lenient?). Society seems to be in a continuous state of uncertainty about its policy towards young offenders.

Let me list a few examples of concerns which are expressed and re-expressed. In 1885 the South Australian Way Commission indicated its doubts about the failure of reformatories to deliver the promised benefits:

> The state deprives these boys of their liberty, on the understanding that it will give them a reformative training; and so far as it fails in doing this efficiently, an obligation, which it has compelled the other party to the contract to accept, remains unfulfilled. (Second and Final Report of Commission Appointed to Report on the Destitute Act, 1881, S.A.P.P. 1885:4:228 p.94)

These words could just as well have been written in 1985; persons who are familiar with the language used by Mr Justice Fortas in *Gault* will recognise the reference to the gulf between rhetoric and reality.

The Way Commission's comments were part of a chorus of criticism of institutional treatment. Before the end of the nineteenth century the view that, wherever possible, institutional committals should be avoided was widely accepted (Seymour 1988:58–63). Thus a commitment to 'diversion' (in the sense of seeking non-custodial alternatives) is by no means new.

In Western Australia in the 1920s there was a bitter battle over the exercise by welfare authorities of their power to release children from institutions. The children's court magistrate saw this use of administrative discretion as undermining the power of the court. Although he did not use the term, he was airing one of the central complaints of those who today support the justice model. Later that decade, the magistrate who led the campaign was complaining of the perception of his court as giving bad children a pat on the head (Seymour, 1988:123, 135).

Another more recent illustration of our uncertainty also comes from Western Australia. In 1976 a report expressed concern about the system's failure to give proper protection to children's rights, and ten years later another report warned of the danger of focusing too exclusively on the justice model and so ignoring children's needs (Western Australia Department for Community Welfare n.d.:7, 1986:3)

My argument is that, given the origins of our courts, it has been and ever will be thus. Australia's children's court systems represent a distinctive mix of justice and welfare. Further, the nature of this mix is constantly being re-examined. At one time there is a call for more emphasis on justice aspects and, at another, for more emphasis on welfare goals. These calls are usually presented as requests for a 'better balance'. And, most important, these calls seem invariably to be ideologically and not empirically based. They are not based on a careful examination of the day-to-day operations of the systems under attack.

Just what does the current emphasis on the justice model mean in practice? In some jurisdictions we have seen a clarification of the law relating to appeals and to the right to trial by jury. There are also now references in some Acts to legal representation and to evidential rules. But none of these changes is likely to alter the character of what continues to be a modified magistrate's court, dealing (rather speedily) with a large number of relatively minor offences.

It might be answered that it is in the area of sentencing that the proponents of the justice model have wrought the most change. There is some truth in this. The newer legislation includes statements of guiding principles, and these now refer not only to the welfare of young offenders, but also to the need to recognise an offender's individual responsibility (*Children (Criminal Proceedings) Act* 1987 (NSW)). This is a departure from welfare principles, but its significance is difficult to assess. In a small number of exceptional cases the new legislation will make a difference. In the past, there were some cases where the courts felt reluctantly constrained to avoid institutional committals (on the grounds that these were not in the offender's best interests). Under the new statements of objectives some of these cases may now result in committals.

But in the majority of cases, I suggest, it will be business as usual. The children's court magistrates have always employed rough and ready notions of tariff, reserving the more severe measures for the more serious offences. And it should not be overlooked that many young offenders have been, and will continue to be, dealt with by way of discharges and monetary penalties. Concentration on potentially 'therapeutic' measures should not lead us to overlook the courts' routine use of criminal penalties. This reinforces my plea for an understanding of the special nature of Australia's children's courts: their police court origins are not far beneath the surface. It is, therefore, wrong to assume that we have recently experienced a significant change in the direction of proportionate sentencing and a crime–punishment model. The fact that we employ procedures under which children face specific charges inevitably prevents any single-minded preoccupation with children's welfare.

Then there is the question of indeterminacy and administrative discretion. The most blatant example of an indeterminate measure—wardship—has disappeared from the criminal jurisdiction of the children's courts. This is an important move in the direction of the justice model. But institutional committals retain a significant degree of flexibility. There is still considerable room for the exercise of administrative discretion. As far as I am aware, none of the Australian proponents of the justice model has advocated procedures under which the courts determine the exact term of a committal.

And finally, although the treatment rationale has been challenged and there is now a good deal of healthy scepticism in the air, we have not completely abandoned the idealism on which the children's court movement was built. The increased concern with the criminal justice aspects of the system are no more than one thread in the pattern. The foundations laid by the childsavers remain. Although welfare workers, probation officers and institutional staff might all readily agree that they cannot unerringly 'reform' their charges, the majority of them would, I believe, assert that their aim is to bring good influences to bear. The measures which they employ— supervision orders and institutional regimes—will continue to combine control and support, whatever the theorists say.

In short, much remains unchanged. An uneasy mix remains just that. Future historians may regard us as having been blinded, not by the rhetoric of rehabilitation, but by the rhetoric of justice.

There is an additional aspect which must be considered. So far I have been examining what we can learn about the children's court systems when we view them against welfare and justice models. But what models should we employ to analyse the misnamed movement towards 'diversion'? Here I am talking about 'diversion' from the courts. The term is, I believe, an unsatisfactory one, for it suggests removal from a predictable and normal course. To talk of diversion in the criminal justice system is to suggest that the expected destination of all cases is the court and that efforts must be made to send some of them to another destination. In fact, what we are talking about is informal alternatives and these have been a feature of juvenile justice systems for many decades. Police cautions have long been one of the recognised methods of dealing with young offenders. What we have witnessed recently have been determined efforts to expand, formalise and systematise informal responses.

The question which needs to be addressed is: how do we characterise such a policy? Is the 'diversion' movement an offshoot of the justice model? If we talk of crime and punishment, the use of informal alternatives can be seen as the systematic and principled extension of a policy of leniency. This leniency can be seen to be a reflection of the view that children are not fully responsible. Alternatively, resort to informal alternatives can be seen as the best method of 'treating' large numbers of young offenders. If we want to help, it has been realised, often we can do this best by leaving the child alone.

At present, I believe, much analysis of 'diversion' is muddled. Some writers clearly see 'diversion' as an expression of the welfare ideology. For some observers, those who provide informal alternatives have taken on the mantle of the childsavers. The use of these alternatives is seen as an avenue to counselling, follow-up and sustained family support. Yet empirical studies clearly demonstrate that they do not work that way. In Australia, police cautions and panel appearances rarely lead to sustained counselling or follow-up. To put it somewhat provocatively, therefore, it can be said that the development of panels and cautioning is a way of formalising a policy of doing nothing. Quite where this fits in the welfare–justice continuum is not clear.

5   Juvenile justice reform and the symbol of the child

KATHY LASTER

Launching the Australian Labor Party's election campaign of July 1987, the then prime minister, Mr Hawke, vowed that, 'by the year 2000, no Australian child will live in poverty'. The political instinct which drove the Labor Party to make such an emphatic statement was the perceived importance of children to the Australian electorate. Children were used as the symbol for the social and economic priorities of the Labor Government. The promise, instantly lampooned, quickly became a political embarrassment. What had been overlooked was that the electorate was smart and recognised that its own commitment to children was rhetorical rather than real. Paradoxically, the politicians' promise drew attention to the ambivalence of this society to its young. The metaphor had backfired.

This same ambivalence is reflected in the law's attitude to juvenile justice. Its guiding principles, legislative formulation and the rhetoric which surrounds its reform, in whatever direction, are a veneer which hides more complex and often contradictory expectations of children generally and young offenders in particular.

Currently, the dominant ideology is 'back to justice' for juveniles. It developed as a reaction to the excesses of the paternalist approach of the childsavers. Young people who do wrong should not be denied the legal protection and rights afforded to adults in similar circumstances. There is no justification for intrusion and deprivation of the liberty of a young person beyond the right of the state to exact appropriate 'punishment'. Within this threshold of punishment, however, young people should be treated as liberally and generously as possible in recognition of their special vulnerabilities and status within the community (Child Welfare Practice and Legislation Review, 1984:357–61).

The philosophy is easily stated and, at first sight, seems a radical departure from what went before. The old paternalist philosophy allowed children, and girls in particular, to be placed in institutions for extended periods 'for their own good' (Cain, 1989). The current approach has decriminalised juvenile status offences (such as 'exposed to moral danger') so that juvenile offenders can only receive a custodial disposition for an offence which would merit similar punishment in an adult (Murray, 1985:78). This has resulted in a reduction in the number of children in institutions and in the length of time they spend there (noted by Luke elsewhere in this volume).

Like all new reforms, the new philosophy has been greeted as an 'improvement' or 'progress' in society's response to young offenders. Yet our gains may well be illusory and short-lived. In practice, while we have improved the lot of many young people, this has probably been at the expense of the small group who, for various reasons, continue to be part of our juvenile justice and institutional populations. Nor is there any guarantee that apparent gains can necessarily be sustained. 'Back to justice' philosophy reasserts the right of individuals to be held responsible for their actions. Given the volatile nature of public attitudes to both crime and young people, it is not difficult to see how such a philosophy could easily be converted into old fashioned retribution in a new guise.

Attitudes to children

Historians of childhood pose a favourite question: When have children had it 'good'? For Lloyd Demause the history of childhood has been marked by progress and evolution, from barbarism to a kind of civilised acceptance of the rights of the child:

> The history of childhood is a nightmare from which we have only recently begun to awaken. The further back in history one goes, the lower the level of child care, and the more likely children are to be killed, abandoned, beaten, terrorised and sexually abused (De Mause, 1974:1).

Few other writers share Demause's optimism. Neil Postman has warned of the disappearance of childhood through the electronic media, particularly television, which has exposed children to adult secrets and destroyed the characteristics which distinguish them from adults, such as their clothing, food, language and play (Postman, 1982). Such a view turns on its head the thesis of Philippe Aries who regarded the Middle Ages as the golden age for children precisely because the idea of 'childhood' did not exist. According to Aries, children enjoyed great liberty during this period because, from the ages of five to seven, they were integrated into the life of the community, sharing in adult work and play. Progressive centuries created the concept of 'childhood' as a separate entity in order to discipline the next generation to the bourgeois need to preserve wealth (Aries, 1962: part 3).

The search for an ideal 'golden age' for children, however, is misdirected. Far more productive is the examination of the factors which seem to govern the attitude of a particular period to its young. Broadly, these vary according to the perceived utility of children for social organisation, prevailing conceptions of the role of the state and the degree of confidence or optimism a society has in its future.

The social utility of children

The most obvious service that children provide to a society is as 'population'. The value assigned to 'population' has, of course, varied. For some societies a large population has been synonymous with prestige, autonomy and self-sufficiency. In Britain and Australia in the late nineteenth and early twentieth century the falling birth rate was viewed with alarm (Hobsbawm, 1969:chapter 9). Legislative measures such as the introduction of *The Infant Life Protection Act* 1890 (Vic.) were designed to reduce infant mortality by regulating the care of children through control over infanticide and baby farming (Laster, 1989:162–3). In the early twentieth century, increasing attention was paid to the provision of assistance to poor families through universal welfare services such as age pensions, health insurance, school meals and compulsory education (Parton, 1985:36–8).

For other societies, a large and healthy young population served the need to preserve military strength (Donzelot, 1979; Searle, 1971). In the classical period, the development of the human phalanx, which relied on the disciplined formation of large numbers of infantry, assured Sparta's survival and shaped its regimented system of stoic community education for young citizens (Sommerville, 1982:24–7).

Children have also been instrumental members of the labour force. Depending on the mode of production of a given society, a ready and large population of children was necessary to achieve economic objectives (Donzelot, 1979). Shifts in the technology of production, however, meant that child labour competed with adult male labour in the middle of the nineteenth century. Support for child emancipation through protective legislation which regulated and controlled the employment of children grew accordingly (Sommerville, 1982).

A large population, however, is not always desirable. Traditional and neo-Malthusians have regularly sought to limit the size of families through methods ranging from birth control to negative eugenics (Tilly and Scott, 1978:170). Too many children at the wrong time pose a threat to social stability. The apparently large numbers of poor children who constituted about 30 to 40 per cent of the British population at the end of the nineteenth century 'constituted a disquieting alien presence in the midst of mid-Victorian plenty' (G. Steadman-Jones cited in Parton, 1985:28; Walvin, 1982).

The response to this perceived threat to social order was the systematic endeavours of the childsaving movement to set appropriate levels of parental control over their children. Failure to meet these standards warranted intervention to 'save' the child from falling into a life of crime (Platt, 1977; Wilson, 1979). The childsaving movement was therefore a practical resolution to the paradox of children being regarded as both important for the social structure but at the same time constituting a threat to social order.

Nowadays, of course, children are not required as cannon fodder. The technology of war has alleviated the necessity for large numbers of foot soldiers. Nor, in this age of mechanised production, is the labour of children required. Indeed, much of our social policy is directed at keeping children *out* of the workforce for as long as possible (Keeves, 1990:57). We now value 'children' and 'childhood' for different reasons. The 2.2 children in a western nuclear family may be critical for the economy, not as producers, but rather as consumers. The Australian Institute of Family Studies has recently calculated that a one-child, single-income family with a weekly income of $578 gross would spend a total of $171.16 per week on a child aged up to one year. This total weekly expenditure would increase to $206.70 for a child aged between eleven and thirteen years (Australian Institute of Family Studies, 1991:57). Much of our economic activity is geared towards servicing the needs of the child in the family and the culture of youth.

Lurking beneath the surface, however, is a fear of the child who is isolated from the controlling mechanism of the family. 'Homeless youth' have become the target of active strategies of intervention and control by both the private and the public sectors (Alder and Sandor, 1989). Front page headlines such as 'Viet Gang Fear', 'The Copycat Cowards: Thug Gang Runs Wild' and 'The Gang Menace' (cited in Warren, 1991:3) exemplify the often hysterical concern at young people who gather in public places or organise outside of the family into 'gangs'. Although we may freely indulge our children and be kindly disposed towards their foibles whilst they remain within the family, community tolerance for the dependent child eking out an existence, through crime where necessary, is low.

These shifting concerns about the relationship between children, families and the state over time underlie the ideology of the role of the state towards families, children and juvenile justice.

The ideology of the state

There has always been a direct parallel between the state's relationship to the citizen and the parents' relationship to the child. In the seventeenth century, for example, Hobbes maintained that, just as with the sovereign, the relationship between father and child is based on the fear of the absolute power of the father over the child. The child serves the father unquestioningly and is in turn served by the protection and support of the father (Hobbes, 1962).

With the Enlightenment, the father could no longer be allowed to have absolute power over his child. Locke, for example, argues that parents should not have absolute power over their children. Each individual is born with 'natural rights' which must be protected. Children, too, must be accorded progressive degrees of freedom depending on their ability to understand the nature of the social contract (Cleverly and Phillips, 1976: chapter 2).

In the nineteenth century the state was progressively held responsible for the welfare of its citizens. The family, though, was still held sovereign and the emerging liberal state faced the paradox of ensuring that the family remained independent of direct political control (Parton, 1985:26). Thus, if the state accepted the liberal philosophy of individual freedom, contract and responsibility, it could not, at the same time, override those same recently-established freedoms by encroaching into the private sphere of the family.

The paradox was resolved through measures which encouraged the self-sufficiency of families while supporting the education of children to shared social values. Failure by individual families to meet these standards then justified intervention by the state. Initially, such intervention occurred unofficially through voluntary welfare and benevolent agencies (Parton, 1985). By the end of the century, however, the state had been forced to accept direct responsibility for such intervention. At the very least, it allowed these agencies to act with the government's imprimatur (Antler and Antler, 1979).

Once the state had assumed responsibility for controlling the actions of children from wayward families, there was no turning back. The history of juvenile justice in the twentieth century has largely been a balancing act between the respective perceived responsibilities of the child, family, community and the state.

Visions of ourselves

It is wrong, however, to see children and the concept of childhood as having merely instrumental value for societies. Children are also a symbol: they represent the intangible values, hopes and aspirations of a society for itself.

Much has been made of the image of the savage or the primitive as the index to the prevailing western cultural mood (Sinclair, 1977; Pace, 1983). It has become almost a cliché that the 'noble savage' represented the antithesis of the perceived moral and physical decadence of civilisation for philosophers such as Rousseau (1984). What is often overlooked, however, is that the rich culture of childhood throughout the ages has presented the same challenge to the adult world (Factor, 1988). Opinions about the meaning and worth of this 'opposite' culture of childhood, however, have differed. At various times, the innocence, gentleness, beauty and spirituality of the child have been idealised. Shelley's formulation is not untypical:

Know you what it is to be a child? It is to be something very
different from the man of today. It is to have a spirit yet streaming
from the waters of baptism; it is to believe in love; to believe in
loveliness, to believe in belief. It is to be so little that the elves can
reach to whisper in your ear; it is to turn pumpkins into coaches, and
mice into horses, loneliness into loftiness and nothing into

everything, for each child has its fairy godmother in its soul
(P. Shelley, cited in Bartlett, 1977: 857a).

At other times, the dominant attitude to children is that they are uncivilised,
perverse and innately defiant. For these societies the discipline of children
in order to make them into good adults becomes the primary objective. In
the words of the eighteenth-century churchman John Wesley:

Do not 'spare the rod, and spoil the child'. If you have not the
heart of a tiger, do not give up your child to his own will, that is,
to the devil. Though it be pain to yourself, yet pluck your
offspring out of the lion's teeth. Make them submit, that they may
not perish. Break their will, that you may save their soul (Wesley,
1986:367).

Such opinions are advanced to justify the 'education' of children out of
'childhood'.
The dominant attitude to children and childhood is also a reflection of
the society's judgement about the achievements of the adult world. Where
there is confidence in the social order, there is little patience with the
'undisciplined' culture of childhood. For societies uneasy about the apparent
benefits of their world, such as urbanisation and technology, and
apprehensive about the future, childhood is a welcome indulgence. It
represents a period of 'freedom' untainted by the dissatisfactions of adult
life. For Margaret Mead these sentiments combined to provide romantic
accounts of 'opposite' cultures and, in particular, their quite different
approaches to childrearing. The Arapesh, for example, cherish their babies,
indulgently providing them with all their wants, and so these children
never learn the 'grasping action of the mouth' because the readily offered
breast does not have to be 'vigorously seized upon or bitten' (Mead,
1967:65). The controversies over the anthropological interpretation offered
by Mead (Holmes, 1987; Freeman, 1987) are really about the validity of
her critique of western society.
Of course, both 'positive' and 'negative' attitudes to children and
childrearing co-exist at the same time in all societies. William Golding
wrote *Lord of the Flies* (1954), his vicious indictment of the 'true' character
of children, at a time when the dominant view was of childhood as a time
of dependence and vulnerability. The main point, however, is that the
symbol of the child is frequently the battleground for competing images of
the contemporary social order.
The symbols of childhood are often most clearly reflected in attitudes to
juvenile justice. The two dominant paradigms are, on the one hand, children
as responsible actors, accountable for their 'deeds' and, on the other, children
as dependent and vulnerable beings with 'needs' (Australian Law Reform
Commission, 1981: 69; Pratt, 1989). Juvenile justice systems lurch between
these models. Both are indicative of wider social attitudes and represent a

compromise between competing images of childhood and underlying perceptions of the social order. Such compromises must inevitably be political in nature.

Implications for Australian juvenile justice

Australia is a young colonial nation. It has had to develop quick and pragmatic solutions to the problem of 'population'. Throughout its history, immigration has been used as the solution to the pressing problem of shortage of labour and the defence of this white outpost in the midst of Asia (Johnston, 1977; Quinlan, 1979:265–6). We preferred to 'import' the able-bodied fully-grown and then let them fend for themselves without much support: this is a land of 'individual' opportunity because, like that other great colony, the United States of America, we have, by and large, been an optimistic culture. Individuals can succeed in the 'lucky country' because they believe themselves to be spared the problems of the old world (Horne, 1964).

These attitudes have combined to create an ambivalence to children which June Factor has called 'benign neglect' (Factor, 1988:31). Children have neither been seen as a great threat to the social order nor as an idealised embodiment of the values which we have lost. Compared with other nations, perhaps mercifully, there has been little incentive to take juvenile justice and welfare particularly seriously. For example, Australia has seen no major shift from the extreme 'welfare philosophy' of the nineteenth-century childsavers to the formal legalism of 'back to justice'. As John Seymour (1988) so persuasively argues, Australian juvenile justice has always been a compromise between these two different perspectives.

We have, however, tinkered constantly with the legislative formulation of this compromise. In Victoria, for example, there has been a host of changes to juvenile justice and welfare legislation (Child Welfare Practice and Legislation Review, 1984: Appendix One). The same pattern can be found in other states. It is therefore quite inappropriate to talk of a real 'back to justice' movement in Australia because we have never given up using the adult system as the model and yardstick for the juvenile justice system. Children's courts in the criminal jurisdiction were, with the exception of South Australia, offshoots of the adult magistrate's court system, and the standard of proof and most of the dispositional options available to the juvenile courts differed little from their adult counterparts (Seymour, 1988).

We cannot, however, afford to be too smug. The systems that we have created are riddled with injustice for young people, which is all the more pernicious because it is frequently subtle. This is demonstrated in the bifurcation of the juvenile justice system, the development of extra-legal mechanisms of punishment and control, and through progressively diminishing resources devoted to young people in trouble in our community.

Bifurcation

There is no doubt that the de-institutionalisation policies of Australian

ents have been successful in dramatically reducing the number of people in various institutions (as referred to by Luke elsewhere in lume). This 'success', however, comes at the expense of a small er of young offenders who continue to be part of our juvenile justice and institutional populations. Bifurcation of the juvenile justice system into those that can be 'saved' and the small proportion for whom custodial alternatives are deemed appropriate are, as John Pratt (1989:244) points out, one of the major trends in penal policy of the last decade. We have traded the greater liberty accorded the majority of the 'de-institutionalised' young offender population for the tough measures required for 'hard-core' offenders. The problem is well illustrated in the fate of the Tasmanian 'homicidal schoolboy'.

In November 1989, a fifteen-year-old Tasmanian schoolboy, Wayne Johnson, was given a holiday from school. He wanted to go swimming with his friends, but his father refused to give his permission. The boy then went to the cupboard and fetched two shotguns—a single barrel and a .22 rifle. He shot his 41-year-old invalid father as he lay in bed, and when his mother came to see what had happened, he shot her as well. Finally, he shot his ten-year-old brother. When he was finished he fired a second round of shots into each body. He then got into the family car and drove six kilometres before crashing into another car and being apprehended by police.

The family lived in a neat masonry block house in an historic little town on the southern outskirts of Launceston. From all accounts the family was 'ordinary' and the boy had not been in trouble before, either at school or with police. The boy pleaded guilty and Judge Crawford of the Tasmanian Supreme Court sentenced him to mandatory life imprisonment.

There was enormous pressure on the judge to deal severely with this horrific crime. He rejected the option of making him a ward of the state, despite the obvious advantages of this for Wayne's rehabilitation. Such a disposition would have meant his release at the age of eighteen, effectively having served only a three-year sentence. With a 'life' sentence the boy may well not even be released after ten years (Tobin, *Sun*, 4 October 1989; Macay, *Herald*, 23 March 1990; Wilson, *Herald*, 4 April 1990). Community outrage is frequently extreme against children who are seen as perverse and whose behaviour challenges the ideology of the family as a loving, caring institution.

Sentencing of juveniles identified as 'hard-core' also shows signs of bowing to political pressure by becoming more punitive. In Western Australia a perceived youth 'crime wave' excited popular outrage at the seemingly light sentence given to a sixteen-year-old driver of a stolen car who caused the death of a motorcyclist. A commercial radio station promoted a 'rally for justice' to demonstrate this community disquiet (*West Australian*,19–22 August 1991). New South Wales has formalised a more punitive approach with the introduction of a 'minimum sentence' for juveniles which prevents their early release. The punitive approach of the

New South Wales courts is unchallengeable. In 1989, for example, the High Court of Australia rejected an application for leave to appeal by a seventeen-year-old New South Wales youth convicted of the murder of his brother and sentenced to a custodial term of sixteen years with a minimum of twelve years, on the grounds that the matter was not one of public importance (*R v Randall* unreported, 1989). This harshness in sentencing undermines the apparent gains of both the 'minimum intervention' and 'de-institutionalisation' philosophies (Youth Justice Coalition, 1990:301).

Homicide, of course, is an exceptional crime. In all Australian jurisdictions (with the exception of Western Australia) such cases are dealt with in the higher courts, outside the jurisdictional ambit of the juvenile justice system. Yet there is clear evidence that even young offenders charged with less serious crimes are being subjected to more punitive measures.

Juvenile justice legislation in all states allows the juvenile court to waive its jurisdiction and have a young offender dealt with by the adult courts. The criteria for the exercise of this 'waiver' vary, but are always in large part a matter for the court's discretion. It is clear that in some jurisdictions, such as Western Australia, the group of hard-core offenders regarded as warranting transfer into the adult jurisdiction is disproportionately high (Edwards, 1982).

More punitive measures might be justified if it were possible to identify the 'hard-core' of young offenders who pose a serious threat to the community. In practice, though, there seems to be no valid or reliable basis upon which juvenile court judges, administrators and others can predict dangerousness or, indeed, amenability to treatment (Feld, 1981). The former label is frequently applied on the discriminatory basis of race (Pitts, 1986; Wundersitz, Bailey-Harris and Gale, 1990), or gender (Hudson, 1989). The category of dangerous youth is also determined according to the nature of crimes which, from time to time, and for various reasons, excite community opprobrium (Cullen and Gilbert, 1982).

More punitive measures for young offenders have crept into juvenile justice practice despite clear legislative statements about the 'specialness' of children and their need to be 'punished' sparingly, and always with the adult tariff as the outer parameter. Thus in Section 139(i) of the *Victorian Children and Young Persons Act* 1989 (Vic.), seven factors to be borne in mind in the sentencing of young offenders are set out. Five of these (including the need to preserve the relationship between the child and their family, provide the child with the opportunity to live in the family home, ensure that the child's schooling remains uninterrupted and minimise the stigma to the child) direct the decision-maker to consider the 'needs' of the child who does wrong. The final two criteria—the degree of responsibility of the child and the protection of the community—are, however, convenient 'catch-alls' which can be used to mete out severe punishment to those unfortunates labelled as intractable. There is no control over the interpretation and application of these two clauses which were intended to allay conservative community fears at the liberalisation of juvenile justice policy.

Extra legal constraints

More worrying than the perversion of the formal legislative framework is the way in which extra-legal mechanisms have developed to control and discipline the behaviour of the young. Insurance companies now, for example, are increasingly initiating civil actions for compensation for damage done by young offenders. Although the latter have already been punished by the children's court, they are required to pay further for their damage to and theft of property. Some of these debts are inordinately high. Breaking a shop window, for example, requires expensive emergency security measures as well as the costly replacement of the window itself. Clearly, young people nowadays escape the harshness of institutionalisation only to face economic hardship when seeking to make good their 'crime'. These cases are mostly settled out of court, and thus remain private agreements between young people, their families and insurance companies, without court supervision, according to a crude philosophy of economic retribution.

Dissatisfied with the liberalisation of juvenile justice, some agencies have developed their own regulatory procedures to deal with minor crime. In most states, public transport authorities now depend upon quasi-enforcement agencies to ensure that young people do not exploit or destroy public property. In Victoria, the powers and methods of these transit police have been criticised (Corns and Simpson, 1988). At the very least, development of such bodies is out of step with the philosophy of 'minimum intervention' espoused by the formal system of justice.

Sometimes these 'informal' methods of control are legitimated by the formal system itself. Charges are brought to the juvenile court. In practice, however, the court accepts the allegations made by these bodies mostly in the absence of the young person. The paradox here is that, for very minor 'nuisance' crimes, the careful balancing of juvenile justice philosophy has been bypassed.

Discussion of the 'juvenile justice system' as a branch of court jurisdiction therefore is simplistic. In practice, the forms of control are subtle and ubiquitous. In many cases, they contradict the objectives and ideology of the 'formal' system.

Rhetoric

The difference between rhetoric and reality is now a cliché of analysis. Juvenile justice systems too often reflect ideology, not practice.

'Back to justice' for juveniles is a reassertion of the community's confidence in legal formalism. Adherence to the requirements of 'due process' or, in the common law jurisdictions, 'natural justice', was embraced as a way of 'saving' children and families from the excesses of 'treatment', loss of rights and unintended extensions of social control by the state (Ketcham, 1977; Pratt, 1983).

Juvenile justice legislation in most states therefore provides a panoply of rights and protections against denial of rights by the state. For example, in Victoria children and families have far greater rights to participation in court proceedings (Section 18(c) *Children and Young Person's Act* 1989), an automatic right to legal assistance in certain circumstances (Section 21) and a variety of appeal procedures open to them to ensure that the justice system remains accountable (Sections 197–200). Such measures, however, have little effect in practice given that 95 per cent of young people choose to 'plead guilty' (Naffine, Wundersitz and Gale, 1990). The 'fairness' of the system, therefore, as a matter of practice, is rarely tested.

Nor could the system of justice cope if the young (or adults for that matter) insisted on their rights in practice. Built into the rhetoric of 'justice' are practical measures designed to ensure that the system itself continues to work 'efficiently'. For most service providers, including the courts, self-preservation and 'efficiency' have characterised their approach to juvenile justice. According to John Pratt (1989), the 'welfare' and 'justice' models of juvenile justice have given way to a third, instrumentalist approach of 'corporatism'.

A pragmatic approach, balancing the demands of ideology against cost, has always underscored juvenile reform in Australia (Jaggs, 1986; Seymour, 1988). We have been less seduced by ideologically-driven explanations for the 'causes' of juvenile crime simply because the childsaving philosophy demanded the commitment of state resources to children 'in danger'. Australian governments were often content to leave the job in the hands of private philanthropists. As late as 1982 a private agency, the Children's Protection Society, was 'contracted' by the then Department of Community Welfare Services in Victoria to be the authorised intervener in cases of child maltreatment and provide emergency accommodation for such children (Child Welfare Practice and Legislation Review, 1983:100, 200). Parsimony also extended to 'treatment' which, as Garth Luke argues elsewhere in this volume, was in reality narrowly defined in most Australian jurisdictions to mean, 'money for trampolines in institutions'.

Nor is there any certainty that the ideological import of 'back to justice' is appreciated by the general public. Although for lawyers it represents a commitment to 'rights', it is probably more popularly understood as reasserting the responsibility of young people for their actions. There is no doubt that for many 'back to justice' is old fashioned retribution in a new guise. Under the new philosophy, young offenders need no longer be regarded as distorted products of poor families, deprivation, injured psyches or social discrimination (Bayer, 1981). Childsaving and the welfare approach at least had the advantage of forcing society to question its own failure— the worse the behaviour of the juvenile, the greater the soul-searching to discover the social 'root' cause (Bayer, 1981:171–3).

A 'new' philosophy of 'back to justice' allows society to abrogate responsibility for the behaviour of its young. In marketing the 'back to justice' philosophy, we have encouraged the community to accept young offenders as individually culpable and warranting punishment. The pragmatic trade-off in Australia has been to present 'back to justice' as a way of minimising intervention in the lives of 'minor' offenders, while reserving punishment for the smaller group of 'monsters' and 'incorrigibles'. There is little public sympathy left for the group most in need of tolerance (Opotow, 1990). 'Back to justice' allows the juvenile justice system formally to express the optimism a society wishes to preserve about its young, while at the same time placating moral indignation about those individual young people who have seemingly abused the community's trust. In practice, there is little support for providing greater resources to improve the lot of this 'deviant' subgroup.

Conclusion

We cannot afford to be complacent about recent reforms to juvenile justice. It is quite wrong to look at legislation and changes in practice as 'progress'. It is equally simplistic to provide critiques of juvenile justice approaches of bygone days according to the criteria of the modern world. The important point about juvenile justice reform is that it cannot be reduced to the perils of welfare positivism versus the clarity of legal formalism. Rather, reform to the juvenile justice system will always be a reflection of ideology. This ideology is, in turn, influenced by volatile community attitudes to difficult philosophical and political conceptions of childhood, individual responsibility, crime and the role of the state.

Australian juvenile justice has mirrored the pragmatism of our short history. This has allowed us to avoid the excesses of ideology-led juvenile justice reform. It is no guarantee, however, of moderation in the future. Nor should it allow us to be complacent about the costs of such pragmatism for the small group of young offenders who are still part of the juvenile justice system.

We need to be very careful about determining our criteria of success for juvenile justice reform. Mostly, we have relied on a crude utilitarian measure—things have improved because there are fewer children caught up in the formal system. This denies the harsh experience of the small number of young people who continue to be part of our system. It also ignores the development of parallel informal control mechanisms over the behaviour of young people which have mushroomed outside the formal system.

For some reason, juvenile justice researchers have failed to heed Foucault's warning about the inevitable failure of all reform endeavours (Foucault, 1977). We need not, however, be as pessimistic about the prospects for change in juvenile justice. Recognising the ideological dimensions of juvenile justice can also be liberating for social scientists. It allows us to extend our criticism of the system beyond its obvious form and content and, more importantly, to influence and challenge the construction of social attitudes towards the young. The heartening message from juvenile justice reform is that, for better or worse, community and political sensibilities can be changed with speed and ease. The prospects for reform of juvenile justice are therefore not all bleak, since history suggests that communities cannot afford to abandon their commitment to children and, more importantly, to the symbolic importance of children and childhood.

6 Welfare and justice

Compiled from workshop transcripts by
LYNN ATKINSON

Pratt's chapter suggests that we return to a purely welfare approach in our treatment of young offenders. This controversial proposition generated much of the discussion at the workshop, summarised here, on the link between theory and practice in juvenile justice. The participants started by looking critically at the various applications of the due process philosophy of juvenile justice (otherwise known as the 'justice model') in Australia over the last two decades.

While greater adherence to due process has reduced some of the abuses of so-called welfare-based systems, particularly the practice of indeterminate sentencing, there has been little or no commitment to exploring the causes of juvenile offending. The aim of justice models is essentially retributive. It was considered that they are easily coopted by conservatives intent on punishment to the exclusion of all else and used in law-and-order campaigns in the popular press.

As Laster pointed out, in Australia the justice model is susceptible to the same demands for greater efficiency sweeping the adult courts of summary jurisdiction. This is especially true in those places where magistrates rotate through both the adult and juvenile courts, playing a similar role in each but with a different group of actors. In these circumstances, the differences between the adult and juvenile jurisdictions are less marked than if specialist children's court magistrates are involved. The efficiency imperative is also likely to pressure more children to plead guilty, and to reduce informal procedures in the children's courts. In other words, the due process or justice model minimises differences between adult and children's courts and emasculates the argument for maintaining separate jurisdictions. The social justice and redemptive, re-educative dimensions of the children's court are thus at risk.

The various, hybrid models of juvenile justice operating in Australian juvenile jurisdictions were thought not to 'work' in the way Pratt portrayed the Scottish welfare model as working. Drawing on Pratt's outline of the

70

Scottish model, the participants sketched some requirements for a satisfactory juvenile justice system which they believed to be fundamental. It should satisfy, and be supported by, the community, it should be cost efficient, and it should not be accompanied by spiralling juvenile crime. These requirements are not being met. Current juvenile justice practice, with its greater emphasis on due process, still fails to satisfy the general public, who remain critical of the state's response to juvenile crime. Youth offending is perceived to be escalating and official responses are considered inadequate. The costs of a retributive system are not being contained. Additionally, from the point of view of the consumer of juvenile justice, the defendant's role under a justice model is increasingly one of observer rather than participant. The defendant is often marginalised by the process and becomes the object, rather than the subject of the proceedings.

The Scottish 'pure welfare' model ('welfare', because it is not punitively cast and based on just deserts; 'pure' because policy and practice converge rather than conflict) was redubbed 'accountable welfare' by the participants. The question was put: If this process were as successful as suggested by Pratt, how could it be adapted to suit local conditions, given that each juvenile justice system has roots in the particular community which both generates and supports it, and is shaped by a number of often conflicting historical and contemporary forces? Perhaps a model derived from, and operating in, a particular location cannot successfully be transplanted to another.

The scene thus set, the workshop participants focused on the task of developing a juvenile justice process (rather than model) for Australian contexts which would recognise the differences between and within communities. They favoured a system which acknowledged and accommodated cultural and locational differences, so the justice process and its outcomes would be more equitable.

The importance of location as a factor in the delivery of juvenile justice, on the national, regional and local levels was further discussed. The Scottish system, for example, as Laster commented, is set within a more stratified society. Cultural attitudes to authority are one of many dimensions of a particular society that will affect the operation and effectiveness of a system of social control.

One participant, Michael O'Connor, raised examples of locational differences in the delivery of justice in the Australian context. A country town in one Australian state, for example, might have police who deal punitively with young offenders through arrests and court appearances while, in another town, community policing principles and informal responses to non-serious crime might be favoured. Some places, particularly those with high Aboriginal populations, are over-policed. Mainstream and Aboriginal legal aid services are available in some places and not in others. In some states and in some locations there are specialist children's court magistrates; others have magistrates on rotation or on circuit from the adult jurisdiction.

The political orientation at both state and local government level can seriously affect policy and practice in juvenile justice. For example, James Hackler suggested that conservative state governments are inclined to encourage and respond to law-and-order campaigners in the electorate, whereas non-conservative governments are more likely to place a higher value on issues of social justice. Thus, while location is a central and overarching feature of difference, other factors, such as the racial and cultural composition of communities, policing strategies, court operations, and politics all affect the way a juvenile justice system delivers 'justice'.

Despite dissatisfaction with the status quo in every Australian juvenile jurisdiction, and the reputed success of the Scottish model, there was concern about the relevance of overseas models to the Australian experience. Rod Blackmore referred to current and potential international influences on legislation in New South Wales: these included the Beijing Rules and the United Nations Convention on the Rights of the Child.

The participants looked to the Scottish model for guiding principles. Did it really work? If so, why? What were the principles that could be applied elsewhere? Would Australian communities and juvenile justice practitioners reacting to past welfare approaches accept an even more welfare-oriented approach? At first, the welfare-based Scottish model was viewed with scepticism and vigorously debated, mainly because of the injustices which hitherto had been perpetrated in the name of welfare. It was pointed out that a common and erroneous assumption among practitioners and policy-makers had been that a 'welfare' model automatically brings justice, because of its premise that it is concerned with the welfare of the child. Christine Alder was concerned that in the recent past Australian welfare-based systems had been punitive in their indeterminate sentencing practices, particularly for girls. Social workers had become de facto gaolers with their discretion to keep juveniles (and girls especially) in detention, for their rehabilitation and supposed well-being. A return to such a coercive and inequitable system clearly could not be part of a reform agenda.

It was suggested that juvenile justice should be premised on the known facts. We know that most juveniles do not re-offend, that the juvenile justice process is, itself, punitive, and that juveniles grow up, and usually out of, crime. These factors suggest that a course of patience with young offenders should be pursued, using the minimum intervention required to rehabilitate the child and satisfy community expectations. These known 'facts' of juvenile justice also raise the crucial question of whether being caught up in the system itself is punishment enough. The Scottish system, it seems, takes this line. Rather than adhering to the welfare ethic of treatment and rehabilitation, with its subtext of punitiveness and its tendency to net-widen, the Scottish system also strongly supports concepts of parsimony and minimal intervention (concepts supported by John Braithwaite). The outcome of 'no further action' is the cornerstone of Scotland's non-judicial children's hearings. This is in line with Feeley's (1979) argument that referral to the system is, in itself, sufficient punishment for most juveniles.

No other informal mechanisms (such as panels and police cautioning schemes) operate within the Scottish system. This, in itself, reduces the possible responses to young offenders, and successfully avoids accusations of net-widening and recruitment. Pratt also pointed out that the narrow range of options available in Scotland has the advantage of ensuring parity of outcomes across the entire jurisdiction.

Because guilt has already been admitted, judicial officers, police, lawyers and social workers are absent from the Scottish children's hearings. The cost saving is obvious. Less money is spent on punishment practices and salaries for professionals, and so resources are 'freed-up' for potential redirection into crime-avoidance programs, such as employment and training schemes. The Scottish system also eliminates problems such as 'police-sponsored' delinquency (good-order offences) and social worker discretion which, in the past, have led to unnecessarily punitive sentences in the name of rehabilitation. To Pratt, the Scottish system can be said to work, because the community is relatively satisfied with it and it does not attract undue media attention. It is inexpensive and has contained, rather than sponsored, juvenile crime.

Concerns were raised about the fact that most diversionary schemes usually require the defendant to admit to the allegations, usually without the benefit of legal advice. To Naffine, this was the Achilles heel of the Scottish system. Pratt disagreed, observing that, in Australia at least, some 95 per cent of juveniles attending court plead guilty anyway, even though most of them have the assistance of a lawyer. Some participants, however, did not accept that the current high rate of juvenile guilty pleas reflected the actual level of guilty offenders. It was thought that there should be greater emphasis on due process of law to ensure that children were not pressured to plead.

Notwithstanding these concerns, some considered that a prior admission of guilt was still the best available means of bringing juveniles before a non-judicial, alternative-to-court tribunal. Others favoured less coercive entrance criteria.

According to Pratt, the Scottish system encourages the active involvement of the defendant in the children's hearing. This contrasts with the offender's mute role as object of admonishment before children's courts. There was also uncertainty about whether, even at an alternative-to-court hearing, youths would have stories to tell and, if they did, whether they would want to speak out. However, as Michael Barry noted, the South Australian experience with children's aid panels suggests that, when given appropriate encouragement from the panellists, children and parents did talk freely about the offending and the family problems which, in their view, precipitated the behaviour. Participants therefore considered that the juvenile justice system should provide the opportunity for them to do so. It was also concluded that it was both desirable and possible to summon an alleged juvenile offender to such an informal hearing without the appearance being dependent on a plea of guilty.

The participants believed the Scottish model had the capacity to offer, and more importantly to deliver, what was termed 'accountable' welfare. Such a system appears to work where previous so-called welfare models have failed. The due-process models which have, to some extent, taken their place are proving inadequate to deal with juvenile crime and criminality, and have become increasingly costly. Premised on the knowledge that most young offenders do not re-offend and that most juvenile crime does not endanger the public, there was considerable support for the establishment within Australia of non-judicial, alternative-to-court tribunals to deal with the less serious juvenile offenders. (Questions of what constitutes serious juvenile crime and how serious charges should be dealt with were not taken up in this discussion.) The participants then formulated fundamental principles to govern such a process of accountable welfare.

First was the principle (emphasised by Braithwaite) of parsimony in intervention and outcome. This includes minimal intervention by the authorities and minimal outcomes in terms of dispositions and record. The group supported a policy that an appearance at the alternative-to-court tribunal should be sufficient in itself, and should not lead to any further sanction or outcome. The current economic problems of the states were seen to complement such an approach in that a recession cannot support expensive net-widening systems. Second, an admission of guilt should not be required to precede the informal tribunal hearing. Third, participants advocated a process which had the flexibility to be culturally specific and to reflect the subjective needs of the consumer. Consumer evaluation of the process was supported.

Finally, the system should aim for maximum participation by the key actors—namely, the alleged offender and the victim. The role of the police was less clear. It was agreed that they were key players at the apprehension stage, but were arguably dispensable at the dispositional stage. The Scottish system did not include the police in the children's hearing; in fact a reduction of police and judicial personnel was one of the platforms of the Scottish model. Some participants argued for the active involvement of the police on the grounds that, as crucial players in juvenile justice, their support for something new is vital to its success. The active involvement of the police in the informal hearing was seen as one way to ensure their support.

Participants also thought it important to promote social justice. To this end, they suggested that juvenile justice should connect with other youth-oriented social policies and programs. Juvenile justice should not be seen merely as a legal issue with legislative solutions, but rather, as Polk has said in his paper, later in this volume, on informal processes, as an issue with a broader structural base, requiring broad-based, creative solutions.

The group then discussed the difficulties of 'selling' their proposed 'minimalist' juvenile justice process to the various state jurisdictions in Australia. An attempt was made, in the closing stages of the session, to address such practical issues. The cornerstone of the proposed process was the principle of parsimony. A suggestion by Braithwaite for achieving this was to set targets for reductions: a ten per cent reduction over a given period, for example, in arrests and sentences to detention. This would then be evaluated to assess outcomes. Would such a process lead to an escalation in crime, as is frequently suggested by the media and the community? The participants assumed this would not be the case, and hence further reductions could be sought. The discussion in this session was concerned with matching juvenile justice practice with an appropriate and consistent philosophy, to achieve greater and more effective justice in the juvenile arena. A flexible, consistent and welfare-based model of juvenile justice was developed by the participants, by utilising overseas approaches to supply guiding principles, rather than precise details to be replicated.

The following recommendations arose from the discussions on the philosophy of juvenile justice:

- That the juvenile justice process should be based on principles of accountable welfare.

- That the primary principle of juvenile justice should be parsimony: in intervention, process, disposition and record.

- That there should be maximum participation of the child and other interested parties in the justice process.

- That there should be no presupposition of guilt at any stage in the legal process.

- That there should be no predetermination of the characteristics or cultural values of any model. The shape and value of the model should depend on the perceptions of the actual participants.

- That, in setting and implementing targets, there should be dialogue between the parties involved in adjudicating and dispensing juvenile justice.

Part III

Policing

7 Police, youth and violence
CHRISTINE ALDER

Police consider their work with juveniles to be one of their more difficult responsibilities. Research, both in Australia and overseas, indicates that, in general, relations between police and young people are strained and frequently hostile. It has also been suggested that police sometimes use violence in their dealings with young people. This aspect of police–youth relations has rarely been acknowledged in the Australian literature. However, the findings of recent studies indicate that it is an issue which can no longer be ignored, as this and the following chapter illustrate.

The policing of homeless youth

The economic circumstances, living situation and age of homeless youth are consistent with key indicators of vulnerability to violent crime in general (Grabosky, 1989; Hindelang et al.,1978; Stafford and Galle, 1984). When violent behaviour is discussed in relation to homeless youth, it is most likely to be in terms of these young people as perpetrators of violence rather than as victims. As the numbers of such young people have increased, so has the conception of them as posing a threat to other members of the general public. As Wilson and Arnold (1986:18) point out, 'the picture of rebellious and violent gangs of youth roaming our streets, seeking out violence and trouble to inflict on bystanders or parents or authorities' is the one most often portrayed by the media. It is also this image of young people on the street which appears to inform police practices. However, both victimisation research and the experiences of professionals working with these young people suggest that the popular conception of homeless youth as perpetrators of violence serves to obscure their experiences as victims of violent crime.

To counterbalance the existing emphasis on homeless young people as perpetrators of violence, in 1989 a colleague and I conducted a study to investigate the nature and incidence of homeless youth as victims of violence after they had left home. The research consisted of intensive interviews with 63 young people, under eighteen years of age, who at the time were in

Melbourne, Victoria, but had nowhere permanent to stay (see Alder and Sandor, 1989; or Alder, 1991 for methodological details). The young people were contacted through hostels, refuges, a drop-in centre, on the street and by word of mouth. A team of young people was employed as researchers on the project (Alder and Sandor, 1990). The investigation was not designed specifically as a study of police violence towards youth. However, a pilot study, as well as the researchers' own professional experiences with young people, suggested the need to anticipate that the police would be one of the sources of violence. A literature review also indicated this as a potential area of concern.

In general, previous studies suggested that the lower the individual's social class, the greater the probability that the individual would have contact with the police (Thornton, James and Doerner, 1982:341). The probability is heightened for homeless youth because they are more likely than other young people to congregate in public spaces. Their general situation means that school or employment are not options and the refuges are closed during the day, so they gather in public spaces. They are thus highly visible and interactions with police are likely to be more frequent than for any other group of young people. That such interactions are not always friendly is captured in the observation by O'Connor and Sweetapple (1988:27) that 'it is on the streets literally, that the struggle . . . between police and young people is at its most explicit and most aggressive'.

There was also some indication in the existing literature of the general strains and conflicts in police–youth relations (James and Polk, 1989). Two pieces of Australian research indicated quite explicitly that violence was sometimes used by police in their dealings with youth. In a 1975 Queensland study, young people alleged that police were brutal, hypocritical, deceitful and remote from the daily lives of youth (Smith, 1975:227). The use of police violence was also discussed in a more recent Queensland study (O'Connor and Sweetapple, 1988).

On the basis of previous research and literature, it was therefore expected that police would be one of the sources of violence against homeless young people. However, the extent, the nature and the consistency of its use, as reported by homeless youth, was not anticipated. Over half (58 per cent) of the young men and 47 per cent of the young women in the research reported having been physically hurt by police (see Alder and Sandor, 1989; or Alder, 1991 for details of findings). The assaults predominantly involved the use of fists and/or hands, but also consisted of kicking and pushing. Verbal abuse and intimidation often accompanied the physical abuse. The young women in particular were almost invariably the victims of verbal abuse in the form of sexual harassment, with accusations being made about their sexual lives and their sexual status. In most instances of assault, more than one police officer was reportedly involved, and most often these officers were males. Incidents began with police–youth contact 'on the streets', but in most cases it was claimed that the physical abuse occurred back at the police station. In general, these incidents were never reported to anyone by the young people for fear of retaliation, or because of their belief that nobody really cared and thus nobody would do anything to help them.

The consistency of the reports of police violence by these young people gave us confidence that we were not simply being told stories. While the sample was relatively small, during the course of the research we worked with, and spoke to, many other young homeless people. Overall their comments indicated that the use of violence by police was understood as a given feature of police–youth relations: incidents were frequently accepted as part of the routine and were sometimes regarded as justifiable by the youth, as indicated by the following comments:

> When I was caught trying to pinch a car they hit me, he hit me with his hand for being a smart arse. I deserved it, they've got their job to do. I try to pinch a car so they give me a back-hander. (Warren)

> A couple of days ago I did get a bit of a beating . . . but that was my own fault . . . I'd been out with a friend, I helped him knock off a car which I shouldn't have done. (Steve)

> How have you been treated by the police? (Interviewer)
> Oh, fairly alright. Portland cops gave me one bashing but that's about it. (Austin)

[quotes from Alder and Sandor 1989:35–6]

In general, rather than exaggerate police assaults, these youths were more likely to underestimate their significance. They were quite likely to report that they were not hurt by police, but rather that 'they just kicked me around a bit' or 'she just slapped me across the face'. Similar findings are reported in the Salvation Army (1989:7) study which concluded that young homeless people took police violence for granted and, in fact, expected to be treated violently.

To check further on the validity of these findings, interviews were conducted with professionals who worked with young people, including youth workers, lawyers, nuns, priests and social workers. These discussions revealed a common understanding that the police frequently use force and violence in their dealings with young people on the street. The extent of these reports and the extent of the incidents reported by the young people themselves indicate that the use of violence is not limited to isolated cases.

Since the completion of the research, the findings have been corroborated by those of other studies. In Victoria, a study of homeless young people in inner urban Melbourne conducted by the Salvation Army, concluded:

> Over half of the young people interviewed who have committed offences claim to have been physically abused by police officers. The alleged incidence of abuse is even higher among the under 16 year olds, 67 per cent of whom claim to have been physically abused by police officers during questioning. The nature of the abuse described

ranges from general punching and slapping around to being hit over the head with telephones, punched in the chest with telephone books to disguise the bruises, hit on the head with the butt of a gun, handcuffed and driven roughly for extended periods in police vans and burnt with cigarette butts (The Salvation Army, 1989:7).

Other research in Queensland (O'Connor and Sweetapple, 1988), Western Australia (White, Underwood and Omelczuk, 1991) and New South Wales (Youth Justice Coalition (NSW), 1990) all report violence as a feature of police–youth relations. Evidence indicates that the levels of violence are even higher for Aboriginal youth. Research conducted in Western Australia (White, Underwood and Omelczuk, 1991) examined the incidence of reports of violence against youth made to youth service workers. It found that those workers who interacted predominantly with young Aborigines reported a 60 per cent higher incidence of complaints relating to police assault than workers who dealt predominantly with non-Aboriginal youth. Similarly, a study which covered New South Wales, Western Australia and Queensland found that 85 per cent of Aboriginal juveniles reported being hit, punched, kicked or slapped by police (Cunneen, 1991).

There is thus mounting evidence that the use of violence by police in their handling of young people is far more extensive than was suggested in the earlier literature on police–youth relations. Most of the research with findings of police violence have been of young, homeless people (White, Underwood and Omelczuk, 1991; Alder and Sandor, 1989; The Salvation Army, 1989), young people who spend a lot of time on the streets (Smith, 1975), or Aboriginal youth (Cunneen, 1991). Such findings indicate that there are class and race issues which warrant further examination. Since most of the initial contact between these young people and police occurs 'on the street', concerns regarding the nature of the policing of youth in public spaces are also raised.

Confrontations and consequences

Confrontations between youth and police most often begin in public places and need to be considered in the context of young peoples' experiences of police harassment. Those who congregate in groups in public spaces appear to be the targets of what may be referred to as 'pro-active' policing; that is, they are questioned and asked to 'move on'. The police objective is to prevent 'potential' trouble and to respond to the expectations of a public which, it is assumed, feels threatened. Young people perceive such a request as a denial of their legitimate right to occupy public space. Their sense of the injustice of the police action becomes a powerful catalyst for hostility towards police, especially for youth whose homeless status testifies to a history of injustice.

From the police perspective, the questioning of young people in public spaces and directions to 'move on' do not constitute 'harassment' but are a legitimate tactic for maintaining order and protecting the public from an assumed threat to their safety. The police themselves may perceive these young people as potentially violent offenders. The National Committee on Violence (1990:36) noted that 'some of the most profound differences in assessments by Australian Police Commissioners were in the perceived level of violence by youth'.

While the perception of young people as perpetrators of violence is buttressed by media reports, it is not necessarily consistent with available statistics. From its review of violent crime in Australia, the National Committee on Violence concluded that, 'despite perceptions to the contrary, violent offending by juveniles is relatively uncommon. Gang violence is not a major problem in most jurisdictions' (National Committee on Violence, 1990:4). Nevertheless, young people hanging about the street are considered as 'trouble' and 'potentially dangerous' by some police officers (James and Polk, 1989).

Unfortunately, the employment of the 'harassment model of maintaining order' (Sanders, 1981:219) fuels the antagonism felt by young people toward police. Homeless young people believe that police are not sympathetic to their position and, in fact, actively dislike them. As one youth said, 'they think we're scum'. The following quote captures the tone evident in many interviews with homeless youth:

> I don't really trust [the police] . . . like, sometimes the way they
> come across to you like you're all hardened criminals—I don't like
> it. They come up to you and ask you questions you don't really want
> to answer, ask you what ya age and all that and ya don't really want
> to tell them that, you want to keep it to yourself. They treat street
> kids like a lower grade of people and I don't like that (quoted in
> Alder and Sandor, 1989:35).

Given the experience of harassment and the expectation of violence, perhaps it is not surprising that the attitude of youth to the police has been described as one of suspicion, disrespect, distrust, dislike, contempt and occasionally fear (Smith, 1975:227). When asked to 'move on', such a young person may not cooperate with the police request. In a public setting in particular, the police officer may then feel the need to assert either police, or his personal, authority: the request to 'move on' develops into a test of power between two males, one a youth and the other a relatively young police officer. It is a confrontation between two young males in a society where aggression and hostility rather than tact and consideration are the culturally expected responses (Youth Justice Coalition (NSW), 1990:234).

Smith argues that the behaviour of young people in this situation is partly determined by their previous experience with police which

> encourages them to operate in a continuous state of rivalry with
> police. This rivalry coupled with peer pressure to appear tougher and
> smarter than police leads to abrasive encounters. These usually take
> the form of open defiance when confronted, or more subtle attempts
> to verbally outsmart police (Smith, 1975:225).

'Acting smart' is, in fact, a common complaint from both police and young people about each other's behaviour (Youth Justice Coalition (NSW), 1990: 234) and becomes part of an ongoing set of expected and anticipated behaviours and responses which aggravate the mutual antagonism.

In this context, young people do sometimes verbally abuse and taunt officers. Such behaviour is a direct display of disrespect and confronts the authority of the police. It has been argued that such challenges to the officers' authority are key precursors of police violence. The police believe that young people are obliged to display respectful behaviour towards them: such behaviour is thought to symbolise the young person's law-abiding attitude and attests to their acceptance of the particular officer's authority (US Commission on Law Enforcement and the Administration of Justice, 1975:241). The failure of young people to show such respect creates a difficult situation for the officer. However, police and young people are not power equals and there are certain expectations and obligations inherent in the police officer's role which are concomitant with their power status. As a superintendent of police in Chicago is quoted as saying:

> . . . the officer must remember that there is no law against making a policeman angry and that he cannot charge a man with offending him. Until this person acts overtly in violation of the law he should take no action against him, least of all lower himself to the level of a citizen by berating and demeaning him in a loud and angry voice (quoted in US Commission on Law Enforcement and the Administration of Justice, 1975:246).

No matter how disrespectful a young person may be, an officer is not justified in making an arrest or taking any other action.

Police use of violence against young people is not always in response to verbal abuse or taunting by the young person. In his study of the police experiences of Aboriginal youth, Cunneen (1991) questions the explanation that police violence is a response to challenges of police authority. He observes that unprovoked violence and harassment may occur without any overt challenge to authority. He argues that in most cases violence serves an instrumental purpose: it is used as a means of 'gaining admissions' or as 'a routine form of summary punishment' (Cunneen, 1991). This explanation is consistent with many of the more serious examples of police violence reported by homeless young people.

The research of O'Connor and Sweetapple (1988) also indicates that police violence cannot be explained simply in terms of disrespect for the officer. They found that the nature of the interaction between police and young people reflected the degree of 'cooperation' shown by the young person. Of particular concern is the finding by O'Connor and Sweetapple (1988:17) that cooperation is evidenced by 'a willingness to waive basic common law rights, or by a prompt confession and a declared intention to plead guilty to the charges'. They go on to note that 'the degree of unpleasantness is directly related to the extent to which the young person tries to enforce their legal rights during questioning' (O'Connor and Sweetapple 1988:21). Our study produced similar findings. As an example, one seventeen-year-old young woman reported to the author that before she was assaulted by police she had requested to make a phone call. The police response was, 'Where do you think you are—America?' Young people are thereby faced with the dilemma of foregoing their legal rights or being abused by the police.

The Youth Justice Coalition (NSW) (1990:235) points out that the assertion of their rights by young people is taken as a challenge to the control of the police. As a consequence, legal advice is rarely available to young people before or during questioning. The Youth Justice Coalition (1990:235) therefore concludes that 'for many young people, "rights" are barely relevant in their everyday dealings with police officers'.

Thus there is evidence in recent Australian research that not only do police use physical violence in their handling of young people, but also this form of violence is often associated with the violation of other legal rights. Both of these forms of abuse of authority have been defined as 'police brutality' in the United States. Carter (1985:322) for example, defines such abuses of authority as:

> . . . any action by a police officer without regard to motive, intent or malice that tends to injure, insult, tread on human dignity, manifest feelings of inferiority, and/or violate an inherent legal right of a member of the police constituency.

In order to operationalise his concept of abuse of authority, Carter suggests a three part typology:
1 Physical abuse/excessive force;
2 Verbal/psychological abuse; and
3 Legal abuse/violation of civil rights.

There is evidence of all three forms of abuses of authority or police brutality in recent research on police–youth relations in Australia (Cunneen, 1991; Alder and Sandor, 1989; O'Connor and Sweetapple, 1988). Some of the material regarding physical and legal abuse has been discussed above. Verbal and psychological abuse is evident in the reports by young women of verbal harassment: language is used which casts a slur on the young woman's sexual reputation (Youth Justice Coalition (NSW), 1990:254). Racist language is also used (Youth Justice Coalition (NSW), 1990:232). Complaints of the use of racist language were made by 84 per cent of young people in a study of Aboriginal youth and police (Cunneen, 1991). To the general public, such forms of verbal and legal abuse are likely to be considered less significant than physical abuse. They probably also occur with greater frequency. For these reasons, Carter (1985) argues that they signify a far more problematic threat to our democratic society.

It is in the context of all three forms of abuse that young people have learnt that you 'never trust a copper' (Smith, 1975:225). They do not expect police to be fair (O'Connor and Sweetapple, 1988:21). However, it needs to be noted at this point that youth hostility and resentment of police is not directed at the role of the police officer as an enforcer of the law but derives from their experiences with individual officers. Youth do distinguish between good and bad police officers (Smith, 1975:228; Youth Justice Coalition (NSW), 1990:236). Smith (1975:228) argues that their hostility is directed at the ways in which local police fulfil their role. Similarly the Youth Justice Coalition observed that:

Dissatisfaction is often expressed, not about police intervention itself, but about its unpredictability and inconsistency in the way people are dealt with (Youth Justice Coalition (NSW), 1990:236).

That is, young people are not simply retaliating against a higher authority; they recognise the need for, and the role of, police officers in our society. Instead, it is their experiences with police officers which produce distrust and disrespect.

Thus, while verbal and physical abuse are sometimes used by officers as a means of asserting their authority, the effect of such abuse is to create even greater resentment and disrespect (US Commission on Law Enforcement and the Administration of Justice, 1975). As a consequence of such police practices, young people not only have little or no respect for police, but they also have no trust in them and therefore do not go to them for help. In *Homeless youth as victims of violence* (Alder and Sandor, 1989), three quarters of the young people reported that they had never asked the police for help. The explanation most frequently offered was 'I wouldn't really trust them'. Furthermore, three quarters did not report incidents to the police in which they were victims of a violent crime, even when the victimisation was serious enough to warrant medical treatment. Added to distrust, the explanation offered for not seeking police assistance was that the police would not do anything anyway, or 'they'd just laugh at me'. Thus, not only is a proportion of the population not being provided with service by our police force, but also a number of violent offences are going unreported.

Considering change

There have been many recommendations regarding the improvement of police–youth relations and the problem of police violence (e.g. Youth Justice Coalition (NSW), 1990; US Commission on Law Enforcement and the Administration of Justice, 1975). These recommendations are as many and as varied as the different levels of the problem and the perspectives on it. Clearly there is a need for legal reform in the area of youth rights and police powers, but this is unlikely to be sufficient unless there are changes to general policing policies, to police understandings of their role and to police attitudes towards young people. To some extent, this can be achieved through police training, and this has been suggested as an important area for change. However, police training predominantly affects new recruits and while it is new young officers who are said to engage in abuse most often, such abuse occurs most frequently in police stations where there are senior officers who are responsible. It has been argued that violence is used 'mainly because of indifference or lack of control by their superiors' (Sykes, Fox and Clarke, 1985:181). Thus, much broader issues of police organisation and general policies are implicated (James and Polk, 1989). Policies need to address not only the causes of the problem of police violence, but also issues of accountability and monitoring and the necessary official sanctions.

Ultimately, police responses to young people, particularly the homeless and the marginalised, have to be considered as part of a general social strategy of control with respect to these young people and to their plight in Australia. This general strategy is consistent with law and order politics as they are emerging in Australia (Carrington,1990). The maximisation of law enforcement resources and the intensification of penal measures are fundamental dimensions of the 'New Right' politics. There are demands for an increase in police powers and a strengthening of police numbers at the same time as financial resources and housing options for young people living away from home are diminishing. In New South Wales, this regime has led to an increase in police powers to apprehend homeless youth under the age of sixteen. Also, amendments to legislation have made homelessness and 'frequenting a public space' grounds for legitimate police intervention (Carrington, 1990). Such policies of attempting to control homeless youth through increased policing have the potential to aggravate further the antagonism between police and youth. In England, Jefferson (1987:50) has observed that 'the greater the contact of any kind with police, the greater the hostility'.

Police perceptions of black and homeless young people, and their justification for the use of harassment and violence, must be understood in the context of our governmental and societal response, or lack of response, to the situation of these young people. As government policies continue to neglect young people in terms of their employment and housing, and their right to a safe, independent and secure livelihood, so they continue to marginalise youth. Police attitudes are but part of broader social and governmental responses which fail to treat young people as responsible, contributing members of our society. As one reads through the recent accounts of police interaction with homeless young people and Aboriginal youth, one is left with the disquieting feeling that perhaps our broadest-based policy with respect to these young people is one of policing, of 'managing the rabble' and of 'street cleaning' (Irwin, 1985). And as a society, we appear to tolerate the use of violence to this end.

Conclusion

It may be argued that the present focus on police violence tends to distort police–youth relations. We need to acknowledge the many police officers who do not resort to such practices, as well as the efforts in some states (particularly New South Wales) to address specifically, and on a broad scale, the problems of police–youth relations, including the use of violence. Certainly, in most states, various programs and policies have been implemented which are intended to be in the best interests of young people. These include cautionary programs, blue-light discos and police–youth clubs. These programs and policies are most often the focus of discussions of policing youth (e.g. Challinger, 1985; Seymour, 1988).

Use of police violence, on the other hand, has been ignored or dealt with only indirectly as 'over-zealous policing' or 'informal sanctions involving physical force'. However, the consistency of the recent findings of police violence in different Australian states means that we can no longer fail to address this problem. As senior police officers in some states have recognised, to ignore this problem is not only to abandon young people to violent victimisation; it also ultimately makes policing itself more difficult. The continued use of police violence against young people ultimately threatens the safety of everyone in our community and undermines the principles of democracy we like to believe are the foundation of our society.

8   Issues of juvenile justice and police

LINDA HANCOCK

In the last decade, most Australian states have attempted to overhaul juvenile justice legislation (see Chapter 1). In the area of policing, the new laws have sought to divert young people from courts, and to lessen the impact on them of criminal justice intervention. Key changes include: the introduction of cautioning systems; statutory limits on police detention of young people; the requirement that police proceed by way of summons rather than arrest; reforms aimed at increasing police accountability in their interviews with youth; and recognition of youth rights and advocacy in their dealings with police.

But despite progressive legislation, there remain crucial areas of police–youth relations that are neither regulated nor open to public scrutiny. Accordingly, police are not accountable. Those aspects of policing to be discussed here concern the use of discretionary powers in the service of systematic or institutionalised discrimination—not against all youth, but in dealings with particular groups of young people. Youth who are especially vulnerable are those marginalised from mainstream culture through class, race–ethnicity and gender, or combinations of all three. There are five major areas of policing where a lack of regulation leads to abuses as detailed below.

1 Discriminatory use of the cautioning system

The use of pre-court diversion schemes has raised questions about net-widening: that is, the extension of police intervention to youth who previously would not have been sent to court anyway. In Chapter 2 Wundersitz also demonstrated the lack of uniformity between states in the use of diversionary schemes.

These issues, however, are not the focus of this discussion. Rather, the concern here is whether diversionary procedures are used in a way which discriminates against certain classes or categories of young people. Research suggests that the use of diversionary schemes (including both panels and police cautions) does not rely solely on offence-based or legalistic criteria, as one would expect if the main intention were to screen out non-serious or first offenders. For example, a Victorian study (Hancock, 1978) found that, when matched on legalistic criteria, youth from higher status, higher socio-economic backgrounds and two-parent families were more likely to receive warnings than were youth from lower class backgrounds, single parent families and lower status areas. This study concluded that police employ a welfare model of decision-making: they allow such extra-legal factors as character, home, appearance, neighbourhood, and socio-economic status to influence their decisions to prosecute rather than to warn (Hancock, 1978:38).

Similarly, Gale and Wundersitz (1989:17) found that Aboriginal youth were consistently more likely than non-Aboriginal youth to be referred to court rather than diverted to an aid panel, and this applied even when the young persons were charged with similar offences and had comparable prior criminal records. This outcome was strongly related to police practices at the point of apprehension: in particular, the study found that arrest was the main factor determining a court referral. Conversely, report-based matters were more likely to be sent to a panel. Hence, more Aboriginal than non-Aboriginal youth were directed to court because of their higher rate of arrest.

Cunneen (1990:4) has also shown that police discretion to arrest and to decide how to proceed after arrest is critical in determining the 'extent to which Aboriginal youth become entrapped within the formal processes of juvenile justice'.

Indeed, in all states where studies have been undertaken, it is clear that the decision to warn or to send a child to court is highly discretionary, and police guidelines are not uniformly followed. For example, in Victoria, under Standing Order 5.3, an officer must endorse on the police brief the reason for not cautioning a first offender (Seymour, 1988:234). Despite such requirements, data from a sample of 399 Victorian court appearances for January to December 1989 show that a substantial proportion (30 per cent) of youth appearing in court were first offenders, whilst only 16 per cent of these youth appeared before court on offences against the person. Even if protection applications are excluded, 24 per cent of youth appearing in court are first offenders, of whom only 19 per cent appeared on charges for offences against the person. It thus appears that substantial numbers of first offenders are not cautioned and that police routinely send certain first offenders to court (Hancock, 1991).

2 The lack of an independent witness at police interviews with youth

Police standing orders in all states require that an independent adult be present during police questioning of juveniles. However, police regulations are no more than guidelines which do not have the force of the law (Seymour, 1988:199). This point was reiterated in a Western Australian children's court judgement in 1990 by Judge Hal Jackson, who noted that police standing orders 'are of no legally binding effect in this state . . . the law to be applied, therefore, is the common law and that is not static' (Legislative Review, 1991:73). Reacting to this, the committee recommended legislation be enacted which would require the presence of an independent party during police questioning of children, with non-adherence to the guidelines rendering evidence inadmissible.

Various studies have questioned the extent to which interviews are, in fact, conducted with an independent adult witness present. Bacon and Irwin (1990) stated that only thirteen out of 25 juveniles in their New South Wales study had an independent witness present during police questioning. An Equal Opportunity Commission study in Western Australia, (1990:40) reported Aboriginal respondents' complaints that the requirement is regularly contravened and police often make no effort to contact parents, guardians or family members. Raynar (1988: 39) noted that, in two Community Services studies of juveniles in Western Australia, there was no independent adult witness present at police interviews in 86 per cent and 94 per cent of cases respectively. And according to Lipscombe (1989:34):

> A 1988 survey of young people at Longmore Remand Centre and the Perth Children's Court found that, even though 50 per cent of juveniles requested a relative or friend be contacted, the police did so only in 29 per cent of instances, and often after questioning was completed. It also found that in 86 per cent of interviews no adults other than officers were present.

In addition, as outlined by Seymour (1988:193), specific issues need clarification such as 'which categories of adults are required to be present during interviews of juveniles? At what stage or stages of the investigative process must they be present? What role do they perform? What are the consequences of a failure to arrange the attendance of a witness?'

In the absence of systematic research into the presence of independent witnesses, evidence is sketchy. What there is, however, indicates there is cause for concern. Moreover, the presence of a 'support person' who is ignorant of the law or intimidated by persons in positions of authority, such as police, may not be sufficient to protect a young person's rights, especially where the penalty for an alleged offence is serious (O'Connor and Tilbury, 1986). Sensitive to this problem, a report of the Legislative Review in Western Australia (1991:74) proposed a system of youth advisers to be available as independent, legally aware adult witnesses for interviews with juveniles.

Given the high proportion of guilty pleas in juvenile courts, there are doubts whether courts adequately question police about the process of evidence gathering and the context of guilty pleas. Drawing on Rees, Cunneen (1990:39) points out that guidelines for interrogating juveniles 'have been structured more to assist the police in ensuring the admissibility of evidence than to protect the young person.'

3 Police use of violence against particular young people

Recent studies based on interviews with young people further support Alder's findings cited in Chapter 7, of alarming levels of reported violence against youth. They also indicated, as did Alder, that youth regard such violence as 'normal' or expected and feel that complaints are useless. For example, a Victorian survey of young people's experiences of mistreatment by police between August and December 1990 revealed 127 incidents of mistreatment reported in 55 cases, with 37 per cent of the recipients being under seventeen years of age. Thirty-three per cent of incidents involved verbal abuse and 29 per cent involved physical abuse. Other mistreatments included being kept in cells (9 per cent), denial of access to a lawyer (7 per cent) and denial of a telephone call (10 per cent). Significantly, in only 36 per cent of cases, no formal action was taken. '[I]t would seem that [police] are aware that they have little accountability in cases proceeded against by way of summons only, or not proceeding at all!' (Federation of Community Legal Centres, 1991:3.5).

In New South Wales, Bacon and Irwin (1990), in a study which investigated youth–police relations under new legislation dealing with powers to pick up homeless youth, found that one third of their sample reported being hit or kicked by police officers, while one half of those taken to police stations complained of being treated badly.

Cunneen's (1990) interviews with Aboriginal juveniles found that most Aboriginal females held in state detention centres had been victims of police violence. This study reported that eleven out of fourteen Aboriginal girls interviewed reported being hit by police. Incidents included complaints of being 'ankle-cuffed' for questioning, 'smacked in the head', 'picked up by the hair and kept hammering my head into the wall' and 'stabbed in the hand with a pen'. One girl who claimed to have been assaulted herself, reported witnessing the sexual assault of another Aboriginal girl by police officers. Given the Youth Justice Coalition (NSW) (1990:254) finding of one girl in fifteen reporting police violence, it appears that violence against Aboriginal girls may be higher than against non-Aboriginal girls.

Racist harassment and violence by police against non-English speaking youth in Victoria is cited in an Ethnic Youth Issues Network report (1990) on complaints of harassment and intimidation by authorities such as police, transit police and shopping centre security officers. The report says victims were predominantly male, aged seventeen and of Asian descent. Violence was used to gain admissions in relation to alleged thefts, or eventuated when youth asserted their rights—as for example, when a youth asked a police officer for his badge number.

Significantly, as shown in the previous chapter, a number of studies also reveal low rates of reported complaints of police violence. The Federation of Community Legal Centre's (1991) report revealed that only 36 per cent of victims reported the incident and of these, only 20 per cent made reports to bodies officially empowered to investigate complaints of police maltreatment. Reasons given for not reporting complaints included: being too frightened, fear of reprisals by police or having threats made against them (46 per cent), the belief that making a complaint would make no difference (22 per cent), and not knowing how to make a complaint (27 per cent).

While various complaint mechanisms exist in each state, these are not necessarily effective. In New South Wales, for example, youth can make a complaint to the police officer in charge, a copy of which must be forwarded by police to the ombudsman. However, critics of the ombudsman's office claim it is not an effective grievance mechanism for young people because of its inaccessibility, the time taken to process complaints, and the lack of a special unit, division or juvenile liaison officer to investigate young people's complaints (Youth Justice Coalition (NSW), 1990:116).

4 Police use of welfare applications

At the point of contact with youth, police have wide-ranging discretion to take no action, to warn or, if sending the young person to court, to choose between arrest/summons or a protection application. These choices are frequently gender-biased. It seems that in those states where pre-court diversionary schemes operate, a higher proportion of females than males are selected for this form of processing: that is, girls are more likely to receive a police caution or a referral to a children's panel than boys. However, if they do go to court, girls are more likely than boys to appear on a welfare or protection application than on an offence charge.

The more frequent use of cautions or diversions for girls can be explained on legalistic grounds. Girls, on average, commit fewer and less serious offences than boys, and have less serious past offence records (see, for example, Wundersitz, Naffine and Gale, 1988). It could, therefore, be argued that they merit less severe treatment.

However, when we analyse why girls are sent to court, we find that since the 1970s the majority have been the subject of welfare or protection applications. Various studies support this. Leaper (1974), in Victoria, found that 62 per cent of protection applications concerned females. Females also predominated in the non-neglect applications of 'exposed to moral danger' (93 per cent female) and 'found wandering' (73 per cent female). Another Victorian study of court appearances in 1975 found that 79 per cent of non-neglect protection applications were female and that 63 per cent of females (compared with 8 per cent of males) were presented to court on protection applications. This study also found that the repercussions of a protection application were more serious for girls than for boys, with girls receiving a higher proportion of supervisory dispositions (detention, probation, supervision order). This occurred despite the finding that girls were more likely than boys to be first offenders and to have committed fewer and less serious prior offences (Hancock, 1980).

In 1983, the majority of young females in Victorian Youth Training Centres were there on welfare applications, mostly on the grounds of 'exposed', 'uncontrolled' or 'inadequate supervision and control'

(Department of Community Services, 1983). The trends are similar in New South Wales. In 1983–84, 85 per cent of girls (2233) were in institutions on protection applications and the remainder (407) were sentenced for offences. By comparison, 56 per cent of boys were in institutions on protection applications (Australian Bureau of Statistics, 1983–84: 6).

During the 1980s there were attempts to limit the vagueness of status offence statutes by specifying criteria which were more objective than vague catch-alls like 'exposed'. The New South Wales *Community Services Act* 1982 adopted the term 'child in need of care' to replace the former 'exposed to moral danger', 'uncontrollable' and 'truancy' provisions. Greater emphasis was placed on referring a young person to the welfare department for counselling and assistance, while coercive intervention was to be used as a last resort (Women's Co-ordination Unit, 1986: 30). Similar changes have taken place in Victoria under the *Children and Young Persons Act* 1989.

In analysing gender-bias in police recommendations, a key question is whether the different outcomes for young females and males are a police construction or a response to actual differences in behaviour. In terms of offending behaviour, we are not necessarily dealing with similar phenomena. Given the more serious offending of males, we would expect more severe outcomes for them. At both warning and court levels in the processing of young people, we would expect more lenient treatment of females, based on legal criteria. However, in the area of non-criminal status offence behaviour, it is evident that policing is a gendered process. Analyses of these processes reveal that paternalistic and biased attitudes to much female adolescent non-criminal behaviour is also shared by parents, social workers, police, court officials and magistrates.

Commenting on the gender-specific punishment of 'protection', Box (1983:170) stated: 'rather than concern themselves with dispensing justice, juvenile courts are often transformed into stern parental surrogates who lock up their naughty daughters for behaving in ways which gain scarcely concealed approval when committed by sons'.

5 Policing youth in public spaces

As Alder commented in the previous chapter, young people often display a public presence which is seen by police as a threat to public order. So police do what they think the community wants—they seek public order and 'clean streets'. Such 'street cleaning' is often related not only to age but to ethnicity. Cunneen (1991:27) cites numerous complaints of police violence in inner-city public areas in Sydney, Brisbane and Perth. There are complaints from Aboriginal youth of being arrested 'for nothing' when they were in a park or walking along the street, and frequent reports of police violence from young people arrested for public order offences. Such incidents have a symbolic significance—they publicly and individually confirm police authority.

It is frequently the case that those police patrolling inner-city streets are recent graduates, barely older than the youth they confront. O'Connor and Sweetapple allude to the element of contest between young police on the beat and youth on the streets: 'Armed with a new status and a new uniform, it sometimes seems that they have taken the role of prescribing a moral standard for their peers' (O'Connor and Sweetapple, 1988:27). Similarly, the report by the Victorian Federation of Community Legal Centres (1991) on police mistreatment of youth found that the highest proportion of complaints concerned young, inexperienced police officers.

This preoccupation of police with patrolling young males on the street is not new and dates from the early days of paid work (Brogden, Jefferson and Walklate, 1988:105). The chief focus is not necessarily on law enforcement. Commenting on the policing of public places, in particular the streets, the Youth Justice Coalition (NSW) (1990:232) notes that the maintenance of order, rather than law enforcement, is the priority. This entails the imposition of authority, the use of discretionary powers (such as stop/search), and the application of broad criminal offences (notably offensive language and disorderly behaviour).

As a direct outcome of policing the streets, much juvenile crime is related to young people's use of public space. Vague offence statutes such as Summary Offences Acts or offences against good order are used, it is claimed, against certain classes of juveniles or in a discriminatory way (Youth Justice Coalition (NSW) 1990; Cunneen, 1988).

Conclusion

Important common features emerge from the foregoing reports in this and the preceding chapter.

- There are very high and unacceptable levels of violence and abuse in police interactions with juveniles. Studies are relatively recent and it is only now that the composite picture is becoming clear. These studies cover a wide geographical area and a diversity of youth, yet the results are consistent.

- The victims of much police abuse are poor or marginalised youth or from ethnic minorities.

- For a variety of reasons (including ignorance of their legal rights, fear of retaliation and cynicism about formal complaint mechanisms) most youth do not complain about police violence or about the lack of adherence by police to guidelines or statutory requirements which regulate police–youth interactions.

- Much of the regulation of police–youth relations appears to be by informal means or police standing orders rather than legislation. Not only are these regulations hidden, but they lack the force of law.

- Despite attempts to regulate police, legislative and administrative guidelines are full of gaps and inconsistencies and lack systematic monitoring and review.

- There is no clear explication in law or in police instructions regarding police powers and the rights of suspects. To date, no state has enacted a statutory list of young offenders' rights or provided legislative support for the United Nations Convention on the Rights of the Child.

- It appears that grievance mechanisms are under-developed and under-utilised in the juvenile justice system. Although there are a number of avenues available to youth to complain about their treatment, these are not effective methods of redress.

- The reforms of recent years have sought to enhance and protect juveniles' rights within the juvenile justice system. There is a general recognition that young people are disadvantaged and dependent and are less likely than adults to speak up for themselves, to know their rights, or to pursue remedies for abuses against them (Youth Justice Coalition (NSW) 1990:110).

- To a large extent, police violence towards young people remains hidden, especially violence directed at minority youth and youth who congregate in public spaces or who adopt an uncooperative stance towards police. Studies indicate that these youth often expect violence or rough treatment by police, or see it as part of 'normal practice'. If they do complain, they report they are not supported, as such treatment is dismissed or regarded as 'normal' by others.

- At bottom, there appears to be a culture that condones police violence. O'Connor and Sweetapple (1988:26) claim that the unlawful behaviour of police is condoned by many adult authority figures to whom juveniles have complained. Similarly, Cunneen claims that such acceptance of police violence is systematic and institutionalised. He notes that 'Breaches of regulations in relation to interviewing Aboriginal juveniles and the use of violence in relation to admissions seem to be condoned as part of "getting the job done"' (Cunneen, 1990:55).

- Those young people most susceptible to violence and discrimination are those who are most structurally marginalised in Australian society: those with the least knowledge and resources to sustain and adequately defend complaints of abuse.

- There is a need to monitor police discretion in areas such as formal cautioning, interview, arrest procedures, custody and the court's admission of evidence. There is also a need to institute effective and efficient complaint mechanisms to deal with young people's allegations about police abuses of power. At the same time, we need to change attitudes: to encourage the recognition of young people's rights to occupy public space, a higher priority among the police for working with juveniles, and special training for police in their dealings with young people.

9 Police action

Compiled from workshop transcripts by
LYNN ATKINSON

The power differential between young people and police, and its effects on justice for juveniles, was a major theme in the workshop discussion summarised here. In particular, the workshop participants were concerned with a major symptom of this unbalanced power relationship: police violence towards youth.

It was recognised by participants that a general problem in Australian police forces was the fact that police misuse their authority to abrogate the rights of individuals. Young people, because they are particularly powerless, are most at risk. The participants believed that police, both in policy and in practice, should recognise that young people, like all citizens, have a right to use public space. Such recognition would enhance opportunities for better relations between police and youth. One suggestion was that police be given a legislative mandate to take no action if that seemed the better course at the time. Incentives to take no action, as well as barriers to taking action, would support the use of such an initiative. Arrest, for example, could be made a troublesome option for police. This would encourage them to proceed against young offenders by way of a report or an attendance notice.

One way to convert negative and often violent police–youth interactions into positive or reasonable relationships was for police to become more involved in local community activities, especially those where use of public space was at issue. One group of participants, however, was wary of extending the reach of the police because of the implications for net-widening. Sergeant Fred Wojtasik, a serving police officer, was one who was reluctant to give a broader reach to police. However, he argued his case on the basis of rationalising available resources.

Participants examined ways of challenging the traditional tendency of police to act at the behest of powerful groups, such as local councils and the media, rather than considering the interests of all the parties concerned. Negotiation between the three groups (young people, those who would bar them from public spaces, and police) was supported by some, so long as this would promote better management of existing situations and enhance the rights of young people, rather than broaden the police role.

Sometimes particular circumstances and decisions aggravate the situation on the street for both the police and youth. For example, James Hackler pointed out that a decision to provide 24-hour access to alcohol in Hindley Street, Adelaide, as a service to tourists has had a spillover effect for the juveniles who frequent the place. It has given them easier access to alcohol and this has, in turn, affected the extent and the way in which they are policed. As Hackler said, there are, broadly speaking, two approaches to this kind of situation. On the one hand, police can adopt a 'get tough' policy with aggressive young police officers being brought in to take a confrontationalist stance. This will inevitably increase the number of apprehensions and charges. Alternatively, police can respond with a preventative, community policing approach, using more experienced officers to defuse and resolve the situation rather than inflame it.

Acts of violence by police may also be used as an alternative to, or substitute for, other 'legitimate' forms of processing. Street kids, for example, may find themselves being assaulted without being cautioned or charged. As Christine Alder noted, none of the street kids she had interviewed had ever been cautioned: 'Despite this wonderful cautioning program operating in Victoria, not one of them was cautioned, because cautioning requires that the parents come down to the police station. But these kids don't have parents. So the police, in essence, exercise summary justice.' They deal with the situation themselves, through the use of violence.

Another major concern of participants was the complacency about violence as reflected in the attitudes of young people themselves, of senior police, of defence counsel, and of the community at large. Christine Alder pointed out that, since most of the assaults recorded in her research had taken place at police stations with senior officers in the vicinity, it would seem that these acts occurred with at least the tacit approval of the apprehending officers' superiors. If defendants do inform their legal counsel of an act of police violence against them, they are often met with a fatalistic response: that complaining is a waste of time, and effectively nothing can be done. Such demonstrations by defence counsel of helplessness and indeed, of tolerance of police violence, help explain why young people themselves accept a certain level of police brutality and why, when it becomes more serious, they seldom complain. While 'street kids' and Aboriginal youth are particularly vulnerable to police violence, most youth are exposed to it, and most youth seem to share the belief that violent policing tactics are both unremarkable and condoned by the community.

The community, as employer of the police, fails to set parameters for acceptable police behaviour which exclude violence. Police are thus able to rationalise their often over-zealous policing of youth on the basis that they are simply responding to public fears. For their part, as Alder commented, academics might complain of police brutality, but they have mostly failed to address it in their research. Instead the question is likely to be subsumed into the less contentious issue of police–youth relations. Alder noted that police violence towards youth may be a response to challenges to police authority. But such challenges, she concluded, do not justify, either legally or morally, a violent police response.

Juvenile defendants appearing in court have experienced police violence directly or indirectly, and have either heard adults claim that they are impotent to deal with it or witnessed them apparently condoning it. As a result, faith in the fairness of the court system, in which the police play such an important part, is likely to have been eroded. Structurally and procedurally, the court replicates the power differential experienced by juveniles who encounter police on the street. A lawyer and a police prosecutor confirmed that young people were disadvantaged in court if they attempted to put the police case against them to the test. David Alcock, a lawyer from South Australia, was concerned that witnesses lacked confidence when giving evidence in court. This lack of confidence was 'more pronounced for a child, much worse for a younger child, and much, much worse for an Aboriginal child'. He noted that, as a defence counsel in the children's court, he is seldom confident that a child witness will give evidence 'that will impress a magistrate sufficiently to at least cast some doubt, if not acquit, the defendant on the basis of full belief in their story'. From the police prosecutor's point of view, Fred Wojtasik found that 'children are very easy to influence. One of the big problems in the court process itself is that it is very easy for a child to make a concession in cross examination which is favourable to the [prosecution's] case'. Compared with the young defendant, the police are knowledgeable about the law, are well organised and have access to considerable resources to prepare and present their cases.

Thus, young people, especially the very young and Aboriginal youth, invariably make poor witnesses under cross-examination, and, all too easily, they can incriminate themselves. This happens not only in court but also after arrest, during police questioning. Paradoxically, some procedures designed to reduce the potential for abuse have either been subverted by the police or have had unintended negative consequences. For example, as Kathy Laster noted, in Victoria all police interviews now have to be taped. This, she claimed, has acted as a 'disincentive to diversion. Now that they have a tape recorder, the chances are they are more inclined to charge instead of letting young people off or not taking notice'. This, Laster notes 'is simply a pressure of circumstances'. It is a relatively painless procedure, especially on a cold winter's night, for police to bring the accused into the station out of the cold, and to sit down and turn the tape recorder on. Prior to this, however, when considerable amounts of paper work were involved, the decision to bring a young person in for charging was less attractive. Thus a reform aimed at ensuring police interviews are conducted with propriety seems to have undermined the use of diversion from the formal juvenile justice system.

David Alcock was less than satisfied with the outcomes of another well-intentioned reform, in this case in South Australia, designed to protect Aboriginal juveniles while they were being questioned by police. In that state, police are now obliged to have a parent or guardian, or an officer from the Aboriginal Legal Rights Movement present when they interview the young accused. David Alcock maintained that often when a defendant attempted to remain silent, divulging only the information required by law, parents subverted this. Because these parents wanted to get themselves and their child home as quickly as possible, in their haste they often encouraged compliance with the police. Thus, Alcock concluded that although the requirement that a third party be present during the interview represents an attempt 'to empower people by giving them the opportunity to invoke their legal rights . . . on some occasions, such moves may be very counter-productive'.

With juveniles so clearly disadvantaged by our formal juvenile justice system, workshop discussion turned to alternatives and ameliorative reforms. Broadly speaking, participants supported maximum use of programs which minimised apprehensions and arrests, and which dealt with those brought into the system in alternative-to-court programs. The New Zealand model of family group conferences was seen as exemplary in rerouting most children away from the courts. There was also support for minimising confrontation between police and young people in public places, by utilising community service personnel in these situations instead. Joy Wundersitz pointed out that such an idea had proved effective in Hindley Street, Adelaide, where a small intervention unit comprising Aboriginal and non-Aboriginal workers took to the street during the critical late-night period when young people congregated and were most likely to become involved with the police. When alerted to the possibility of trouble, the police would call on the intervention unit to approach the youth and try to defuse the situation, rather than have the police move in and run the risk of escalating the matter to the point of arrest and charging.

Linda Hancock favoured the adoption of community policing squads and practices which, she argued, provided positive ways of policing youth. These squads were also regarded as good role models for other police, helping them to become practitioners of humane, preventative policing. However, undermining this educative role is the low regard in which community policing squads are held within police forces. As Hancock pointed out, their low status was linked to the nature of their caseloads. These largely involve women and children, and 'work with children and families gets accorded a low status generally'. There was, however, some anecdotal evidence in Victoria of the positive effects on police of participation in a community policing unit. It was also argued by Michael O'Connor that successful community policing might require a change of perspective in Australia—rather than police using the community to carry out police work (as happens for example in Neighbourhood Watch) the community should use the police. Michael Hogan suggested that the community and the police should have equal responsibility and capacity to drive community policing policy. He recommended that more mechanisms for negotiation with young people be developed, perhaps through local youth services. He also advocated more camps for local police and young people (like those which had operated previously for some Sydney inner-city youth), to enable them to explore their mutual expectations.

Workshop participants considered ways of reforming the police, of monitoring them, and of making them accountable for their policing of young people. It was recognised that many police are themselves concerned about police–youth relations, and about police violence. The participants highlighted a number of positive, police-initiated programs which have been established as an alternative to confrontationalist policing. Garth Luke cited the example of New South Wales, where police officers who have a track record of using sound community policing techniques when dealing with Aboriginal youth, have been appointed as General Duties Youth Officers. The aim is to increase the numbers of these appointments so that there is one General Duties Youth Officer attached to each patrol. It was recognised, however, that such preventative policing can conflict with routine policing. Michael Hogan cited the carrying of guns as a case in point. Regulations in New South Wales provide that all officers, irrespective of personal preference, must wear a gun, even though this conflicts with the principles and practices of preventative community policing. In practice, the problem was solved informally: authorities now turn a 'blind eye' to the non-wearing of guns by the General Duties Youth Officers.

Concerns were expressed about establishing a specialist police unit for youth because it could become marginalised within the force, as has happened with community policing units. Were this to occur, the ability of these units to reform police attitudes and behaviour towards young people would be limited. Eventually, the group gave its support to a specialist police–youth unit concerned with training and policy making which would influence recruits and officers at all levels. Such a unit would operate in conjunction with street-level initiatives, like the widespread deployment of General Duties Youth Officers.

While strong police policy statements were considered an important means of curbing excessive police discretion and circumscribing police behaviour, it was noted by Michael O'Connor that such statements need monitoring to ensure that they are taking effect. For example, for police to exercise restraint with regard to young people on the street (a radical departure from the norm), a strong policy statement and monitoring program would be required.

Participants discussed the role and effectiveness of crime prevention programs. One problem with these programs is the uncertain nature of funding. Linda Hancock described one pilot program in Victoria which received funding for only twelve months. It was established to minimise the juvenile justice response to young people in crisis or at risk, and involved social workers accompanying police when they are called out to such events. The aim is to resolve the issue immediately, by accessing support groups who provide a 24-hour, around-the-clock service. Combining the resources of police and Health and Community Services, this team, (like the South Australian Hindley Street intervention unit) was designed to spread the responsibility for youths in distress to authorities other than the police. Limited funding for these programs raises questions not only about their long-term effectiveness, but also about monitoring and evaluating such strategies in the short-term. It also raises questions about the genuineness of the government's commitment to change.

There was concern that as long as the police, and their community sponsors, accept violence as the norm, future steps to make police accountable will fail. Police will merely continue to find ways of subverting any such measures which are introduced. Legislative controls on police accountability were not favoured, on the grounds that they are easily subverted and have not worked in the past. The success of police-complaints authorities and of ombudspersons was also questioned, because in practice, these bodies or agents are inaccessible to young people. It was argued that police complaints tribunals did not get to the heart of the matter because of the legal protections available to police officers who prefer not to give evidence to these tribunals. With this kind of reputation, it is not surprising that complaints tribunals see few young complainants.

While police subverted some procedures intended to protect young people, others failed because of faulty design. Linda Hancock explained how police in Victoria were deterred from filling in a short questionnaire intended to provide data for a central register of young people at risk, because of a 'fifty page coding guide [they] have to go through in order to fill out the four page questionnaire'.

Other mechanisms to encourage greater police accountability were discussed. Michael O'Connor described how, in rural areas of England, the local police officer attends the community's parish meetings. This makes that police officer more accountable to the community at the local level. Adequate record-keeping by police was considered an important means of ensuring accountability. It was remarked that police in Australia keep minimal records of people in their custody, for example. By contrast, as Michael O'Connor noted, in Britain detailed information is recorded on those in custody. It includes such data as who they have asked to see, whether they have seen a lawyer or doctor, been interviewed, or eaten food. The custody form is completed not by the officer dealing with the prisoner, but by a custody officer. The form and the information contained in it are also checked by senior police. They are seen as a tool of management, benefiting both police and those in custody.

In terms of the police custody of juveniles, firm guidelines for detaining youth, easing restrictions on bail, and the use of court attendance notices were seen as fundamental safeguards. Police attitudes to bonds for youth were also perceived to be a problem requiring urgent review. It was recommended, for example, that a duty solicitor be present at the police station when decisions about bail are being made. Ultimately, the group concluded, there should be a presumption of no custody for juveniles. While this provision would not make it impossible to detain children in custody, it would make it very difficult, and each detention would have to be justified. Finally, it was noted that police stations were inappropriate places for youth to be detained.

Participants agreed that the community should consider how, and for what purpose, it wants its youth policed. The community has a responsibility to give the police clear guidelines about what is acceptable police practice. However, police must not be alienated by the reform process and, indeed, they should be party to it.

In summary, workshop participants addressed three key questions in this session. Why is it so easy for police to abuse the young? What is the effect on youth of police violence? What can be done about it? The responsibility for stemming police violence towards youth was thought to extend beyond individual police, and beyond the police hierarchy. The community at large was judged to be tacitly supportive of current police behaviours because it has failed to intercede effectively, even when faced with clear evidence of police brutality. Police violence is sustained by widespread tolerance, if not approval, and by the unequal balance of power between young people and the police.

Youth perceptions of the juvenile justice system as a whole, and their sense of being dealt with justly, are strongly influenced by their poor relationships with police. The community and the police need to work in concert to create appropriate boundaries within which the police can conduct their business legally and humanely.

The following recommendations on the policing of youth were made:

- That police acknowledge there is a problem of police violence towards youth. The problem is either not recognised at present or it is rationalised to a level of acceptability.

- That there be an independent review in each state of police violence to young people and of other matters bearing on police–youth conflict.

- That police recognise and support the rights of young people to use public space, and that, through negotiation, they promote reasonable relations with youth in public areas.

- That measures to ensure police accountability are set in place. These would include the establishment, by legislation, of tribunals to which individuals and agencies acting as advocates can seek redress and police policy statements, whose outcomes are monitored, to curb the misuse of police discretion.

- That specialist units in the upper echelons of police forces be established to coordinate street-level initiatives for juveniles and to address matters of policy and training in youth matters.

- That police are given a mandate and encouragement to opt for inaction or no further action when dealing with young people.

- That a duty solicitor be available at police stations.

- That stringent restrictions apply to keeping youth in custody. If custody is necessary, young people should not be kept at police stations.

- That community policing be promoted, but in such a way that the community defines the style of policing.

Part IV

Informal processing

10 The search for alternatives to coercive justice

KEN POLK

Like any other set of social institutions, the juvenile justice system is undergoing constant development and change. In recent years, this has taken the form of challenges to the idea that correcting juveniles is possible within the traditional 'correctional' institutions and programs. Some now argue that the justice system may be able to help young people best by establishing programs located away from the training schools, by introducing procedures which reduce the stigma said to attach to programs operated within the justice system, and by utilising personnel who are not associated with juvenile justice agencies. The purpose of the present discussion is to examine the specific forms that these alternatives could take, and to assess their potential for alleviating the problems which bring youngsters to the attention of juvenile authorities.

The idea that correctional institutions could bring about the rehabilitation of juvenile offenders probably reached a peak of optimism in the 1950s and early 1960s. In these years, there was a flowering of the 'rehabilitation ideal', which argued for the development of treatment within institutional settings. A typical approach to the task was to determine for each youthful offender the level of personality development, and then provide individually-tailored treatment regimens within the correctional institution appropriate for that level (Warren, 1976).

The mid-1960s through 1970s saw a sustained attack on establishment corrections and, indeed, on the very idea of correctional treatment and rehabilitation itself. The sources of this attack were multiple. Partly, it was a result of problems within the justice arena. Not only were juvenile delinquency rates sky-rocketing, but also the many evaluations that were being conducted on programs run inside the juvenile institutions suggested, in general, that neither the old and traditional methods, nor even the new experimental treatment programs were effective in reducing the level of delinquency. As a consequence, reformers began to examine the exceptional powers given to juvenile authorities, raising questions about the appropriateness of the common practice of denying routine due process to juveniles. In short, a mood developed that the juvenile justice system was a 'tarnished superparent', and that 'nothing works' (for a review, see Empey, 1982). The attack was, in fact, on a much wider front. These were the years of the civil rights protests, and of the development of student unrest. One focal point was the Vietnam War, which served to widen the constituency of protest by young and old. In general, then, there was a climate of opposition to established institutions and established ways, both inside and outside of justice systems.

The responses, too, were varied. Labelling theorists called attention to the harmful consequences to youths of being caught up in the official system of justice. Lawyers called attention to the exceptional threats posed by the denial of due process to juveniles. Professionals working with young people argued for new programs which would avoid the dangers of processing within the justice system, most often (in the early years at least) by locating the desired services explicitly outside of that system.

Consequently, from the late 1960s onward, alternatives to traditional processing proliferated. Their general aim was to lessen the coerciveness and stigma found in the workings of the juvenile court or state training schools. The form of these new approaches tended to differ, however, depending on where they were located.

One set of procedures that became popular in the early 1970s were what were termed 'diversion' programs. Here the intention was to respond to young people who had come to the attention of either police or the juvenile court and deflect them out of the system before any official action was taken. Diversion programs are located toward the 'front end' of the justice system: they are intended to provide a mechanism for removing potential offenders from the system at an early point of contact.

Somewhat deeper into the system, there were various attempts at 'deinstitutionalisation' or 'decarceration' whereby juveniles destined for stays in correctional institutions were offered some form of community program. This entailed the use of halfway houses or community centres rather than youth training centres.

Others argued for 'decriminalising' some forms of juvenile 'misbehaviours', so that conduct such as truancy or running away from home would not provide grounds for arrest and court processing. If truancy were not a part of the juvenile code, then police would not have the authority to apprehend or intervene, and thus the problem would have to be dealt with by some agency outside the boundaries of juvenile justice.

All of these alternatives shared the basic premise that programs designed to help troublesome young people are best located beyond the framework of the traditional juvenile justice system (for a discussion, see Empey, 1982). Cohen (1985) has coined the global term 'destructuring' to refer to the process of reducing the size and reach of justice agencies.

In the twenty or so years that have passed since the initial bloom of this period of 'destructuring', the debate has become more diverse and complicated. One stream of writers has pointed out that destructuring may have quite different results from those initially intended, including the ultimate contradictory trend of 'widening the net' of justice rather than closing it. That is, rather than reducing the reach of juvenile justice, that system's boundaries actually may have been inadvertently expanded (see for example, Klein, 1979; Austin and Krisberg, 1981; Polk, 1984a, 1987; Cohen, 1985, 1987).

Others have assumed that there is truth in the adage that 'nothing works' in terms of rehabilitation in correctional institutions. They have urged that, since we cannot rehabilitate, we ought both to try to reduce the over-reach of juvenile justice, and to ensure that, within that system, justice and fairness prevail (in some forms this is known as the 'justice' model, e.g. Hudson, 1987).

Yet another group of writers, committed to the classic liberalism implicit in the rehabilitation ideal, argue that treatment can work. Under the right circumstances, classic treatment programs and programs cast in such frameworks as diversion will rehabilitate young offenders (e.g. Binder and Geis, 1984). Such professionals want to restore faith in the ability of the juvenile justice system to correct.

Then there are the advocates of 'new left realism', who reject the 'impossibilism' popular with some commentators. Such writers attempt to establish a new agenda for reform, one which recognises the importance of crime control to the communities most affected by crime (Matthews, 1987). Since it is mostly the working-class communities which suffer from the everyday impact of crime, new strategies and targets of crime prevention need to be constructed which confer power to control crime on the community itself.

In Australia, the juvenile justice systems operating in the various states reflect a mix of the various ideologies. At their core is the youth correctional system, including the provision of youth training centres for those seen as the most difficult of juvenile offenders. At the same time, both for program and budgetary reasons, the correctional agencies usually wish to establish community-based programs as alternatives to placement in the institutional settings. In Victoria, for example, there has been a consistent move in recent years to reduce the number of youthful offenders in the state training schools. Simultaneously, there has been an increasing use of alternatives, such as attendance centres and community programs.

What are the implications of this attempt to shift from institutional to community-based programs for delinquent young persons? Is this movement of corrections into the community a healthy shifting of responsibility back to communities and neighbourhoods where the problems originate, or does it represent a move to extend the formal net of social control outward from the limited base within the justice system into the community itself?

In attempting to answer these questions, the following discussion will focus on two central issues. The first is the nature of adolescence and what are perceived to be adolescent problems. Here the concern is with such issues as: Why is there seen to be a need for a juvenile justice system at all? What is it about youthfulness that has required an entirely separate system of justice for young people? The second issue concerns the general historical patterns of social control of adolescent behaviour that have evolved over the past decades. This entails an analysis of the guiding ideas that have driven the systems which emerged to control youthful misconduct.

The problems of youth

One must comprehend and balance the many competing theoretical perspectives on juvenile justice with a clear statement of what it is about young people, and specifically the problems they pose for social control, that requires their special treatment. The idea of adolescence is a relatively recent invention, as is the derivative notion that there is a separate and distinct class of adolescent problems. Conflicts between young and old are ancient, but the idea that juveniles constitute a separate class of persons, with unique needs in terms of the bureaucratic organisation of social control, is an idea that began to crystallise roughly a century ago.

The long-term trends toward industrialisation (which continue today in the form of post-industrial developments) were accompanied by a radical reshaping of social life. As the modernising economies expanded their industrial capacities, people shifted from country areas into the cities and new forms of family life emerged. At the same time, drastically altered forms of class relations appeared. Dense working-class communities evolved in the developing cities of the middle and late nineteenth century.

All of these trends had (and in their modern forms, continue to have) special implications for young people. In the earliest phases of industrialisation, the young were often recruited for the new jobs in factories. As the pace of industrialisation quickened, however, there was a progressive push of the very young out of the labour force. A major feature of the late nineteenth and early twentieth century was the removal of very young children, under the age of twelve, from direct forms of economic productivity. Disconnected from earlier family-based forms of economic production, and removed from the newly emerging class of industrial workers, the first wave of marginal children began to 'roam the streets'.

The social control response

The developing, newly-urbanised societies were thereby confronted with the basic problem of what to do with a large pool of idle children, especially working-class children. The resultant strategies were two-pronged. At one level, there was what might be called a 'developmental control strategy', which saw the emergence of mass public education. Such schooling, especially in working-class communities, was designed initially to provide the minimal level of literacy and numeracy required for the new working roles being created. In addition, it sought to socialise the young into appropriate compliance with the new order. It also occupied their time. At a second level, there was a need to address what were seen as unacceptable forms of troublesome and deviant behaviour among such young people. (Bear in mind that this was the time when Australia saw the emergence of the phenomenon of the 'larrikin'.) Prior to this, there were no special provisions for children above the age where criminal culpability could be assumed. Children, as was true of adults, had been fully exposed to the attempt to control the dangerous classes of the seventeenth and eighteenth centuries through the terror of a vastly expanded system of execution in England. With the shift away from that policy, they shared with adults first, the fate of transportation and then, the experience of incarceration in what Irwin (1985) has termed the 'fortress prison'.

The control mechanisms directed at young people of the lower classes consisted of what can be termed the first great form of diversion, the emergence of separate juvenile courts at the turn of the century. It is interesting how rapidly these developed throughout the English-speaking countries, with most jurisdictions putting in place such institutions somewhere between 1895 and 1915. These institutions provided a set of 'coercive control' mechanisms which can be viewed as a form of back-up to the wider 'developmental control institutions', such as schools, which were being established at about the same time.

The existing adult courts and prisons, premised on regimens of punishment, harsh discipline and penance, were deemed inappropriate vehicles for the correction of the young. Although still based on the capacity of the state to impose coercion, the juvenile court became an explicit device for widening the mandate of control, from forms of strictly defined crimes to a wider set of concerns about the 'conduct' of young persons thought to be in social 'danger'. Thus what later became known as the 'status offences' were introduced into the juvenile court codes. These included, as grounds for adjudication, such phrases as 'being in danger of leading a lewd or immoral life', 'endangering one's own welfare', or 'being in need of care and protection'. In other words, from its inception the juvenile justice system was both a diversion (from the adult system) and an exercise in net-widening (in the sense that the boundaries of controlled behaviour were widened). Its stated purpose was that of protecting the interests of the child. It reflected the state's concern to provide for the 'proper' upbringing of a much-needed future workforce with basic literacy skills and commitment to such values as hard work and industriousness.

From that point on, the history of approaches to young offenders— shifting from enthusiasm, to reform, and ultimately to dismay—has been well documented (e.g. Empey, 1982). When early findings of social science began to demonstrate the inadequacies of custodial institutions as centres of rehabilitation and correction, the first response was to bring about internal reorganisation within these institutions. One such endeavour was the

Highfields project (McCorkle, Elias and Bixby, 1958) which was designed to use the peer pressures operating in such institutions as a positive force for rehabilitation. This form of treatment was referred to as 'guided group interaction'.

When these reforms, in turn, failed to deliver their promises, social scientists began to focus on the coercion inherent in custodial environments. They sought alternatives which would lessen the amount of control inside such institutions. One major option was to move some corrective programs closer to the 'community'. This approach was utilised in the Provo experiment (Empey and Rabow, 1961) which shared many of the assumptions of the guided group interaction of the Highfields project, but located the treatment in a community rather than an institutional setting.

When a full attack was mounted against the formalised juvenile justice system in the late 1960s and early 1970s, the various forms of destructuring (diversion, deinstitutionalisation, decriminalisation, etc.) began to evolve which, in essence, represented a second great wave of 'diversion'. As in the century before, many of these were attempts to pull back from the existing coercive system of justice, while at the same time, widening the net of justice in terms of both the forms of intervention considered and the kinds of persons who would carry out such interventions. Since the beginning of the 1970s, many millions of dollars have been spent on diversion programs (such as youth service bureaux or police cautioning programs) and on various attempts to establish community-based programs (such as halfway houses or attendance centres) as forms of deinstitutionalisation.

Reflecting their different legal traditions, the specific forms that these alternatives have taken have varied from country to country. In the United States there was a long period of flirtation with the various forms of 'destructuring', followed by a confusing period in which various approaches operated. This included a call for the 'justice model', a plea by some for a return to the 'rehabilitative ideal', and for others, continued tinkering with new variations on the theme of destructuring.

It is my perception that the destructuring phase came somewhat later in England, and that it was never as widespread. It has been followed in the 1980s and into the 1990s by what appears to be competition between the 'justice' model and a continued expansion of various forms of destructuring models (with continued emphasis on deinstitutionalisation and diversion, for example).

Destructuring also came relatively late to Australia, although the timing varied from state to state. Western Australia, for example, introduced a diversionary system of children's panels in the mid 1960s, with South Australia following suit in 1972. A formal police cautioning scheme became operational in Queensland in the 1960s, but similar schemes did not take a firm hold in Victoria and New South Wales until the mid to late 1980s. Deinstitutionalisation of youthful offenders appeared as a significant policy thrust in the mid 1980s, but again, there were some regional variations, with this move taking place in South Australia in the 1970s. Overall, though, what has happened in Australia (given that professional knowledge slips rapidly over national boundaries) is that the destructuring alternatives are being put in place at the same time that the justice model is being considered.

The question of net-widening

A suggestion often made in critical reviews of such destructuring efforts is that they may have an effect quite opposite to that which is intended. Throughout the 1970s there were persistent concerns that diversion in particular may actually widen, rather than narrow, the reach of the justice system (Klein, 1979). What is the current status of that argument? To what extent can it be said today that diversion programs are net-widening? Several observations can be offered in response to this question.

First, we must consider the nature of youthful misbehaviour that triggers the response of the juvenile justice system in the first instance. There continues to be a constant evolution of the problems of economically disadvantaged young people, with the more obvious forms pressing themselves upon the consciousness, and conscience, of the nation. There is in Australia, as elsewhere, an emergent youth 'underclass' which has been dispossessed by the economic transformations. There is little room in the economy for those individuals with not much to offer in the way of qualifications, skills or experience who are trying to enter the adult world of work. Accordingly, the state is now confronted with various forms of youthful distress. These include such problems as long-term unemployment, homelessness and, spinning off from these, troublesome behaviour ranging from the trivial to the serious.

Because, historically, a significant proportion of youth problems have come to be defined in such social control terms as 'runaway', 'truancy', or 'children in need of care and protection', as well as the use of terms such as 'delinquency', it is expected that the juvenile justice system will be central in program responses. Put another way, these youth problems are not viewed fundamentally in economic terms, but in terms of the need to impose coercive procedures to 'control' the 'misbehaviour'. The state thus continues to base its strategies of social control on procedures which are segregative and exclusionary rather than integrative and inclusionary.

An alternative and positive approach to social control would be located in such developmental institutions as the school. Integrative (in contrast to segregative) policies would be designed around procedures which pull all participants, including those perceived as moving toward the margins, into the mainstream of activity (see Polk, 1984b and Knight, 1985; and the discussion of Braithwaite, 1989:176). For example, a group of young people (including some known to be in trouble) could form part of a consultant team to work with teachers on a program of alcohol education in the school. Such mechanisms are designed to pull all young people toward the centre of school activity. Hence, they stand in sharp contrast to the negative, exclusionary approaches of the justice process which result in the segregation of 'offenders' and their symbolic and stigmatising designation as different from others. Yet it is precisely these segregative and stigmatising approaches that are extended into the newly-formed community-based alternatives. While the ultimate power of the juvenile justice system derives from its capacity to impose coercive sanctions (institutionalisation), most proposed policy options seek to find an appropriate response which avoids the more obvious manifestations of legal coerciveness. This endeavour is an attempt to cope with the problem of social control of youth by means of a 'community-based' strategy, rather than with an institutional one. Provision must be made, of course, for the persistent few that are seen as dangerous offenders. As Pratt (1989:247) puts the matter:

The 'hard core' will still be locked up; but a delinquency management service is now provided in the community for that troublesome segment of the youth population not dangerous enough to lock away but too disruptive to ignore.

Pratt argues that, at least in England and Wales, a 'corporatist' model of juvenile justice is emerging in which there is increased centralisation of policy, a heightened level of government intervention and an expanded web of 'co-operation of various professional and interest groups into a collective whole with homogeneous aims and objectives' (Pratt, 1989:245). Working within this model, community interventions are generated which 'blur the boundaries' between strictly justice agencies and other community institutions, resulting in the creation of teams consisting of social workers, probation officers, youth workers and teachers.

The melding of juvenile justice into this network, however, has a price. Its required emphasis on control and surveillance dictates the nature of such cooperation. Rather than seeing the generation of separate inclusive, integrative strategies within such developmental spheres as schools and employment training centres, these services become coopted within a logic of segregative, coercive social control. In Pratt's words:

Instead of a shift from the inhumanities and injustices of the last institution, we find these features of the carceral system now being reproduced in the community—in those projects that are supposed to be *alternatives* to the institution (Pratt, 1989:252).

As Austin and Krisberg (1981) have pointed out, however, the resultant widening of the net of juvenile justice can take many forms. It can include the establishment of *different* nets (where new programs supplement rather than replace previous programs), *denser* nets (where the alternatives increase the intensity of intervention) and *wider* nets (where persons who previously would have been ignored become swept up, thus increasing the total number of persons under control).

One of the fundamental reasons for this widening of the net of social control is the inability of the state to provide effective economic and educational solutions to problems generated by the constant pressures exerted on young people by technological change. Given that failure to put in place positive, developmental options, the state falls back on two strategies. It defines the resultant problems as issues of social control, and then puts in place widened social control programs.

As such interventions expand outward from strictly juvenile justice agencies and functions to the community, the development agencies within the community (including schools and recreational agencies) become penetrated and, to some degree, are taken over by the logic of the juvenile justice system. Instead of schools providing improved educational and economic options for all students (including the economically disadvantaged), special units are created to manage the behavioural problems posed by the underclass. Potentially, this can lead to schools becoming involved in a variation of what Irwin (1985) has called 'management of the rabble'.

Conclusion

The conclusion that is offered, then, is that diversion, and its related forms of destructuring involving young offenders, will continue to represent an expansion of the coercive control mechanisms of the state. This assumes that ongoing technological advancement will continue to put economically disadvantaged young people at risk. There are two distinct strategies which could deal with such problems. One is an economically or educationally based developmental approach. This would emphasise the importance of integration and inclusion which calls for an opening up of opportunity and advancement. The answer to homelessness and youth alienation would be to improve access to challenging education or training programs, and/or to employment programs that open up pathways to conventional life. Such inclusive strategies play only a minor role today in the youth policies evolving in nations such as Australia, the United Kingdom or the United States.

Instead, there is a reliance on the second approach, which emphasises segregative, coercive control strategies in which the juvenile justice system is the central organising agency. Though many of the presenting behavioural problems do not constitute law violations, this approach defines them in terms of social control. And so, (true to its history) the system moves toward non-coercive, community-based solutions which aim to 'nip the problem in the bud'. The net of control is widened to scoop up clients previously ignored or dealt with elsewhere, new agencies are coopted into the coercive control enterprise, and new forms of control intervention evolve (Polk, 1984a).

This is not to argue, however, that the agents of juvenile justice should cease to seek alternatives to coercive, custodial institutions. It is perfectly reasonable to examine control policies and argue, where appropriate, for the least restrictive alternatives. In fact, in recent years, in Australia there has been some interesting theorising about ways of sanctioning within the justice system that minimise penalties (for example, the suggestions of Freiberg, 1986, and the notions of 'shaming and reintegration' of Braithwaite, 1989).

We agree with Matthews (1987:357) when he argues that focusing only on the pessimistic message (regarding the widening of social control) may lead to 'the premature abandonment of a search for alternatives to incarceration'. It is *theoretically* possible both to divert (or decarcerate) and to restrict net-widening in such endeavours.

It may seem odd that programs which purport to be alternatives to formal intervention could have such net-widening effects. But, as argued elsewhere (Polk, 1987) the reason that the system of justice expands is because the programs are, in most cases, funded by the justice system, personnel are drawn from that system, the flow of clients tends to be controlled by that system and, more importantly, the theories of delinquency and youth problems which guide diversion are justice system theories. Thus, rather than seeing net-widening as an unanticipated consequence of such destructuring initiatives as diversion (as Cohen, 1985, has suggested), the expansion of social control should be viewed as a logical result of the basic ideas and intentions of those who create such programs.

Ultimately, the basic problem is the inability of the contemporary state to give priority to policies of positive, inclusive development for young people generally, and the economically disadvantaged in particular. The basic features of integrative strategies are easy to identify. They are premised on the importance of providing access for all individuals to challenging jobs, training and education. Thus, school and work programs will be at the core of any integrative strategy. These developmental activities in the main would be designed to heighten the youngsters' sense that they have something to contribute to the community. Such contribution is easy to demonstrate when young people (including some who have been identified as troublesome) play out such roles as tutor, recreation aide, community researcher, or environmental advocate. Such integrative approaches provide both the immediate gratifications of jobs and wages, and contribute to the longer range development of youth by providing training, skills and experience.

The failure to consider positive programs for youth has caused the range of problems associated with the state employing coercive social control, based in the criminal law. Once this happens, it follows that the juvenile justice system will be called into action. The new dispossessed, 'dangerous class' of youth becomes managed by a broad set of control mechanisms which are forced to widen out to incorporate new forms of misbehaviour (many far removed from violations of the criminal law), then new clients, with new forms of collaboration with community agencies, and then new programs. Diversion becomes one of the devices for carrying out this widening of social control.

11 Informal processing: the South Australian experience

MICHAEL BARRY

Informal processing is present in any justice system. At its most basic, it exists when police choose not to define a particular incident as criminal, or to ignore that behaviour, or to warn the alleged offender without any formal action being taken. Without doubt, by far the bulk of informal processing is exercised at this level in most justice systems.

However, when informal procedures become institutionalised (such as in South Australia, with its system of children's aid panels and screening panels), such processing is no longer anonymous. Regardless of disclosure safeguards, the informal process becomes an inherent component of the justice system. This fact cannot be disguised by the apparently benevolent ideals which underpin and justify these informal processing mechanisms. Nor is this observation restricted to the panel system as it operates in South Australia; it can also be applied to institutionalised police cautioning programs such as those operating in Victoria, Queensland and New South Wales, and to other diversionary programs such as the Family Group Conference system in New Zealand.

The panel system operating in South Australia has been criticised both inside and outside of the jurisdiction. Much of the criticism has focused on the claim that panels have widened the net of social control. It is argued that, because these panels were designed to have a beneficial, welfare-oriented, early interventionist approach to youth offending, their introduction encouraged police in South Australia to channel a greater number of early offenders into the system. In previous times, such offenders may have been 'let off' with a simple, on-the-spot warning.

Wundersitz (1989) has confirmed that when children's aid panels commenced operation in 1972, there was a significant increase in the total number of children brought into the system for processing: that is, a net-

116

widening effect occurred. Another marked increase occurred after 1979 when, under the new *Children's Protection and Young Offenders' Act*, screening panels were established to decide the most appropriate venue to which children should be referred. This Act also extended children's aid panels so that they could deal with youths up to the age of eighteen years.

These results indicate that the introduction of panels in South Australia actually increased the reported crime rate amongst juveniles in this state, without any direct relationship to underlying crime levels. Aid panels ensure that trivial offences committed by children are brought into the justice system and hence become incorporated within official crime statistics. If such panels had not existed, many of these matters would probably have been treated by on-the-spot police cautions, which do not form part of official crime statistics.

This may help to explain the finding (see Chapter 2) that South Australia has the second highest detected offence rate per thousand youth population in Australia. It seems unlikely that South Australia is a more criminal state than any other. Rather, it is probably due to the particular method of processing which this state has chosen to adopt.

The proponents of diversionary systems often lose sight of the implications of net-widening. For example, they usually base their claims for the success of these systems on the fact that the majority of children subject to such informal processing do not return to the justice system. I have been guilty of the same sin, arguing that aid panels have worked because some 87 per cent of children who have appeared before aid panels since their inception in 1972 have not subsequently appeared before a children's court (Department for Family and Community Services Annual Report, 1991).

Not only does this claim ignore the statistical aberrations which tend to inflate the 'success' measures, but more significantly, it disguises the fact that the introduction of panels almost certainly introduced a whole new group of minor offenders to the system, for whom the very act of detection and apprehension by police probably would have been sufficient to ensure that they did not offend again. For many of these young people and their families, the panel appearance itself was probably redundant, given that the primary impact was almost certainly achieved at the point where the young person was caught by police. Again, the same criticism can be applied to all other diversionary mechanisms, including institutionalised police cautioning systems.

Apart from net-widening, informal processing has other deficiencies. All such systems, for example, favour the compliant, the affluent and the intact family. Conversely, they punish the non-compliant, the disadvantaged and those from disrupted families. For such youths, their personal, family or cultural experiences do not encourage them to consider the state as a benevolent authority. Hence, they do not comprehend or appreciate the advantages inherent in diversion, and so do not respond to them appropriately. It is well known, for example, that marginalised youth, such as the chronically unemployed and Aborigines, often fail to appear at an aid panel hearing. Referral to court, with all its attendant disadvantages (such as a permanent criminal record), inevitably follows.

Furthermore, the delivery of institutionalised informal justice normally relies on white, middle class concepts such as respect for established authority, an acceptance of the existing socio-economic status quo, and an acceptance of the notions of contrition and remorse. Informal processing also relies on a preparedness to discuss with strangers intimate family details which are perceived by the authorities to have contributed to the alleged offence of the child. For some cultural groups, this is seen as unnecessary and an unwarranted intrusion on their privacy. Their subsequent failure to comply with requests for such family details may then be interpreted by the panellists as an unwillingness to cooperate, which in turn, may result in a harsher outcome for the child.

Yet, despite these deficiencies, there are some positive aspects. Even net-widening has not, it seems, produced the dire consequences it may have done. For example, although Wundersitz did find inferential evidence that net-widening occurred after both the 1972 introduction of aid panels, and the 1979 inception of screening panels, in both periods this net-widening was restricted to a very short period. A pattern of rapid increase was followed by stabilisation and decrease which, she concluded, 'suggests that the expansionary effect of the panels did not continue indefinitely. Instead, once the new target population of pre-delinquents had been identified, it henceforth stabilised' (Wundersitz, 1989:37). In other words, the panels were not progressively net-widening.

The Wundersitz study covered the period from 1972 to 1986, as illustrated in Figure 11.1. This graph is a dramatic representation of her findings, particularly in relation to the 1979 innovation of screening panels. However,

Figure 11.1 Rate of appearance per 1000 youth population, July 1972 to June 1990

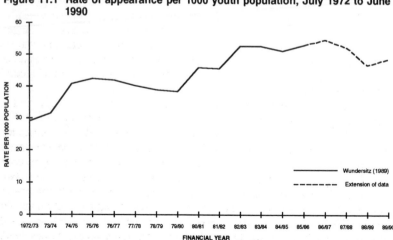

it is interesting to note that when this graph is extended to cover the more recent years, there has been a further downward trend in total appearances. The exception is the 1989/90 and 1990/91 financial years which went against this trend. It should be noted, however, that even though the rate of appearance did increase in these last two years, it is still lower than that recorded in the final year included in the Wundersitz study (1985/86).

What conclusion can be drawn about this apparent reduction in appearance rates? It seems unlikely that it represents a reduction in the real crime rate, given that total reported offences in South Australia increased over this time period. The more likely conclusion is that the reduction represents a further stabilisation in the operation of the panel systems (as predicted by Wundersitz) and, more importantly, a stabilisation in the police adjudication decision on whether to proceed with a matter. It seems that more common sense is now being used when deciding how minor offences and first offenders should be dealt with. As a result, more of these minor offences do not enter either the formal (court) or informal (panel) system.

Another feature should also be noted. Proponents of the net-widening theory argue that, because institutionalised forms of informal processing bring an increased number of young people under the net of social control, this should result in the greater penetration of this new group of offenders into all levels of the criminal justice system. That is, according to the 'labelling theory', it could be argued that net-widening would ultimately result in greater numbers of young people being subject to the most severe penalty—namely, incarceration.

However, the South Australian experience has been contrary to these expectations. The average number of children in detention has continued to diminish over the period since the net-widening reforms were introduced. Figure 11.2 illustrates this comparison. In 1972—the year in which aid panels were introduced—there was an average of 250 youths per day in institutional care. However, during all of the subsequent net-widening phases (from 1972 to 1989) this figure declined to less than an average of 50 youths in institutional care per day in 1989. Thus, the ultimate 'damage' feared by the theorists has not been realised in South Australia. Innovations which unintentionally widened the net of social control at the front-end of the system have not produced a corresponding increase in custodial populations. In fact, the reverse has occurred.

Another advantage of the panel system in South Australia is that it fulfils some form of social contract between the justice system, the police and, more indirectly, the community. Panels have had the unintended consequence of generating much better relationships between the police and the Department for Family and Community Services which, in turn, have encouraged real compromise and consensus between these two agencies. As a result, although we have more young people being drawn into the formal processing system, there are fewer going to court and fewer getting locked up. The whole panel system, particularly children's aid panels, is, in effect, a marketing tool whereby these results can be achieved.

Figure 11.2 Average number of youths per day in institutional care compared with the number of individuals per 1000 youth population processed by the juvenile justice system.

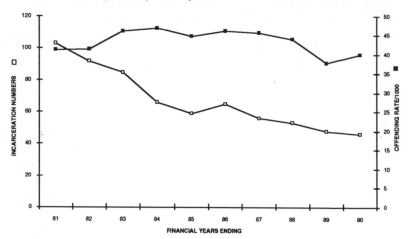

Note: The author wishes to thank Kym Thorpe, Department of Family and Community Services, for his assistance in the preparation of these graphs.

Conclusion

Not many people in South Australia would consider that children's aid panels fulfil a rehabilitative function. They do not believe that putting a police officer and a social worker in a room with a frightened parent and a frightened child actually has the cathartic effect of stopping crime. Most of us acknowledge that the majority of these youths probably would have stopped offending at the point of detection. However, in the absence of an effective police cautioning system, panels do ensure that the trivial cases are diverted out of the formal court system, thereby enabling the latter to focus more on the tougher end of the offending spectrum.

It could be argued, however, that if a state is going to opt for an institutionalised form of informal processing, it cannot afford to be half-hearted about it. The informal system has to be there for almost every offence, for every age group, and without rigid rules. Otherwise, there will only be a small subset of offences and a small group of offenders who will be dealt with by the panels. This is clearly illustrated by comparing the only two states in Australia which have panels operating at present. In South Australia, all young people are eligible for a panel appearance, and as a consequence, some 60 per cent of cases are dealt with in this way. By contrast, in Western Australia, where there are rigid criteria governing access to panels, less than 20 per cent of cases are dealt with in this way. The remainder end up in the court system.

Some of the issues relating to the concerns for due process that are raised by the operation of informal mechanisms, have been dealt with in earlier chapters. No further discussion will be undertaken here except to comment that they are probably best described by a comment from Alcock (1990, personal communication), who characterised screening panels as 'the last kangaroo court in the British criminal justice system—the only venue where two non-legally trained people sit and make important decisions about an individual's criminal history without the opportunity of any representation by any person, including the young person themselves'. This is one of the challenges facing informal processing mechanisms: to ensure that they are attentive to children's rights, and that they do not encourage or facilitate inappropriate admissions of guilt.

Where, then, does that leave panels? Wundersitz (1989:42) argues that 'if the problems associated with the panel system can be identified, the task of law reformers should be to overcome these deficiencies through modification of the existing mechanism. To abolish one or both may be counterproductive, especially since, as prior experience has indicated, any new scheme designed to replace them would probably also produce unforeseen, harmful side-effects'. Seymour (1988) also warns that tampering with a system is likely to produce unintended and probably undesirable consequences.

This expression of caution, however, is not an excuse for inaction. The other part of the message is that administrators should take steps to ensure that informal processing mechanisms work effectively. In particular, I would argue that the panel system in this state, especially at the screening level, should be further refined to ensure that the more trivial offences and offenders are removed entirely from informal panel processing where the intervention and resources of the state are neither warranted nor required. More importantly, the informal processing mechanisms must be constantly monitored to ensure that they do not discriminate unintentionally against the most disadvantaged in our society.

12 Alternatives to court

Compiled from workshop transcripts by
LYNN ATKINSON

The meaning and function of diversion, as a part of informal processing, were discussed at length by workshop participants, as were the Australian manifestations of this approach. In Australia, as Ken Polk pointed out, diversionary schemes are primarily intended to steer young offenders *away from* the courts and from the additional consequences associated with a court appearance, such as the acquisition of a criminal record. By contrast, in most United States jurisdictions, the emphasis is on diverting youths *into* programs.

Garth Luke spoke about the police push in New South Wales for a system of infringement notices for some designated offences, and the mandatory use of cautions in certain other cases. Police support for the initiative was thought to be connected with a reduction of paperwork. A scheme like this, if implemented, would divert considerably more trivial matters from court than is currently the case. Polk spoke of a diversionary scheme in San Antonio which similarly relied for any popularity it had with police on their dislike of paperwork. This scheme, operated by the Youth Service Bureau, had the added advantage for police that it was conveniently located on the way to the courthouse. The incentives of convenience and less paperwork therefore encouraged the police to reroute juveniles, otherwise destined for court, to this alternative.

The participants sought to identify the types of informal agencies which police would be willing to use in a diversionary way, and which were demonstrably helpful to juveniles caught in the justice net. Youth advocacy agencies, which take practical steps to redirect troublesome youth into interesting activities, meet these criteria, as does the Victorian Aboriginal community initiative to deal with drunks picked up by the police. The use of such agencies would shift the authority for dealing with matters away from the justice arena, and the emphasis would be on service, rather than on control. Such agencies can also be useful resources because they respond in a practical way to situations where police and young people have traditionally come into conflict. It was pointed out, however, that programs like this do have a high attrition rate because, as Polk commented, blame attaches to them when things start to go wrong. This was not seen as necessarily a bad thing: new agencies, with new staff and more creative ideas simply take their place.

Because some programs achieve their diversionary aim more successfully than others, their benefits are believed to justify the costs. In South Australia, for example, despite the initial net-widening effect which occurred after the children's aid panels were established, the primary aim of diverting large numbers from court has been achieved. According to Michael Barry, relations between social workers and the police have also improved, which he regarded as a bonus in the overall 'success' story. Such cooperative arrangements between welfare officers and police were viewed, however, with concern by other participants, who regarded them as further evidence of the omnipresent justice system infiltrating and ultimately capturing diversionary systems.

Successful diversion schemes in Australia should be less costly, less time-consuming and less punitive than the alternative of formal processing through the children's court. Workshop participants also noted that punitiveness in the court system extends beyond the sentences handed down: a structure which alienates young defendants appearing before the court, and adjournments which increase the number of appearances at court, ensure the process itself becomes a substantial part of the punishment. The official diversionary schemes set up in most of the states are arguably less punitive in terms of the process and certainly less punitive in terms of outcome. In most cases, once the child has been warned and counselled, the matter usually ends there. No further outcomes are imposed and there is no lasting criminal record.

However, a recent informal initiative in New South Wales, described by Michael Hogan, clearly departs from these particular standards of success. The new local community aid panels (CAPs) in New South Wales, as Hogan pointed out, 'are organised by local police but they require the co-operation of the courts in referring matters to them'. They involve a local solicitor and a police officer who devise 'useful' activities for young offenders, the completion of which is meant to mitigate their sentences in court. They have no statutory base and there are no regulations governing their operation. A more serious drawback, however, is that CAPs do not divert young people from court. Instead, children must first appear before the court before they can be referred to the panel. And, following the CAP hearing, a second court appearance is required for reporting back. It is at this second court appearance that the charge will be dealt with. In effect, it involves double processing, which is both punitive for the offender and costly to the system.

Because the scheme has no legislative standing, there are no legal penalties for non-compliance with orders from the CAP. Nevertheless, non-compliance can have a de facto impact at sentencing. Despite their emphasis on socially responsible activities for young offenders (such as donating blood), the CAPs, in effect, hand down community service orders before conviction. This is carried out under the banner of rehabilitation rather than punishment. Because they target first or minor offenders, CAPs are likely to be successful in the sense that many of the youths with whom they deal will probably not reoffend. However, according to the criteria for success listed earlier in the discussion, the CAPs do not measure up: system costs are not diminished; the number of court appearances for individual defendants are apparently increased, not reduced, and the number of young people dealt with overall in the children's courts is not reduced.

Police support for the CAP initiative contrasts with their antipathy towards the police cautioning scheme in New South Wales, which has been considerably less successful in diverting young offenders from court than the cautioning schemes operating in Queensland and Victoria. One possible explanation for police support of the CAPs lies in the opportunity it gives to police to exercise the 'treatment' option, especially since there is the powerful added safeguard of a double dose of court appearances. Clearly, if a program involving police is to be successful, it must at least have their support. However, if a scheme is coopted by the police, and fails to meet the other important criteria for success (such as actual diversion from the courts; less punishment; non-acquisition of a criminal record) that scheme, although supported by the police, merely becomes self-serving, rather than 'successful'.

Participants agreed that models of successful diversion should include appropriate and adequate screening measures to determine the clientele. In the Australian context, diversionary schemes usually target and ensnare juveniles at the 'soft' end of the offender spectrum: first, minor and often younger offenders. A successful screening procedure should minimise net-widening by setting aside cases involving trivial offences (particularly those relating to breaches of public order), so that no further action would be taken. Further, the screening procedure should direct a substantial number of more serious cases to the diversionary scheme, leaving only very serious property offences and offences against the person to be dealt with in the courts. In a cautionary note it was pointed out that there will always be a need to protect the public against certain offenders. Ken Polk spoke of the formal justice system as a scarce and very expensive resource, too costly to be invoked for trivial matters, but to be used when the situation requires it. He pointed out that the Dutch regard prisons as an expensive resource 'not to be wasted'. Why not, he asked, treat the justice system as a whole in the same way?

One of the problems noted by Joy Wundersitz in current screening procedures is their inability to ensure equal access to diversionary schemes for Aboriginal juveniles. John Braithwaite's idea of introducing a well-resourced, expert third-party advocacy group into the regulatory framework (outlined later in this summary), has relevance here.

It was also argued that, because the diversion process begins after the police have responded to an incident, an early screening mechanism or 'circuit breaker' was needed which would stop further action on trivial, particularly police-generated, charges once the police had become involved. Michael O'Connor suggested that an independent person be located in the police station so that if a juvenile were brought in on a trivial charge 'a discussion can stop it from going any further'. The aim, as he saw it, would be to intervene before, rather than after, a report was lodged by police. Another suggestion was that a youth worker–coordinator be located at the police station to deal with juveniles brought in by police. This person would screen incoming cases for no further action, referral to other agencies, referral to the court diversion program or, for serious cases, a referral to the formal juvenile justice system. Ken Polk supported the idea in principle, but thought it would not solve the problem since, no matter how trivial the offence, the police would continue to respond to pressures to 'clean the streets'. What was required, he argued, was a fundamental change in public attitudes and police policy.

A suggestion for intervention at a later stage was for the children's court prosecutor to have the authority to screen trivial cases out of the formal process and, preferably, out of the juvenile justice system altogether. A variation on this would be to have a prosecuting unit to which an application could be made by the defendant to have a trivial matter (the sort that now often results in a court dismissal) thrown out. It was pointed out that this should happen before the matter proceeds to court, to prevent the defendant from being caught up in the punitive court process.

Apart from the benefits usually associated with informal processing, there were others which were noted. Participants remarked on the capacity of diversion schemes to reflect and uphold the values of particular communities and to meet their needs. In this context, John Braithwaite argued that, in providing alternatives to formal legal processing, we should be seeking to identify particular community groups and constituencies and giving them more power and resources to provide advocacy services.

Braithwaite went on to outline a way to achieve a solution of empowerment. The juvenile justice system at present involves the defendant in a grossly unequal relationship with the state. Braithwaite proposed transforming this relationship by including an expert third party who would represent, lobby, advocate for, and empower particular youth constituents. For example, feminist groups might assist girls involved in crime and Aboriginal groups might help Aborigines involved in the juvenile justice system. Under such a tripartite arrangement, these advocacy groups would be funded by government, and would work to diminish state control over their young constituents, and to address their clients' specific needs.

While supporting this in principle, Kathy Laster argued that there were problems associated with enlisting the services of advocates from the youth's own ethnic background. She asked, 'Who, in the ethnic community, would be an appropriate person to place in that position? And, after they had been there a while, would they still be in touch with that community, or would they get brought into the system and adopt its values?' There is the additional question of whether the young person would regard them as an empowering agent or part of the system.

Laster also noted that, in certain situations, having a system which reinforced ethnic values may not always be acceptable to the young person involved. By way of illustration, she cited the case of girls from patriarchal communities who, in many cases, would prefer to be dealt with formally by the court, rather than by way of informal mechanisms which tried to reinforce the values of their own community. By seeking to impose such cultural assumptions as 'the father has a right to keep his daughter at home', informal procedures could potentially disempower the young person.

Another perceived benefit of diversion was that it might help reduce the sensational reporting of children's court cases. In other words, the more cases diverted away from court, the fewer opportunities there would be for reporting juvenile hearings. There would therefore be less ammunition for media-driven law-and-order campaigns. Since several states appear to be in the grip of sensational media reporting of juvenile crime, it was considered that any measures which take youth out of that distorting spotlight would promote greater justice.

Participants also considered the relationship between diversion and incarceration. Successful diversion schemes can drastically reduce the number of youths passing through the courts and into detention centres. As Michael Barry pointed out, funds could be released to develop creative solutions at the 'hard' end. However, the fact of crowded courts and detention centres in some jurisdictions (despite the presence of diversionary schemes), suggests that this is not always the case. Instead, diversionary schemes run the risk of absorbing available resources and community goodwill and taking them away from those who most need them—namely, the serious and recidivist offenders. Ken Polk also noted that, while it might be cheaper to divert a child from court, rarely do diversion schemes replace costly institutions: these tend to remain, and so in practice, overall costs are actually increased. In effect, diversionary schemes become accessories, rather than alternatives, to formal processing.

Some of the negative features of diversionary schemes include their failure to attend to the underlying structural and economic problems confronting large sections of the youth population. Diversionary schemes (even those which have minimised net-widening or restricted it to the 'soft' end of the justice continuum) also increase the reach, if not the depth, of state control. Multiple diversionary schemes in the same jurisdiction are problematic for similar reasons. As John Pratt pointed out, in England in the 1980s diversionary programs were well resourced but, because of their sheer numbers, they often lacked the clients to sustain them. There were claims of client poaching by self-serving diversionary programs struggling for existence and a piece of the funding pie. This creates subtle pressures for net-widening, with the welfare model creating and rationalising the need for clients.

Pratt outlined one diversionary scheme, however, which approximated the group's informal definition of success, and which seemed to avoid most of the major costs of diversion. The New Zealand Family Group Conference (FGC) diverts the vast majority of cases away from the juvenile court. Once the case has been screened by the youth justice coordinator and referred to an FGC, the local community, the family of the offender and the victim (if they so choose) are involved in designing appropriate sanctions. These are intended to affirm community values, to help the offender, and to provide, in many cases, restitution to the victim. The particular circumstances of the youth are discussed and addressed as far as possible with existing resources. Like most other youth court diversion programs, however, participation in the scheme relies on a prior admission of guilt by the offender.

The New Zealand scheme favours solutions which empower offenders. And yet it also confronts offenders with their responsibilities—either to the victim or to the community. In turn, community responsibility for the condition of marginalised youth is neither underestimated nor undervalued. The scheme derives from an attempt to deal with offending by Maori youth, and was premised on the need to reinforce or inculcate in these young people respect for traditional Maori values.

Participants expressed interest in the FGC scheme, but Jeanette Lawrence wondered whether it would be relevant to white Australian working-class culture. She also questioned the wisdom of giving the family responsibility for determining outcomes for the youth when it may have been the family which was at fault in the first place. It was also argued that all diversionary schemes, including the recently established FGC, should be subject to monitoring and evaluation. Participants discussed the possibility of legislating for mandatory monitoring and evaluation, to assess, for example, whether the scheme under investigation was servicing its target group and how; whether unacceptable levels of net-widening were occurring; whether the community was being exposed to more danger; and whether there were cost savings. Ken Polk suggested that legislative guidelines should be particularly concerned with formulating targets. He advocated a system of information which could be fed back to the agencies responsible for diversionary programs.

It was agreed that there needs to be some sort of central record-keeping system for diversionary interventions. This was considered necessary to ensure that multiple offenders receive an appropriate sanction, and for the purpose of monitoring and evaluation. Where police keep their own records of informal dealings with offenders—an unofficial warning or reprimand for example—it was considered that the status quo should remain, with these records being kept separate from the formal record-keeping system.

An assessment should also be made of the costs of reduced legal protection, an inevitable byproduct of informal processing. James Hackler commented that our society is committed to due process, to the detriment of creative informal justice programs. The point was contentious, and signalled how difficult it is to balance competing demands within juvenile justice. Nevertheless, it was agreed that the operation of diversionary schemes needs to be carefully monitored to prevent injustices and to ensure that excesses in the name of welfare do not recur.

In summary, the discussion on informal processing focused on diversionary schemes which reroute juveniles from the court system. It sought to identify the components of a successful diversionary scheme, conceding that compromise and trade-offs were perhaps inevitable. Participants made the following recommendations:

- That there be clear specification of the types of informal processing that are possible—which types are in place and which might be needed. That there is a need to look beyond police cautioning and panels to identify what additional forms are possible and where on the juvenile justice continuum the intervention should take place.

- That there should be as extensive a role as possible for diversion, without significant net-widening. Although some net-widening is inevitable, this must be minimised.

- That there should be effective screening mechanisms established to decide the appropriate course for a particular case. Particular emphasis should be placed on screening cases for no further action.

- That, after police have become involved, there should be a circuit-breaking mechanism to prevent trivial cases going to court or being formally processed.

- That appropriate measures of success should be developed to evaluate informal mechanisms, with priority and resources allocated to data collection and evaluation. Agencies administering diversionary programs should both contribute to, and be given feedback from, this data base, to enable them to monitor the effects of their programs.

- That the potential threat to due process should be evaluated, and ways of overcoming such threats be developed.

- That central records of diversionary interventions should be kept for the proper administration of justice and monitoring and evaluation. However, there should be strict controls on confidentiality.

Part V

The courts

13 Influences in reform of juvenile courts

ROD BLACKMORE

Juvenile courts, in whatever state or country, are creatures of legislation specifically designed to separate children's cases from the mainstream forms of justice that would otherwise apply. It is natural, therefore, that reformers will target legislation as the first area for change, although I would argue that for matters of procedure—as distinct from the powers juvenile tribunals may possess—there are other areas of priority to be grappled with than necessarily tampering with or creating wholesale slaughter of existing laws. The history of juvenile justice in my own state of New South Wales— which is by no means entirely paralleled by developments in other states or countries—indicates that there have been many influences, apart from legislation, which have exerted a significant effect on the way in which juvenile cases have been treated.

The former legislation, the *Child Welfare Act* 1939 (NSW)—itself no more than the revamping of two previous statutes which first provided for children's courts in 1905—remained in force for nearly 50 years. The process of reforming that legislation took nearly twenty years, and (contrary to international principles enshrined in the 'Beijing Rules') left the courts with fewer powers than before. Many participants in the system feel that the court's powers were needlessly eroded and that the present court is hamstrung by over-restrictive provisions such as the mandatory application of children's sanctions to young adults over whom it has residual jurisdiction. As we will see, the current legislation (the *Children's (Criminal Proceedings) Act* 1987) has helped to create a more distinct specialist court. It has spelled out guiding principles, and removed euphemistic and nineteenth-century terminology.

Role of the court

Diversion from prosecution has been a feature of a number of juvenile legal systems in the second half of this century. Each of those systems, however, retains a juvenile court with established principles of due process, procedural fairness and separation from adult-oriented provisions. The children's court, which should never be seen as less than a court of law fulfilling its part within the framework of criminal justice as a whole, has two essential functions. First, it serves a *judicial* function. It determines, when necessary, the question of guilt or innocence of an offender in accordance with the precepts of the criminal law, and it weighs and determines other conflicting evidence which comes to the court in the way of submissions, reports and opinions. Second, it has an *empowering* function. It imposes appropriate orders which are the authority upon which persons may act in carrying out the directions of the court. In earlier years, the concept of a welfare approach to young offenders was shown to be more punitive than an approach based on acceptance of responsibility coupled with a provision to provide guidance and assistance. In New South Wales in the early 1970s, offenders and non-offenders as young as fourteen years of age were frequently detained for indeterminate terms averaging 8.5 months, ostensibly 'for their own good', and at the whim of the administrators. By the end of that decade, largely as a result of the court having asserted itself, magistrates began to impose specified terms. As a consequence, the custodial population was reduced by 45 per cent and shorter terms came into vogue.

Under the present 'truth in sentencing' legislation (which has abolished remissions), detained offenders tend to be older and are sentenced for more serious offences. In the first year of the operation of the new sentencing laws (1989–90) the average length of detention was only 4.3 months. Now, non-offenders do not suffer detention with delinquents, although there is a perceived need to retain a form of control while counselling takes effect.

'Back to justice' reform does not mean (as some commentators have supposed) that every case has to be established by confronting an accused juvenile with witnesses in the adversarial setting. Even though the juvenile possesses a right to insist on their innocence, it has been a longstanding sentencing principle that a genuine and appropriate plea of guilty, promptly entered, may be accepted and regarded as strong evidence of contrition which may be received as mitigating the offence. Moreover, in New South Wales, a recent legislative provision has required criminal courts to give reasons for not reducing sentencing orders when an offender has promptly pleaded guilty. There remain, of course, safeguards against pleas inappropriately entered which are either not supportable by available factual material, or which have been entered as a matter of convenience. A proper plea of 'guilty', therefore, is not inconsistent with principles of 'due process', even though, in the eyes of a number of critics of the system, it is a dirty word.

As courts of first instance, juvenile courts, wherever they are established, are subject to the hierarchy of the superior courts. This provides both a safeguard for offenders against harsh or unlawful judgements, and a brake on courts which might choose to adopt generous interpretations of their legislated powers. The ability of juvenile courts to influence their own future as part of a system of juvenile justice is thus considerably, although not entirely, limited. Again, using New South Wales as an example, the comparatively recent creation of 'community aid panels'—a diversionary concept which enables young offenders to receive a more lenient outcome through provision of additional mitigating factors—has been an informal initiative of the courts demonstrating disenchantment with the lack of formal (government) programs.

Effects of diversion

It is demonstrable, I would argue, that the involvement of many young offenders in the formal part of juvenile justice characterised by the court system, is far from necessary. This has been recognised in many jurisdictions by the provision of various forms of diversion, ranging from the exercise of police discretion, cautioning by police, screening and aid panels, and 'family conferences'. There remain, however, offenders for whom these diversionary schemes are impractical or ineffective, and for whom a tribunal with formulated principles and powers of intervention are necessary. There is scope for determining, within the setting of the local judicial system, just what the nature of such a tribunal may be. Justice systems with a few tiers serving small populations might well integrate juveniles into lower court criminal justice or into a family court model. The larger the population to be served and the greater the number of tiers of the judiciary, the greater is the opportunity for thorough specialisation in the form of a children's court. The reality is that, in most justice systems, compromises will have to occur, particularly in smaller communities which lack appropriate physical facilities and expert personnel. These deficiencies are best overcome by the setting of clear guiding principles and codes of practice rather than by complex regulatory provisions which only serve to make the process less intelligible for young offenders, submerge the real merits and issues of cases, and provide technical grounds of appeal.

Even within a formal juvenile court system, 'diversion' remains a continuing option with the commendable goal of preventing even greater penetration by offenders into that system. Accordingly, detention is necessarily an order of last resort. Juvenile tribunals, pursuant to international principles, should be provided with a wide variety of measures which can be tailored to individual requirements. This will ensure that the last resort is not easily reached.

It is possible, nevertheless, for repeated diversion to be counter-productive. Young offenders do become adults. If their only learning experience has been one of repeated diversion which does not achieve acceptance of responsibility, the degree to which they will be expected as young adults to accept the consequences of continued offending (and with which they have had no coping experience) may well prove to be overwhelmingly destructive.

Ideals

In a paper I wrote during 1990 I noted that a number of surveys, research papers and reports on the role of the children's court and its personnel, had made suggestions for improvements in the court system. An almost ideal situation, if those suggestions could be implemented, would include the following features:

1   Availability of an independent adult. On apprehension of a juvenile by police, an adult would always be available, whether of the juvenile's own family or choosing, or from lists of willing volunteers.

2   Suitability for police caution or other diversionary process, such as referral to a community aid panel. These diversionary measures would receive priority of consideration before a decision to prosecute.

3   Citation to appear at court (not involving a determination whether to grant or refuse bail) would receive priority whenever feasible once a decision to prosecute had been made.

4   Service of summary of police case upon the young defendant would be effected at the time of processing by police, together with a copy of the formal charge(s) and information concerning rights to free legal aid (including where to contact the solicitor rostered on the list that day).

5   Legal aid solicitors would actually be available for consultation prior to the day on which the defendant is required to attend court.

6   Rostered solicitors would have arrived at court at least an hour and a half before the commencing time, giving priority of interview to those who might be in custody who had also arrived from their place of detention in good time.

7   Uncontested adjournment applications would be dealt with by the court registrar prior to the normal sitting hour, freeing the court itself for the substantive business of the day.

8   The defendant would be given ample time to instruct the solicitor so that the defendant's version of events could be fully canvassed, advice given on plea, and time spent explaining the court process.

9   An opportunity to view the courtroom prior to appearance would be made available to juveniles and their families, with explanatory material (given either orally by a court officer, in written or diagrammatic form, or by a video presentation in the waiting area) assisting understanding of the roles of the various persons to be encountered in the court and the procedures that might be expected.

10 A listing by appointment system would obviate undue waiting for families before cases are called. All courts would have full, comfortable, graffiti-free facilities with refreshment amenities for both defendants and other persons required to be in attendance.

11 Special qualifications (e.g. Diploma in Juvenile Justice) would be possessed by all court personnel, including magistrates, solicitors, prosecutors, and probation (guidance) officers.

12 Simple language procedure would entail an outline by the prosecutor of the allegations, and an explanation of the charge(s) personally to defendants by the magistrate—indicating how the outlined facts might relate to the formal charges.

13 Plea would be indicated by a defendant (with the advice of the solicitor), and upon a positive response to enquiry as to the defendant's understanding of necessary proofs and other ramifications of the proceedings. At all times the defendant would be guided through the proceedings by the magistrate, being assisted by the advice of the solicitor.

14 Available court time for each matter (in uncontested matters) could usefully be up to an hour or so. This would enable the facts of the case and other matters relevant to sentence to be probed in some detail, and the hearing of the solicitor's submissions. The defendant and family would be directly involved throughout. Accordingly, no more than five uncontested cases per day would be listed to ensure the attainment of these goals.

15 Background and assessment reports sought by the court would always have been filed at least the day before the proceedings, and have been read by the magistrate and all interested parties out of court.

16 Realistic assessment of the ways in which a defendant might evidence responsibility for the offence, and of a program offering necessary guidance and assistance, would be contained in reports. Reports would not argue the case for just one recommendation, but would canvass all viable options available to the court, indicating the relative merits of the various dispositions.

17 Direct dialogue between the magistrate and defendant would be the norm, prior to finalisation of the proceedings.

18 Sentencing would involve patient explanation, in simple terms, to the defendant of the nature and effect of the court's order and would secure the defendant's understanding. An order in more formal terms might also then be announced.

19 Consideration of appeal or the opportunity to resolve any remaining queries in an offender's mind would be undertaken by the legal representative out of court.

20 Office processes relating to offenders would be similarly comprehensible.

21 In contested cases, instructed solicitors would always appear to undertake the hearing. They would have taken further instructions at some time prior to the hearing day, and would have notified the court and prosecution of any intended change of plea or adjournment application. Prosecuting police would also have notified the defendant and the court of any intended adjournment application or other inability to proceed.

22 Overlisting of defended cases would not occur so that there would be no possibility of a listed case not being reached. Nor would there be underlisting, so valuable sitting time would not be lost.

23 Court facilities would include adequate libraries and access to sentencing and other data on computer files.

24 A range of advisory bodies to the government on the subject of juvenile justice, and other associated tribunals such as boards of review, would exist (with adequately remunerated members meeting regularly).

Each of these suggestions could hardly be disputed in principle. Some commentators on juvenile justice would suggest that each of these features should be spelt out in great legislative detail—that courts should be prevented from proceeding until they had observed all requirements. The existing legislation already abounds with such strictures. These often create greater problems than the ones they seek to cure. It is the brain child of theoreticians who have little concept of practical realities. In examining each of the above recommendations, anyone with practical experience of juvenile justice will realise that there are occasions when the ideal cannot be achieved. For example, we lack the resources of time and personnel. Another problem is the symptomatic apathy of typical young offenders and their families.

The rights which comprise due process of law—the right to be heard, the right to representation, the right to participate in the proceedings and in decisions which affect an individual, and the rights against self-incrimination—necessarily require some flexibility in their implementation. The justice system is not one which can achieve absolute priority of resources over other competing societal needs, particularly in straightened times. The extent to which the court can influence positive changes in juvenile justice is constrained by the resources available to it and by the approach adopted by the various professionals involved in their own court-related roles. Legislation should set out clear but broad statements of principle by which the courts and other participants in the system will be bound. More detailed elaborations of principle may usefully be contained in 'codes of practice' adopted by those participants.

Political and community influence

The most insidious influences on the court system, usually imposed by way of legislation or regulation, are political ideologies. No doubt parliamentarians are responsive to community pressures and to their party views of social issues. There have been many calls for a bipartisan approach to issues of juvenile justice, but many of those who make the calls have extreme minority views for which they lobby heavily. A consequence is that changes are wrought in some cases without wide consultation and without an appreciation of practical implications for the system. Legislative change is exposed to some public scrutiny, but greater change without public scrutiny can be wrought by administrators, especially in the area of service provision. The position of courts in endeavouring to carry out the terms of the legislation, which is their jurisdictional and doctrinal base, can be one of enormous tension with a bureaucracy which sees itself as autonomous, and which may have quite different aims from those of the courts.

The media are also influential. Reports of disturbances in detention centres and of violent or persistent crimes committed by juveniles lead to questions in parliament and encourage other groups to lobby for change. In the main, however, these reports are frequently treated as minor crises which are soon forgotten as some new matter seizes the public's attention.

'Research reports' by individuals or private groups may also be a temporary, and sometimes costly, sensation. Reports of enduring worth are usually those which have been specifically created by the government to review the current system and which, accordingly, have involved wide consultation with the public and with those who are actual participants in that system. All states and countries reviewing their juvenile justice systems have undertaken major exercises of this kind. This has led to the realisation that not every proposal has the chance of adoption. Indeed, there is not one absolute truth which can be enshrined forever in legislative form. Necessarily there are many 'truths' which, in a later review, may not find the same degree of support. This longer process, as opposed to ad hoc tampering with children's laws, at least provides some stability of action for the court, instead of lurching from one fashionable dogma to another.

International influences

Critics of juvenile justice are frequently parochial in their considerations. It is a worthwhile exercise to see how local procedures measure up against international standards. Australia has been particularly active in contributing to consultations on the United Nations minimum standards of juvenile justice (the 'Beijing Rules') and the draft 'Convention on the Rights of the

Child', and has strongly influenced a number of those provisions. Despite this contribution to a consensus of international thought, local legislation may fall short of minimum standards in a number of areas. These include scope of discretion (rule 6), right to legal aid (rule 15), provision of social inquiry reports (rule 16), proportionate reaction to the gravity of offence and the needs of the juvenile and society (rule 17), and availability of extensive disposition measures (rule 18). The trend in this country has been to limit, rather than to expand, the powers of juvenile tribunals, ostensibly to prevent excesses of authority. But such restraints on the courts have not served to promote the safeguards of the legal system as a whole.

When implemented in Australia, as inevitably will be the case, the Convention on the Rights of the Child will apply not only to protective legislation for children but also to that relating to criminal behaviour. Article 3.1 provides:

> In all actions concerning children, whether undertaken by public or private social welfare institutions, courts of law, administrative authorities or legislative bodies, the best interests of the child shall be a primary consideration.

It is interesting to compare this provision with the idea of engendering in the child responsibility for a wrongful act. Is the provision one which will require a return to the 'welfare' rather than a 'justice' approach to young offenders, or do the best interests of the child include the notion of responsibility accompanied by the need for guidance and assistance? There is, of course, a difference between 'a primary consideration' and 'the paramount consideration'.

Accountability of services

It is futile for courts to have even limited powers to make orders which may never be carried into effect. The recipients of those orders—the juvenile offenders, and their families—quickly recognise the hypocrisy involved when, for instance, they are told there will be 'supervision' but nothing remotely perceived to be supervision occurs; or they are told that a breach of conditions or reoffending will lead to a reinstitution of the original proceedings, and that never takes place. Recently I discussed these issues with a group of long-term prisoners, each of whom had a considerable juvenile record before ending up in the prison system, and who are eager to be able to inform present juveniles of the futility of prison existence. Those prisoners, without exception, said they had regarded the whole juvenile justice system as nothing more than a joke, even when it led to the 'last resort' of detention. The reason they gave was that nothing was ever done which tackled the causes of their behaviour.

These problems exist largely because the court is dependent upon other external services to ensure that the terms of its orders are carried out, and these are services in which it may be difficult to ensure any accountability, let alone an accountability to the court. The problem is a legacy of the era in which the 'welfare' of the child was thought to be the sole consideration, and it was considered appropriate for 'welfare officers' to be responsible for all post-court intervention. These officers dealt with, and assumed, expertise in the areas of child protection before the enormity of the problem of child abuse was revealed. They also dealt with non-offending problematic children, truants (who were thought of as little different from delinquents) and juvenile offenders.

With the current 'specialisation' of responses to offenders (there being little specialist work done with troubled adolescents or truants, but much concentration on abused children), there is a need for a body of specialist guidance officers pursuing clear policies consistent with those under which the court is bound to operate. This would ensure that legislative policies affecting the court are followed through. Guidance officers should be accountable directly to the court, rather than being in the employment of, and at least notionally responsible to, a department concerned with welfare. This is not to suggest that the welfare needs of juvenile offenders should be neglected. Rather, the suggestion is that those needs be met by other appropriate specialist personnel.

Movements of the pendulum

Influences upon the court vary. They move from the extremes of the 'law and order' lobby to the cottonwool approach of dewy-eyed social workers. Most jurisdictions I have observed are retaining a reasonable balance between these polarities, and it can only be hoped that those who are able to exert influence, whether by legislation, administratively, or by the use of policy discretion, will refrain from dramatic changes which are confusing to both the community and the participants in juvenile justice, especially those most affected—the young offenders. Proponents of change must be sensitive to the need for cost-effective expenditure. This demands preventive community work and a concentration of allocation of personnel who are involved in face-to-face work with children. Anything further which can be achieved to refine the system should ultimately be regarded as a bonus.

Whatever changes are achieved within the total system (which may see different categories of young offenders being dealt with in a variety of ways), it would seem that there will always be a place for the children's court to continue exercising its judicial functions. It is therefore incumbent upon all participants in the court process to adopt practices which ensure that basic principles of justice are met. No amount of restrictive regulation of court personnel will achieve this. The basic principles have already been formulated. What is required is the will for their implementation.

14 Children's courts: to be or what to be?

MICHAEL HOGAN

The effect of recent legislative changes around Australia has been to move children's justice closer to the adult model. It may now be timely to ask, 'Is there still a role for a distinctive juvenile court?'

A warning

From the outset, some reservations about the subject matter of this paper need to be stated. Indeed, it is necessary to issue a warning. The intention is not to suggest that we sidestep the question of whether there is still a role for a distinctive juvenile court. That would be irresponsible. It is always worth asking whether we are getting value out of an institution that deals with some 50 000 young people a year and which involves the direct expenditure of public funds in the order of anywhere from $10–20 million per annum. Such an institution must be able to justify its existence. And its supporters are obliged to articulate its defence.

This debate on the need for a children's court is more advanced in the United States and the United Kingdom than in Australia. We would do well to be prepared for it. As Gardner (1987:148) stated, the 'advocates of a separate punitive juvenile justice system have yet to respond to those calling for a merger into the criminal system'. The point to be made in this chapter is that we must be very careful in framing and approaching the issue. It is an area that requires a sound conceptualisation and understanding of the recent history of juvenile justice.

There is a danger of a misguided view emerging—namely, that the reforms of the 1980s have been a fundamental mistake because they led to a greater focus on crime and punishment in the juvenile sphere. Some mistakes have been made in Australia. Perhaps the American rhetoric was too readily used here and certainly some of the pitfalls should have been realised. The intentions of the reformers have, to some extent, been distorted.

And yet it is wrong to think, as some do, that the 'back to justice' movement *merely* supplied the philosophical justification for the application of sterner measures.

Certainly, the question of whether we created the conditions for a swing to punitiveness and retribution in the juvenile justice system is a vexed one:

> the realisation that the pendulum may have swung too far toward 'desert' and that this may not in fact be 'just' is beginning to dawn (Freiberg, Fox and Hogan, 1988:84).

The shift of children's justice closer to the adult model

While the general proposition that the juvenile justice system has moved closer to the adult model may be correct, it does not give an adequate picture of the history and nature of recent changes to juvenile justice law and practice.

Extent of change

There certainly has been considerable change. All the States and Territories have either passed new Acts or substantially amended existing legislation, or they are in the process of reviewing their juvenile laws. Child welfare and juvenile justice jurisdictions have been separated; ideologies made explicit; and new procedures and programs introduced. However, the degree of change should not be exaggerated. Much of what has been done in the legislation reenacts provisions from earlier Acts, or merely updates the language. Some changes were marginal; some were substantial.

As many have pointed out, Australian children's courts are essentially offshoots of adult criminal courts of summary jurisdiction. They have always been close—in terms of the substantive criminal law, the criminal standard of proof, the rules of procedure, the sanctions and the transfers to adult courts (Seymour, 1988:110; Freiberg, Fox and Hogan, 1988:10). In many country areas, the magistrate simply changes hats to determine matters involving a juvenile. Rehabilitation was, and remains, an important if less pervasive aim of adult sentencing. Though the shift to formal justice in the juvenile sphere was not substantial, still we may ask whether it was sufficient to undermine the rationale of the children's court?

Change was not a simple, consistent shift to 'justice'

The changes in the new juvenile legislation did not involve a simple or consistent shift to 'justice'. Seymour (1988:245) has said of the Australian Law Reform Commission's *Child Welfare Report*, which got the reforms rolling:

> The Commission concluded that it is not practicable to make a choice between a 'punitive' and a 'therapeutic' approach. Both

approaches must be accommodated. Any system designed to achieve
social control must take children's needs into account. Similarly,
any system which wishes to offer help to the young cannot repudiate
the tasks of the criminal law.

Consideration must also be given to the intentions of the reformers in New
South Wales and elsewhere. Put simply, these included:

* reducing the numbers of children in institutions;
* reducing the numbers of children going to court for minor and first
  offences;
* reducing the numbers of children committed to institutions without having
  first been through a community-based sanction; and
* reducing the great disparities between courts across New South Wales.

These goals have, for the most part, been met. They were motivated by a
concern for the welfare of young people in the juvenile justice system as
much as a concern for 'justice'. Indeed, improved 'due process', which is
one element of the 'justice' approach, was partly seen as a way of enhancing
the delivery of 'welfare'.

While it is not a case, like Canada, of swinging with the pendulum
from one extreme to another, the changes have featured procedural
and substantive elements aligned with the direction indicated by just
deserts, diversionary, and decarcerative ideas (Freiberg, Fox and
Hogan, 1988:11).

The reforms were a mixed bag. In New South Wales they attracted criticism
at the time as being 'too soft'. Most of the provisions identified by the then
opposition have since been amended.

Change was contradictory

Likewise, the legislative changes were not free from contradictions. Seymour
(1988:245) continued that 'it must be frankly acknowledged that the
objective is the synthesis of principles which will sometimes be in conflict'.
In trying to accommodate 'welfare' and 'justice', the Acts were to a large
degree articulating the two existing primary ideologies.

The position taken by various players was also contradictory. In New
South Wales, some children's magistrates have eschewed the tariff system
of a sanction hierarchy—a sign of the 'justice' aim of proportionality—and
have objected to the imposition of limits on their discretion. Yet there have
also been moves to make children's courts more like adult courts. Some
have sought powers to sentence juveniles to imprisonment, and thus have
objected to the lowering of the time limits associated with sanctions such
as recognisance and probation. There has also been support for wider

gateways to the adult system, both in relation to the transfer of juveniles for sentence and trial to higher courts, and administrative transfers to adult prisons. The fact that politicians of the Right continue to criticise juvenile justice legislation for giving young offenders too many rights is indicative of the contradictions of a label such as the 'justice model'.

Legislative change as a consequence rather than a cause

Legislative changes, and subsequent amendments, have taken place in the context of a new conservatism which now prevails across the broad spectrum of political, economic and social matters. Juvenile justice has not been exempt. An element of this conservatism has been the resurgent classicist view of crime as a simple product of individual free will. More potent has been political expediency and pragmatism, and the media misrepresentation that contributes to a 'law and order' climate, wherein the traditional target— youth—becomes again a perceived threat and a cause for 'tough' responses.

The point is that the move closer to an adult model was more a consequence than a cause of a greater focus on crime and punishment. We can only speculate what might have happened had the reforms not been introduced when they were, given the current law and order climate. In some senses I feel that the current New South Wales legislation, with its concern for children's rights, is already anachronistic.

'Extraneous' influences

Although the children's court is the 'hub' of the juvenile justice system, it is by no means the governer of its own destiny. It is subject to the policy and budgetary decisions of police, justice and welfare ministers—for its clientele, for its own resources and for the programs which implement its sanctions. If insufficient funds are provided to make available adequate bail arrangements and community-based programs, it is difficult for the children's court (and the public) to be confident that, if it takes the more risk-laden but rehabilitative approach to sentencing, it will be properly implemented.

It is also necessary to consider the macro-economic and social dimensions of youth crime. Diminishing public expenditure on social programs and services profoundly affects the life chances of young people who are potential candidates for the children's courts (see, for example, O'Connor and Callahan, 1989).

Changes wrought by other legislation

To complicate the picture, some of the most significant changes have been wrought by subsequent legislation, designed for adults, but applied also to juveniles. The best example of this in New South Wales has been the *Sentencing Act* 1989. For imprisonment and detention orders, a minimum term must now be imposed, with a 25 per cent additional term. The Act abolished remissions and it abolished an exemption for juveniles from the ruling that sentences under six months should not have a probation period. We have also seen in New South Wales, as in most other jurisdictions, increased penalties in the *Crimes Act 1990* (NSW) for offences for which young people are commonly charged (such as car theft) and the introduction of new offences (such as those in our new *Summary Offences Act 1988* (NSW), together with the reintroduction of imprisonment as a penalty for public order offences. This last change has been couched in the language of 'getting tough'. All of these changes have had a major impact on young offenders. Indeed, they have done more to undermine the rationale for a separate juvenile court than any shift in the primary legislation itself.

The contested nature of the changes

Those who have been involved in the reforms and subsequent amendments to juvenile justice legislation will be well aware of just how contested was the process during the 1980s. They will know of the fights within and between government departments, of the unsuccessful attempts to convince the relevant minister that proposals coming back from Cabinet bore little resemblance to what went in, and the compromises accepted to get the legislation 'up'. For example, the 1985 draft Cabinet Minute for the New South Wales reforms contained recommendations for a statutory base for police cautioning. These were not accepted for the reason of 'not wanting to be seen as soft on juvenile crime'.

Some jurisdictions (such as New South Wales and Victoria), have been through extensive consultative processes but the results have been realised only very slowly or not at all. Other provisions have not even had the benefit of development through consultation or debate. The point is that reforms have met with opposition from both within and outside of the government, and have been modified accordingly.

The recent history of the politics of juvenile justice awaits a full telling. This brief trespass into the area has sought only to give some account of the reforms as a background to discussion of where the children's courts now stand.

What to do with the children's courts?

The choices

As always, there is a range of options. To reduce them to the bottom line, these entail either abolition or retention of the children's courts. Each option could take a number of different forms. One 'abolitionist' possibility is to repeal the legislation and let the adult courts of summary jurisdiction deal with young offenders, alongside and no differently from adults, except in so much as youth is a mitigating factor. A variation would be to give the juvenile justice jurisdiction to the same courts—with the protective rules but without the special venues. A retention option, but with similar consequences, would be, for example, to drastically curtail the children's court's jurisdiction in this area by lowering the age limit to fourteen.

A quite different abolitionist option would be to hand over young offenders to the family court, and deal with them less for their deeds than for their needs. A comparable retention option would be to repeal the reforms, or reintegrate juvenile justice and child welfare into the children's court. Another option would be to retain the status quo or, alternatively, to retain it in the essentials but refine and reorientate it.

The rationale

Before contemplating *whether* to abolish the children's court and start again, or whether to keep it and reshape it, we should reconsider the rationale which underpins it. The very fact that we have any court dealing with young offenders is to invoke the logic and language of guilt, responsibility and of just deserts. The justification usually put forward for the establishment of children's courts at the turn of the century was the desire to save children from the contamination and stigma of association with adults. Fundamentally, the rationale was that the very nature of children and their situation demanded a different jurisdiction. And this is still the case. Freiberg, Fox and Hogan (1988: 67) offer the view that:

> There is almost universal acceptance of the principle that juveniles are not to be equated with adults. It is part of modern wisdom that children progress through a number of developmental stages and that, during these stages, children think, act and feel differently from adults. Therefore it is regarded as unrealistic and unjust to hold them to the same standards or treat them in the same way even though, ultimately, they will be expected to adhere to adult law-abiding values.

and go on to say:

> Acceptance of the reduced culpability of the young has been translated into the system of structural mitigation of responsibility that is embodied in the present juvenile court system. Special juvenile justice legislation urges recognition of the 'unique physical, psychological, and social features of young persons in the definition and application of delinquency standards' (Freiberg, Fox and Hogan, 1988:209).

As well as acknowledging the characteristics of the individual young offender, the early children's court acknowledged the social context of the young person. This was in keeping with the argument of the 'positivists' that crime is not necessarily the product of free will, but the result of the interplay of 'certain social realities [which] make a nonsense of the notion of untrammeled personal freedom' (Harris, 1985:37). As the Australian Law Reform Commission Report points out, this view was 'pervasive but not paramount in relation to adults, but it holds greater sway in relation to juveniles' (Freiberg, Fox and Hogan, 1987:67). The climate may have changed, but the reason for a children's court has not.

The critique

Nonetheless, there have been strong calls for the abolition of the juvenile court. In the United States, the most vociferous calls appear to come from those pushing for integration with adult courts. It should be noted that these suggestions have not been substantially acted upon. Winzer and Keller (1977:1132-3) argue for abolition because:

> reforms eliminate the unique features of the juvenile court's approach to such deviant behaviour and transform the system into one that focuses, as well it should, on questions of crime and punishment, guilt and innocence.

Giller (1986) has summarised the assumptions underpinning the argument for abolition in the United States:

1 Juvenile courts repeatedly fail to apply the statutory protections that have been mandated.
2 Criminal courts would provide wider protection of juvenile rights than do juvenile courts.
3 The proposed rationale for criminal sanctions, which is 'a shift from treatment to proportionality', parallels the criminal court model more closely than it does the traditional juvenile court approach.
4 A juvenile court model based on proportionality and punishment is incompatible with other components of the juvenile court workload . . . such as for the abused and neglected.
5 The criminal justice process now accommodates the juvenile justice system practices of intake and diversion as well as more diversified sentencing alternatives.
6 A juvenile's criminal court representative would be free to function in an adversarial role.

Giller (1986:166) goes on to find support for these propositions in the United Kingdom.

At approximately the same time, a vigorous move for abolition has been apparent in British social service circles but here, the idea has been to hand over young offenders for disposition to a family court with an integrated jurisdiction over children. The study group of the English Association of Directors of Social Services, the Association of County Councils Working Party on Juvenile Courts, and the National Association for the Care and

Rehabilitation of Offenders have voiced a number of objections to existing children's court processes. They have criticised the lack of a clear philosophy, the adversarial nature of proceedings, the domination of lawyers, the high number of prosecutions, the delays, the punitive sentencing and the inadequate recruitment and training of magistrates (NACRO, 1986).

The lessons

There is considerable evidence in Australia to support similar complaints against children's courts. But I am not sure they can convince us of the need for abolition. Nor can they convince us of the superiority of the alternatives, whether they be local courts or family courts.

There are clear lessons to be learned about the way we conceive and argue for reform, and for the retention of children's courts. Clarke's critique of the 'back to justice' movement in the United Kingdom is useful. He takes its proponents to task for seeing the *Children and Young Persons Act* 1969 as an 'incursion of "welfarism" into the field of juvenile justice', and warns of the dangers of using 'justice' as the basis for a progressive politics of juvenile justice. Clarke (1985:407) argues that:

> the presentation of juvenile justice as the site of an opposition
> between the principles of justice and welfare is ill-conceived, and
> leads to potentially dangerous political consequences.

He is not convinced

> that the current juvenile justice system is a war between these two
> abstract principles. Rather, it needs to be seen as a system which
> criminalises working-class youth, and manages the delinquent using
> a patchwork of processes and disposals which draw upon justice,
> retribution, rehabilitation and welfarism (Clarke, 1985:419).

This is an important reminder that we need to look beyond courts, and beyond welfare and justice. Clarke is in favour of greater political accountability through local boards. He prefers this to legal accountability.

The clock cannot be turned back but we can ensure that there are some checks and balances. It is important to note that other jurisdictions (such as the United States) which have pursued greater individual responsibility, have also moved to increase 'system accountability'. The *Model Juvenile Delinquency Act* 1987 adopts what is described as the 'individual responsibility/system accountability model'. The premise of the 'system accountability' aspect is stated thus:

> The state cannot intervene in an individual's life unless it is willing
> to justify itself publicly. At least two conditions are necessary to
> ensure system accountability: the guiding principles of intervention
> must be reasonably explicit and clearly stated; and the public must

have an opportunity to determine how well they are being followed.
Setting standards, and making visible how conscientiously they are
being applied, is the first step towards some accountability.
Recognising this visibility and accountability of decision-making
should replace closed proceedings and unrestrained official
discretion.

Similarly, the Australian Law Reform Commission Sentencing Report
(ACRC, 1988) adopts a 'structured decision-making' approach to regulate
sentencing processes and practices for adults.

Conclusion

We must argue vociferously for retention of the children's courts. We
should not countenance inadequacies and abuses that seriously detract from
the aims and principles of reform legislation. We must seek to enhance
effectiveness and equity in children's courts.

Children's magistrates must themselves indicate a willingness to look
beyond punishment and retribution. If not, they may put their collective
judicial heads on the chopping block. They must play a role in ensuring a
viable and different system that is fair, responsive, equitable and effective.

The following might be considered as desirable refinements to the existing
system:

- Spell out clearly the rationale of the children's courts. (This is necessary
  in the light of the characteristics of children, their situation and their
  offending.)
- Develop, make more specific and prioritise the principles made explicit
  in juvenile justice legislation.
- Regulate more closely the dispositional process, given that the vast
  majority of children are dealt with as guilty pleas.
- Continue to decrease the reliance upon courts and increase the utilisation
  of diversionary procedures. (This, however, requires that diversion be
  controlled, so that we do not re-create the informal, arbitrary and coercive
  practices of the past.)
- Monitor much more closely the procedural and sentencing practices of
  children's courts through integrated statistics and regular consumer
  evaluations.
- Provide systematic pre- and on-going training to judicial officers.
- Provide comprehensive information to young offenders, their families
  and the public by using interpreters, explanations and written copies of
  orders, through such innovations as Victoria's Children's Court Liaison
  Office.
- Make a real and effective commitment to the participation of the youth
  in the court process. This will require the courts and lawyers to exercise
  their roles in such a way as to avoid marginalising their clients.

- Make use of the knowledge and expertise of the courts in developing local social and situational crime prevention programs.
- Establish formal mechanisms for consultation about the children's courts with professional, consumer and community groups, such as the Children's Court Advisory Committee in South Australia.
- Improve the quality of representation through better resourced, better trained and more accountable lawyers, with a mix of specialist salaried personnel and private and community-based services.
- Develop ways of improving the supervision by the courts of pre-court and post-court treatment of young people in the juvenile justice system.
- Consider adopting the arrangements in South Australia and Western Australia where the jurisdiction is headed by a judge. (This would relieve the pressure to transfer young offenders to adult courts and would improve the status of the court.)

As for a new ideology for the children's courts? Why not 'social justice'—with its commitment to equity, fairness, rights, and access to services. This might be more difficult to 'hijack' than 'justice'.

15 Theory vs practice: a case study

GARTH LUKE

Juvenile justice literature is replete with theoretical analyses of the justice system. One example is Hudson's book, *Justice through punishment: a critique of the 'justice' model of corrections* (1987). Hudson argues that the justice model, or back-to-justice movement, has been the dominant intellectual base for justice and corrections policy in recent years, and that this movement has done little more than provide a rationale for more severe punishment. She puts the case for closure of institutions as the only effective way of reducing incarceration.

In this chapter I will focus on the developments in New South Wales during the 1980s. In doing so, I would like to show how simple models of the justice system often fail to explain the changes that take place, and how some of the back-to-justice ideas have, in fact, been useful in reducing levels of incarceration in New South Wales.

The origins of current practice in New South Wales

Hudson contrasts the legalistic justice model with that of therapeutic welfare. She identifies the following characteristics of the justice model or back-to-justice movement: proportionality of punishment to crime; determinate sentences; an end to judicial and administrative discretion; an end to disparity in sentencing; and protection of rights through due process (Hudson, 1987:38).

As earlier chapters have shown, the real world of juvenile justice in New South Wales, as in most other states in Australia, has always been much more complex than such dichotomous models would imply. There never really was a golden age of welfare in this state. There was a mixture of welfare and justice, cures and punishments, somewhat indeterminate sentences and some attempts to provide psycho-therapeutic programs at day attendance centres and some institutions. In practice this was balanced by a more basic faith in the value of discipline, as shown by the dominance of institutional staff in the hierarchy of the department responsible for juvenile justice services, the Department of Youth and Community Services (YACS). Within the institutions themselves, the substitute for disciplinary regimes in the 1970s was usually not rehabilitative therapy, but rather the 'keep 'em occupied' use of trampolines and videos.

The issue of juvenile justice is an emotionally and politically-charged one. The result is that policy and practice decisions are the culmination of many different perspectives and influences, and rarely entail simple translations of theoretical models or the wishes of one group of people. In addition, there is little agreement about the causes of delinquency. Empirical data can be, and often are, interpreted in different ways with many different implications. For example, high levels of recidivism amongst institutional residents have been cited as evidence of both the failure of institutions and of the need for them.

Nonetheless, justice-based critiques of the system did gain some support in New South Wales, and in the late 1970s and the early 1980s new legislation was developed. The *Community Welfare Act* (NSW) passed in 1982 but not gazetted, separated welfare and criminal matters. It also contained provisions for diversionary community panels and statements emphasising the use of institutions as a last resort. But it could not really be seen as a pure back-to-justice document. There was still an emphasis on treatment-oriented pre-sentence reports, on the option of psychological counselling for young offenders, and a juvenile cautioning scheme which had the option to divert youths from court to treatment.

Attempts at major changes in New South Wales date from 1983 when a left-wing Labor minister was made responsible for the Department of Youth and Community Services. In some ways, with the release of the Houston Report (1983), this was also the closest the state came to a clear welfare model. This report, written by a committee of senior welfare and court staff, documented and costed a number of treatment and rehabilitation programs in anticipation of their implementation. Unfortunately, it was little more than a 'wish list' of treatments which failed to acknowledge the dearth of evidence that such programs actually rehabilitated offenders.

There may have been a time for this report, but the early 1980s was not it. The new minister's senior adviser on juvenile justice matters was a founding member of the Prisoners' Action Group which advocated gaol abolition. He was more concerned with the elimination of social injustice than with the provision of new treatments for offenders. The new minister's priorities were clear. Rather than a back-to-justice model, he favoured a 'get-kids-out-of-institutions' model.

He commissioned a number of senior young offender staff to consider just how many children could be removed from institutions, and what services would be needed to maintain them in the community. This report (commonly called the Pryke Report (1983)), recommended various changes to *administrative* procedures. It sought to reduce the number of beds in institutions; to replace some of these beds with accommodation in community homes; and to upgrade probationary supervision. The emphasis was not on the sort of legislative changes promoted in the justice model, but on the more pragmatic administrative issues. The Juvenile Justice Unit (JJU) of the Department of Youth and Community Services was established to implement these changes. Simultaneously, further review of the legislation was undertaken. For the next few years government policy was largely initiated by the staff in the JJU and the legal staff in the Community Welfare Act Unit. While there was a back-to-justice influence (as evidenced by a strong emphasis on diversion from court and institutions, the diminution of the welfare approach of YACS staff in the court, and greater consistency in sentences), the real concern was to develop a juvenile justice system which recognised both the failure of institutions (rather than rehabilitation in general) and the need for greater equality in treatment. The search was for practical ways of achieving a sustainable decarceration and greater equality of treatment between rich and poor, black and white. Much of the strategy involved administrative rather than legislative change, and was drawn from practical successes elsewhere as well as theoretical critiques.

Even then it would be a mistake to think that the final outcome closely resembles the recommendations of YACS staff. There were several reasons for this divergence between the theory and the practice of juvenile justice:

- The number of policy and research positions was so small that adequate planning and promotion of programs was restricted.
- Significant financial constraints were imposed which limited the programs that could be provided.
- Political decisions were made to resolve current crises (e.g. adverse publicity on institutional leave practices).
- A public scare about non-institutional alternatives was generated by government opposition members. (If any particular model informed these actions, I am inclined to think that it was one written by Machiavelli.)

The juvenile justice program that finally emerged was, therefore, a complex product of many factors. It was nothing like a pure representation of any particular model. In John Pratt's (1989) terminology, it had bits of welfare, justice and corporatism all rolled into one, and was finally shaped by the hands of the politicians.

By 1987, the juvenile justice system in New South Wales featured police cautions, specialist staff with diversionary responsibilities, an enhanced probation scheme, intensive counselling-based day attendance programs, community service orders as an alternative to institutions, and a monitoring system which highlighted diversionary successes and failures. In 1988, legislation was passed which provided for the separation of welfare and justice matters, a clear hierarchy of penalties, and a requirement to consider a pre-sentence report before incarceration.

In summary, the New South Wales system which emerged is the result of a number of different theoretical, practical and political factors. One could put a label on this, just as a cheap astrologer is able to distil the myriad of life experiences into just twelve over-generalised categories. One could, but would it be useful?

The contribution of the justice model

The changes to juvenile justice in New South Wales from 1983 onwards served to reduce the number of children in institutions from 660 in 1983 to 400 in 1988. While there may be reason to believe that the justice model tends to condone punishment (e.g. the emphasis on just deserts), and that it may have been used by some people as a justification for heavier sentences, this has not been the case in New South Wales.

It appears that the ideas of the justice model have contributed to the success of decarceration by highlighting the risks of too much welfare intervention, and by helping to provide some tools for reducing intervention. One such tool is the diversion scheme. Cautions have been used appropriately as alternatives to a court appearance, while community service orders have provided an alternative to incarceration. This is contrary to the experience in many other jurisdictions where such diversion schemes have increased the levels of formal punishment. Institutions have become a 'last resort' with only the older, more serious and more experienced offenders sentenced to detention.

It is important to realise, though, that these successes were not dependent upon legislative changes. They were, in fact, achieved before the introduction of new legislation in 1988. They were also not simply dependent upon a reduction in institutional bed numbers, as the trend towards decarceration was observed in regions that retained institutions as well as those that closed them.

There appear to be two reasons for the success of the diversion program. The first is the introduction of staff who had a clear responsibility and commitment to divert children from custody. These staff have actively presented the non-custodial alternatives to the court in each individual case. The second is the ability of the Juvenile Justice Unit to monitor the system in detail and to provide feedback to diversion workers, sentencers and the police. By contrast, the adult corrections system in New South Wales has simply provided sentencing alternatives and left it up to the courts to use them if they feel so disposed. As with so many other jurisdictions in which this has been tried, the results have been disappointing (Luke, 1990).

Conclusion

This chapter began with the observation that the justice model has come to be associated with punitive sentencing practices. New South Wales, however, tells a different story. Here there is no evidence of a significant increase in the levels of punishment since the 1970s. To date, the only increase in punishment has come about as a result of the 1989 'truth in sentencing' legislation which abolished remissions for children and adults. This has resulted in an increase in actual time in custody of about 30 per cent. While this may appear to be significant, it must be realised that it only returns custodial sentences approximately to their levels before the extreme remissions scheme commenced in the early 1980s (Cain and Luke, 1991).

In any case, the recent move towards 'truth in sentencing' has less to do with the debate about justice versus welfare and more to do with the struggle between judicial and administrative power and what is seen by the public as fair and just. Truth in sentencing was the outcome of energetic public debate in New South Wales. Perhaps, as Hudson (1987) suggests, there are some legislatures where justice policy is largely shaped by debates around different explicit theoretical models. In New South Wales, however, truth in sentencing was supported because people thought it was ridiculous for offenders to be sentenced to ten years and serve only three. Similarly, when people perceive a substantial increase in the seriousness of crime (whether correctly or not), then the justification for a more punitive response is not, and does not need to be, framed in terms of justice theories. This is not to say that there is not going to be a punitive backlash in New South Wales. But those leading this crusade operate from simple notions of law, order and discipline, and will continue to justify their aims in these terms.

Finally, it is at this practical level that the durability of the New South Wales reforms will be tested—not at the level of theory. While the reformers of the 1980s were able to achieve considerable change, they were not successful in moving many resources away from the institutions. In the early 1990s some 85 per cent of recurrent funding for juvenile justice services is still going into custodial programs. Unless this changes, it is likely that community programs will not be able to provide the level of supervision and assistance that will allow them to be seen as viable alternatives to incarceration.

16 Court outcomes and processes

Compiled from workshop transcripts by
LYNN ATKINSON

The trend towards formal justice for juveniles in the last two decades has served to reduce the differences between adult and juvenile criminal courts in Australia. Nevertheless, and in varying degrees from one state to another, substantial differences remain in the philosophy and practice of the adult and juvenile jurisdictions. Social justice, in principle at least, is still a priority of juvenile justice. There is also an emphasis on informal processing for offences which would merit a court appearance in the adult jurisdiction. This discussion started from a point of consensus: that there is a need to maintain the distinctiveness of the children's court. From here, the participants' views diverged as they discussed the nature and impact of that distinctiveness.

Arguments for and against a distinctive juvenile justice system are usually grounded in a comparison of the adult and juvenile courts of summary jurisdiction. John Braithwaite challenged the sense of this comparison. He pointed out, for example, that in the adult sphere, although white-collar crime is a more extensive and costly field of criminal activity than blue-collar crime, it is seldom dealt with formally in the courts. Rather, informal, non-punitive processes are the norm. Given the prevalence of white-collar crime and the amount of investigative and preventative resources involved (Braithwaite referred, for example, to the massive number of staff employed by the Taxation Department alone), the response to white-collar (rather than to blue-collar) crime in fact provides the appropriate model with which to compare responses to juvenile offending. White collar crime is dealt with in an informal and inclusionary way. So both the adult criminal court and the juvenile court can be seen to deviate from this norm. Ideally then, the debate about juvenile justice should cease to focus on comparisons with the adult court. Instead, it should consider the particular purpose and distinctive features, of informal processing for children.

Throughout the workshop, it had been agreed that the children's court should be used only to deal with serious cases which are inappropriate for diversion. There was some debate about where the line marking serious offences should be drawn: should it include, for example, some property offences, such as car theft, or should it exclude all but violent offences against the person? There was some concern that academic criminologists trivialised serious offending by young people, and underestimated its impact on and cost to the community. It was pointed out that the notion of a serious crime varies from one historical and cultural context to another. In any case, irrespective of how 'seriousness' is defined, it was agreed that the children's court should be a humane institution of last resort, able to respond to serious offenders. As such, the court is essential, but it should not be the primary focus of juvenile justice. This raised the question of how and for whom should such a court operate.

The discussion focused on the impact of the children's court on the offender, although victims (both individuals as well as the community) were also thought to have a direct interest in proceedings. Ian O'Connor noted that, with its shift towards due process, the children's court has become familiar and comfortable for the adult players and decision-makers involved in juvenile justice. A major benefit of due process, that of efficiency, is often over-emphasised by the adult players in the system. Meanwhile, juvenile defendants have remained ignorant and powerless. The changes have not benefited them, nor have they lowered the crime rate. Young defendants tend to have a poor understanding of what it means to plead guilty and an incomplete grasp of the court process. They are involuntary parties to a system which discourages participation. Despite many changes in legislation in recent decades, young people attending court are still mystified and are still being dealt with in a hasty and dismissive way. And because they are involved in a non-educative process, there is no disincentive to reoffend.

The courts, it was argued, have lost opportunities to deal with the root causes of offending and to encourage preventative measures. Ian O'Connor gave an example involving social inquiry reports. Because courts are uniquely privy to a wealth of information contained in such documents, which deal with the underlying problems facing the youth population, it was considered that they could conceivably tackle these issues, or at least bring them to public and official notice. Kathy Laster gave an example of how this might work. If there were judges in the children's courts (as is the case in the South Australian and Western Australian jurisdictions), they could be empowered to make declarations about broad matters of policy and practice. Such declarations would not be enforceable but they would carry great weight. This power would enable judges to confer with, say, directors of public housing, welfare and education departments, in order to seek explanations for particular youth problems which come to light. They could raise such issues as why a particular group of offenders lacks adequate housing, or why a particular group does not attend school. Instead, the courts (and indeed the system as a whole) continue to individualise youth crime and so do little to develop a solution which takes account of, and is framed by, broader youth issues.

Social background reports, on the other hand, were seen by Michael O'Connor as potentially damaging to defendants. Judgements about a young client's involvement in, or level of responsibility for an offence, particularly if there were cooffenders, are often made in these reports by the social workers preparing them. These reports usually remain unquestioned by lawyers and by the court. Michael O'Connor was disturbed that well-meaning, soundly based principles of juvenile justice (for example that defendants should participate in proceedings concerning them), did not necessarily work well in practice, and that the 'gloss' and rhetoric of social background reports can effectively hide such failures.

The discussion then turned to the structure and operation of the ideal children's court. The scene was set by John Seymour with a hypothetical situation involving a recidivist offender in need of positive intervention. The group debated how an ideal children's court would deal with the situation.

The determination of guilt was seen as pivotal in deciding how the case would proceed. Safeguards, such as access to legal advice, would ensure that any admissions of guilt were informed and soundly based, rather than merely pragmatic. In other words, a testing of the allegations was seen as crucial. Deals made outside the court, in theory at least, would not determine the plea. To this end, it was suggested that the police version of the offence be read out in court to test the defendant's agreement on the matter, before the plea was taken. Those admitting to minor offences would be processed in such a way as to minimise further action. Those pleading not guilty would have guilt determined when the case was ready.

Conceding the benefits of continuity of personnel, participants suggested that an appropriately structured court could perform the functions of adjudication and sentencing. However, they believed these separate functions of the tribunal should remain discrete. It was suggested that adjudication should take place in the morning and that there be a lunchtime adjournment before the afternoon sentencing session. A duty social worker at the court would prepare reports after adjudication and assist in decisions about dispositions. At the sentencing stage, it was envisaged that there would be greater participation and involvement of the defendant, and more negotiation between all parties, including the young accused.

Because of their role in determining appropriate pleas (and also, in effect, guilt or innocence), it was ultimately, and for some participants, somewhat reluctantly agreed that magistrates, lawyers and prosecutors, albeit with changed roles, would continue to be the major players in the ideal court system.

It was decided, however, that the ideal children's court, because of its commitment to social justice, should have specially trained personnel working in the system. Prosecutors in the new scheme should not be police officers, but should be specialists. Mandatory training would extend to magistrates, lawyers, prosecutors and others such as social workers attached to the courts. Judy Cashmore advocated that an important objective of specialist training in youth issues would be to raise the status, and hence performance and commitment, of those lawyers and prosecutors working in the children's court. Traditionally, such work has been devalued. One novel idea to broaden the experience and minds of court and judicial personnel came from a European jurisdiction where some court and judicial personnel have been known to swap roles. In the example given by James Hackler, a magistrate familiar with a particular case would, on occasion, leave his or her bench to defend an accused youth whose lawyer had failed to arrive.

Consistency and fairness of sentencing were also deemed essential in the ideal children's court. Those jurisdictions with two tiers of judicial officer, that is, magistrates and judges (as is the case in South Australia and Western Australia), were believed to have advantages for equity. As David Alcock pointed out, in South Australia a system of reconsideration operates whereby the senior children's court judge can reassess an order made by a magistrate. This helps to keep the tariff within reasonable limits and counteracts any tendency by a 'maverick' magistrate to hand down excessive sanctions. This is particularly necessary in jurisdictions where much of the children's court work is handled by non-specialised magistrates, who are more conversant with adult sentencing principles. As a lawyer specialising in children's matters, Alcock spoke from experience: 'One minute you're asking a non-specialist magistrate to sentence an adult to six months imprisonment for stealing a car, and then next comes a juvenile who has stolen eight cars and you ask for a fifty dollar good behaviour bond. Those leaps of faith are often very difficult for country and suburban magistrates exercising children's jurisdiction'.

The two-tier structure involving judges and magistrates not only allows for reconsiderations, but also enables more matters to be contained within the juvenile jurisdiction which might otherwise go to the higher courts. Because magistrates have limited sentencing powers, juvenile jurisdictions without judges are limited in the types of offences they can deal with. Alcock pointed out that if all serious offences (that is, offences which carry a term of more than two years imprisonment) had to be referred to the appropriate court in the adult jurisdiction, this would effectively bar many young people from special and distinct juvenile justice. In particular, it would affect Aboriginal young offenders because they are so over-represented at the 'hard end' of the system. Furthermore, Aborigines from remote regions would be disadvantaged by not having access to a locally convened court.

A model children's court would ensure that the lawyers operating within it were accountable. At present, lawyers with no training in or understanding of youth issues, and with no relevant children's court experience, often represent their firms on duty counsel rosters. Under the regime devised by the workshop participants, this would not be possible. Indeed, the participants recommended that children's court lawyers should lose some of their autonomy and become specially trained employees of the court. It was also argued that, because a youth appearing before the court for the first time needed information, the defence counsel, if made an employee of the court, could be one important source of such information.

Australian children's courts are modelled on magistrate's courts, perhaps mistakenly so, as the earlier part of the discussion suggests. While informal procedures and practices have been introduced at times, particularly when the welfare model was in its heyday, children's courts remain modified versions of the adult courts. A more informal physical arrangement was advocated by Fred Wojtasik, on the grounds that this would reduce the level of fear in juvenile defendants and enable them to understand the process and participate more freely. It is important to ensure, however, that informality does not mask important differences between the players. The umpire's, or magistrate's role, the prosecutorial and defence roles do need to be clearly differentiated.

The vexed question of a criminal record was also raised. Unlike adult courts, juvenile diversionary schemes usually dispense with enduring records. Even in the children's courts there are high numbers of discharges without conviction. Beyond this, juvenile records have limited currency anyway, if and when the offender appears in the adult jurisdiction. Thus, many children can, in theory at least, put an offending incident behind them. In practice, however, even the 'non-records' of panel appearances and cautions which are kept for administrative purposes are available to certain agencies. The question, then, is what is to be done with records and who is to have access, rather than whether they should be expunged. Juveniles, like adults, are often refused employment because their involvement with the justice system becomes known to the prospective employer. John Seymour also pointed out that there is something illogical about trying to pretend that an incident did not take place by erasing any record of it.

The discussion addressed other problems associated with children's courts. For example, participants wanted more resources for youth programs and for supervision of bonds. If young offenders on community based orders remained unsupervised and programs did not address real employment and training issues, then magistrates would be disinclined to use those particular dispositions.

The question of orders for restitution from young offenders was also raised. Wojtasik said that in South Australia juveniles can be ordered to pay compensation of up to $2000 in six months. Clearly such an order is unlikely to be complied with, the provision for civil proceedings to recoup the money notwithstanding. In this context, participants considered the juvenile system excessively punitive compared with the adult system, especially considering the dismal financial and employment status of most youth concerned. Kathy Laster found the source for such punitiveness in society's confused images of children, with the good being idealised and the miscreant being punished and targeted for moral instruction. Punishment and instruction about the value of hard work and the dollar are implicit in youth restitution orders.

Though there is, in theory, provision for restitution and compensation to victims, in practice there is widespread non-compliance with these orders. The fact that juveniles do not pay is a source of public grievance and leads to condemnation of the children's court. While there is provision for offenders to undertake community work in lieu of fines levied by the court, there is no alternative provision to help the victim if the offender is required, and fails, to pay compensation. Restitution and compensation was seen by Alcock as being virtually meaningless in practice—a 'ridiculous legislative provision'.

Defendants in country areas caught up in the juvenile justice system can be exposed to greater punishment and disadvantage than those in the city. For example, Michael Hogan recalled 'actually seeing [country] solicitors get up and recommend that their client be "put away"'. Michael O'Connor described how young people in one country town would be detained by police for a night or two rather than released on bail: 'The police [there] are undermining the system. What they're often doing is putting the youth in [the lockup] for one or two nights . . . If it's a Friday night they go into the police station [lockup] and on Monday [in court] the police don't oppose bail. What the police are saying is "We're giving them two days inside".' If bail is granted in this particular town, a curfew is invariably imposed. On the other hand, victims' rights often have greater currency in country areas because of the small-town familiarity between the victim and the adult actors in the juvenile justice system.

Another theme to emerge in this discussion related to youth who in earlier times would have been subject to intervention within the juvenile court system through care and control orders. With the new emphasis on due process, these youths—the homeless, runaways, the unemployed—still exist, but they are no longer incarcerated simply for their own welfare, and no longer generate welfare statistics. Some participants were extremely doubtful that this section of the youth population was being adequately catered for. Ken Polk argued that children's courts have a traditional brief to control the troublesome youth of the 'dangerous classes'. The merely troublesome, rather than the criminal, are no longer officially within the jurisdiction of justice-oriented children's courts. The question he asked was, where is this population and what is happening to them?

Polk introduced the metaphor of the welfare 'rug', under which this population has been swept as a result of changes in the juvenile justice system. The participants tried to assess the whereabouts of the 'rug', the nature of it, and who should take responsibility for it. Garth Luke believed the 'rug' was an irrelevant concept, mainly because of changed attitudes which obviated the need for a cover-up. He believed most of the youth previously incarcerated for care matters had simply gone home, including the young women who were especially targeted for custodial care and control orders. Most participants, however, considered that the extent of youth poverty and homelessness was clear evidence that a large 'rug' does exist and that the young people swept beneath it do not receive adequate services.

Linda Hancock suggested that youth housing refuges absorb some of this particular youth population. Just as the policy of decarceration for psychiatric patients shifted the hospital population into the community, to places like boarding houses, so too, has part of the decarcerated youth population been absorbed, for better or worse, by the community. It was, however, pointed out that for this population of youth, institutionalisation may simply have been deferred. Although no longer subject to orders from a welfare-based children's court, and not necessarily caught in the criminal justice net, the very fact of living for years on the streets, in poverty and unemployed, means that adult incarceration becomes all but inevitable.

What connection does this poorly-resourced 'rug' population have with the formal children's court system? The juvenile justice system, it was argued, must focus on outcomes as well as processes. There was some agreement that, because of their overriding concern with social justice and rehabilitation (which represents the main philosophical difference between the children's and adult courts), children's courts need to be concerned with this group of young people. They should aim for a social justice as well as a criminal justice response to juveniles. Resources, particularly those freed up through the decarceration of the welfare population, should be spent on this forgotten, hidden and under-resourced population. Laster highlighted the community's ambiguous response to youth when she pointed out youth funding priorities. Research into child witnesses (the 'good guys') is currently a magnet for funds; marginalised youth, on the other hand, continue to attract few resources.

The discussion on children's courts concluded with the following recommendations:

- That the most important characteristic of the children's court is to test the allegation. This could be better achieved within the existing magistrate's court format by having the prosecutor state the facts at the beginning, before a plea was entered.
- That the prosecutorial function be handled, not by police, but by a new service, which would have special responsibility for children.
- That the main participants—i.e. prosecutors, lawyers and magistrates— would all be specialised personnel who had undertaken a course in juvenile justice.
- That defendants be provided with more information about the tribunal, its personnel and procedures, which would enable them better to participate in proceedings.
- That the role of defence counsel be expanded to take responsibility for this educational component.
- That there be a duty social worker in court to participate at the sentencing stage.
- That, to overcome delays, the testing of the allegation occur in the morning, with sentencing in the afternoon, after the young offender had discussed the matter with the duty social worker.
- That sentencing involve negotiation between, and the participation of, all parties.

Appendix

The data sources used in compiling the figures for Chapter 2 include:

South Australia:
Youth Offending files maintained by the Department for Family and Community Services. These also provide the raw data for the section on juvenile offenders in the South Australian Office of Crime Statistics publication, *Crime and Justice.*

Queensland:
Australian Bureau of Statistics: *Law and Order.* Cat. No. 4502.3.

Western Australia:
(a) Australian Bureau of Statistics: *Court Statistics: Children's Court, Western Australia.* Cat. No. 4503.5.
(b) Department for Community Services: *Annual Reports.*
(c) Crown Law Department: *Annual Report, 1989/90.*

Tasmania:
(a) Australian Bureau of Statistics: *Children's Court Statistics, Tasmania—1986:* Cat. No. 4505.6.
(b) Australian Bureau of Statistics: *Court Statitics, Tasmania 1988.* Cat. No. 4508.6.
(c) Department for Community Welfare: *Annual Reports.*

New South Wales:
New South Wales Bureau of Crime Statistics and Research: *Court Statistics* (to 1986) and *Lower Criminal Courts and Children's Court Statistics, 1987, 1988.*

Victoria:
(a) Australian Bureau of Statistics: *Court Proceedings Initiated by Police* (final issue, 1986).
(b) *Victorian Police Statistical Review 1987–89.*
(c) *Children's Court Statistics, Victoria 1989, 1990* Attorney General's Department.

Bibliography

Alder, C. 1984 'Gender bias in juvenile diversion', in *Crime and delinquency*, 30; pp. 400–414

—— 1991, 'Victims of violence: the case of homeless youth', in *Australian & New Zealand Journal of Criminology*, 24, pp. 1–14

Alder, C. and Polk, K. 1982, 'Diversion and hidden sexism', in *Australian and New Zealand Journal of Criminology*, 15, pp. 100–108

Alder, C. and Sandor, D. 1989, *Homeless youth as victims of violence*, Criminology Department, The University of Melbourne

—— 1990, 'Youth researching youth', in *Youth Studies*, 94, pp. 38–42

Andrews, R. H. and Cohn, A. H. 1974, 'Ungovernability; the unjustifiable jurisdiction', in *The Yale Law Journal*, 83, pp. 1383–1407

—— 1977, 'PINS processing in New York: an evaluation', in *Beyond control: status offenders in the juvenile court*, L. H. Teitelbaum and A. R. Gough, Ballinger, Cambridge, Mass.

Antler, J. and Antler, S. 1979, 'From child rescue to family protection: The evolution of the child protective movement in the United States', in *Children and Youth Services Review*, 1

Aries, P. 1962, *Centuries of childhood: a social history of family life*, Alfred A. Knopf, New York

Asquith, S. 1983, *Children and justice: decision-making in children's hearings and juvenile courts*, Edinburgh University Press, Edinburgh

Austin J. and Krisberg, B. 1981, 'Wider, stronger, and different nets: The dialectics of criminal justice reform', in *Journal of Research in Crime and Delinquency*, 18, pp. 165–196

Australian Bureau of Statistics, 1983–84, 'Children in care', in *Catalogue No. 44100*, June, 1985, Canberra

162

Australian Institute of Family Studies, 1991, 'Update: costs of children in Australia', in *Family Matters*, 29. p. 57

Australian Law Reform Commission. 1981, *Child welfare: Report no.18*, Australian Government Publishing Service, Canberra

Bacon, J. and Irwin, J. 1990, *If I had a gun I would shoot the lot: a report on young people and police*, Youth Justice Coalition, Sydney

Bailey, V. 1987, *Delinquency and citizenship*, Clarendon Press, Oxford

Bartlett, J. 1977, *Familiar quotations: a collection of passages, phrases and proverbs traced to their sources in ancient and modern literature*, Macmillan, London

Bayer, R. 1981, 'Crime, punishment, and the decline of liberal optimism', in *Crime and Delinquency*, 27, pp. 169–190

Binder, A. and Geis, G. 1984, 'Ad populum argumentation in criminology: juvenile diversion as rhetoric', in *Crime and Delinquency*, 30, pp. 309–333

Bordow, A. (ed) 1977, *The worker in Australia: contributions from research*, University of Queensland Press, St Lucia

Borowski, A. and Murray, J. M. (eds) 1985, *Juvenile delinquency in Australia*, Methuen, Sydney

Bortner, M. A. 1982, *Inside a juvenile court: the tarnished ideal of individualised justice*, New York University Press, New York and London

Boss, P. 1967, *Social policy and the young delinquent*, Routledge and Kegan Paul, London

Bottoms, A. E. 1984, 'Juvenile justice 75 years on', D. Hoath (ed), in *75 Years of Law at Sheffield 1909–1984*, Sheffield University Printing Unit, Sheffield

Bottoms, A. E. and McClean, J. D. 1976 *Decisions in the penal process*, Routledge and Kegan Paul, London

Box, S. 1983, *Power, crime and mystification*, Tavistock, London

Brady, M. 1985, 'Aboriginal youth and the juvenile justice system', in *Juvenile delinquency in Australia*, Allan Borowski and James M. Murray (eds), Methuen, Sydney

Braithwaite, J. 1989, *Crime, shame and reintegration*, Cambridge University Press, Cambridge

—— 1992, Reducing the crime problem: a not so dismal criminology, in *Australian and New Zealand Journal of Criminology*, 25: pp. 1–10

Braithwaite, J. and Biles, D. 1979, 'On being unemployed and being a victim of crime', in *Australian Journal of Social Issues*, 14: pp. 192–200

Brogden, M., Jefferson T. and Walklate, S. 1988, *Introducing police work*, Unwin Hyman, London

Cain, M. (ed.) 1989, *Growing up good: policing the behaviour of girls in Europe*, Sage, London

Cain, M. and Luke, G. 1991, *Sentencing juvenile offenders and the Sentencing Act 1989*, Judicial Commission of NSW, Sydney

Campbell, T. 1983 *The left and rights*, Routledge and Kegan Paul, London

Carney, T. 1989, 'Young offenders and state intervention: issues of control and support for parents and young people', in *Australian and New Zealand Journal of Criminology*, Vol. 22, March, pp. 22–39

Carrington, K. 1990, *Youth: the right police?* Arena, 91: pp. 18–24

Carter, David L. 1985, 'Police brutality: a model of definition, perspective and control', in *The Ambivalent Force*, Abraham S. Blumberg and Elaine Niederhoffer (eds), Holt, Rinehardt and Winston, New York

Cavenagh, W. 1957, 'Justice and welfare in juvenile courts', in *British Journal of Delinquency*, 7, pp. 196–205

Challinger, D. 1985, 'Police action and the prevention of juvenile delinquency', in *Juvenile delinquency in Australia*, Allan Borowski and James M. Murray (eds), Methuen, Sydney

Chappell, D. and Wilson, P. 1969, *The police and the public in Australia and New Zealand*, University of Queensland Press, St Lucia

Child Welfare Practice and Legislation Review, 1984, T. Carney Chair, Report: *Equity and social justice for children, families and communities*, Victorian Government Printer, Victoria

Clarke, J. 1985, 'Whose justice? The politics of juvenile control', in *International Journal of the Sociology of Law*, 13, pp. 407–421

Cleverley, J. and Phillips, D. C. 1976, *From Locke to Spock: influential models of the child in modern western thought*, Melbourne University Press, Melbourne

Cohen, S. 1985, *Visions of social control: crime, punishment and classification*, Polity Press, Cambridge

—— 1987, 'Taking decentralizaion seriously: values, vision and policies', in *Transcarceration: essays in the sociology of social control*, J. Lowman, R. J. Menzies and T. S. Palyes (eds), Gower, Aldershot, Hants

Community Services Victoria. 1986, *Discussion paper on the redevelopment of services for young people convicted of committing offences*, Community Services, Melbourne, Victoria

Cooper, J. 1970, 'Social care and social control', in *Probation*, 16, pp. 22–25

Corns, C. and Simpson, B. 1988, 'Policing Victorian public transport: extending the police domain', in *Australian Journal of Social Issues*, 23, 4, pp. 287–299

Coventry, PACE (n.d.), *Intensive intermediate treatment project*, Church of England Children's Society, Coventry

Cullen, F. and Gilbert, R. 1982, *Reaffirming rehabilitation*, Anderson, Cincinnati

Cunneen, C. 1988, 'Some thoughts on culture, space and political economy, in *Understanding crime and criminal justice*, M. Findlay and R. Hogg (eds), Law Book Company Ltd., Sydney

—— 1990, *A study of Aboriginal juveniles and police violence: commissioned by the National Inquiry into Racist Violence*, Human Rights Commission, Sydney

Cunneen, C. and Robb, T. 1987, *Criminal justice in North-West New South Wales*, New South Wales Bureau of Crime Statistics and Research, Attorney-General's Department, Sydney

Dannefer, D. and Schott, R. K. 1982, 'Race and juvenile justice processing in court and police agencies', in *American Journal of Sociology*, 87, 1113–32

Debele, G. A. 1987, 'The due process revolution and the juvenile court: the matter of race in the historical evolution of a doctrine', in *Law and Inequality*, 5, 512

De Mause, L. 1974, *The history of childhood*, Psychohistory Press, New York

Department for Community Services 1991, *Laws for people—The Report of the Legislative Review, 1991*, Western Australian Department for Community Services

Department for Community Welfare 1961, *Annual Report*, Government Printer, South Australia

Department of Health and Social Security 1971, *Care and treatment in a planned environment*, HMSO, London

Devon and Cornwall Constabulary 1984, *Exeter Joint Services Youth Support Team*, Exeter

Ditchfield, J. 1976, *Police cautioning in England and Wales*, HMSO, London

Donzelot, J. 1979, *The policing of families: welfare versus the state*, Pantheon, New York

Edwards, E. 1982, *The treatment of juvenile offenders: a study of the treatment of juvenile offenders in Western Australia as part of an overall review of the Child Welfare Act*, Department for Community Welfare, Perth, Western Australia

Eggleston, E. 1976, *Fear, favour and affection: Aborigines and the criminal law in Victoria, South Australia and Western Australia*, ANU Press, Canberra

Empey, L. 1982, *American delinquency*, Dorsey Press, Homewood, Illinois

Empey, L. and Rabow, J. 1961, 'The Provo experiment in delinquency rehabilitation', in *American Sociological Review*, 26, pp.679–695

Equal Opportunity Commission. 1990, 'Discrimination in government policies and practices', in *Report No.8 Review of police practices, Main Report*, Equal Opportunity Commission, Perth, Western Australia

Ethnic Youth Issues Network. 1990, *Report to Ethnic Affairs Police Liaison Committee*, May, Unpublished Paper, Melbourne

Factor, J. 1988, *Captain Cook Chased a Chook: children's folklore in Australia*, Penguin, Ringwood

Farrington, D. P. 1984, 'England and Wales' in *Western systems of juvenile justice*, M.W. Klein (ed.), Sage, Beverly Hills, Calif.

Farrington, D. P. and Bennett, T. 1981, 'Police cautioning of juveniles in London', in *British Journal of Criminology*, 21, 2, pp. 123–135

Federation of Community Legal Centres. 1991, *Report into mistreatment of young people by police*, Federation of Community Legal Centres, Victoria

Feeley, M. 1979, *The process is punishment*, Russell Sage, New York

Feld, B.C. 1981, 'Legislative policies toward the serious juvenile offender: on the virtues of automatic adulthood', in *Crime and Delinquency*, 27

Final Report of the Royal Commission into Aboriginal deaths in custody, in *National Report by Commissioner Elliott Johnston*, AGPS, Canberra

Fisher, C.J. and Mawby R.I. 1982, 'Juvenile delinquency and police discretion in inner city areas', in *British Journal of Criminology*, 22, pp.63–75

Fisk, M. 1980, *Ethics and society: a Marxist interpretation of value*, Harvester Press, Sussex

Foucault, M. 1979, *Discipline and punish: the birth of the prison*, Penguin, Harmondsworth

Freeman, D. 1987, 'Quest for the real Samoa—comment', in *American Anthropologist*, 89, 4, pp. 930–935

Freiberg, A. 1986, 'Reward, law and power: toward a jurisprudence of the carrot', in *Australian and New Zealand Journal of Criminology*, 19, pp. 91–113

Freiberg, A., Fox, R. and Hogan, M. 1988, 'Sentencing young offenders', in *Law Reform Commission, Sentencing Research Paper No.11*, Alken Press, Smithfield

Friedmann, W. 1967, *Legal theory*, Stevens and Sons, London

Galaway, B. and Hudson, J. 1990, *Criminal justice, restitution and reconciliation*, Criminal Justice Press, New York

Gale, F. and Wundersitz, J. 1989, 'The operation of hidden prejudice in pre-court procedures: the case of Australian Aboriginal youth', in *The Australian and New Zealand Journal of Criminology*, vol. 22, March, pp. 1–21

Gale, F., Bailey-Harris, R. and Wundersitz, J. 1990, *Aboriginal youth and the criminal justice system: the injustice of justice?*, Cambridge University Press, Cambridge

Gardner, M. R. 1987, 'Punitive juvenile justice: some observations on a recent trend' in *International Journal of Law and Psychiatry*, Vol.10, 2, pp. 129–151

Giller, H. 1986, 'Is there a role for a juvenile court?' in *The Howard Journal of Criminal Justice*,15, pp.161–171

Golding, W. 1954, *Lord of the Flies*, Faber and Faber, London

Grabosky, P. N. 1989, *Victims of violence*, Australian Institute of Criminology for the National Committee on Violence, Canberra

Graham, G. 1988, *Contemporary social philosophy*, Basil Blackwell, Oxford

Hammond, G. 1989, 'The law and ideas', an inaugural lecture presented in the University Hall, Old Arts Building, University of Auckland, New Zealand

Hancock, L. 1978, 'Police discretion in Victoria: the police discretion to prosecute', in *Australian and New Zealand Journal of Sociology*, 14, pp. 33–40

—— 1980, 'The myth that females are treated more leniently than males in the juvenile justice system', in *Australian and New Zealand Journal of Sociology*, 16, pp. 4–14

—— 1992 *Follow-up study on young people and prostitution*, unpublished paper

Hancock, L. and Chesney-Lind, M. 1985, 'Juvenile justice legislation and gender discrimination', in *Juvenile delinquency in Australia*, Allan Borowski and James M. Murray, Methuen, Sydney

Harris, R. J. 1985, 'Towards just welfare: a consideration of a current controversy in the theory of juvenile justice', in *British Journal of Criminology*, 25, 1, pp. 31–45

Harris, R. and Webb, D. 1987, *Welfare, power and juvenile justice: the social control of delinquent youths*, Tavistock, London

Hindelang, M. J., Gottfredson, M. R. and Garofolo, J. 1978, *Victims of personal crime: an empirical foundation for a theory of personal victimisation*, M.A. Ballinger, Cambridge

Hirst, P. Q., 1986, *Law, socialism and democracy*, Allen and Unwin, London

Hobbes, T. 1962, *Leviathan: or, the matter, form and power of a commonwealth, ecclesiastical and civil*, Collier, New York

Hobsbawm, E. J. 1969, *Industry and Empire: From 1750 to the present day*, Penguin, Harmondsworth

Holmes, L. D. 1987, *Quest for the Real Samoa: the Mead/Freeman controversy and beyond*, Bergin & Garvey Publishers, South Hadley, Massachusetts

Horne, D. 1964, *The lucky country: Australia in the sixties*, Penguin, Harmondsworth

Houston, M. et al. 1983, *Report on services for young offenders*, Department of Youth and Community Services, Sydney

Hudson, B. 1987, *Justice through punishment: a critique of the 'justice' model of corrections*, St Martin's Press, New York

—— 1989, 'Justice or welfare'? A comparison of recent developments in the English and French juvenile justice systems', in *Growing up good: policing the behaviour of girls in Europe*, M. Cain (ed), Sage, London

Irwin, J. 1985, *The jail: managing the underclass in American society*, University of California Press, Berkeley

Jaggs, D. 1986, *Neglected and criminal: foundations of child welfare legislation in Victoria*, Phillip Institute of Technology, Victoria

James, S. and Polk, K. 1989, 'Policing youth: themes and directions', in *Australian policing: contemporary issues*, D. Chappell and P. Wilson (eds), Butterworth, Sydney

Jefferson, A. 1987, 'Beyond paramilitarism', in *The British Journal of Criminology*, 27, pp. 47–53

Johnston, R. 1977, 'The immigrant worker', in *The worker in Australia: contributions from research*, A. Bordow (ed), University of Queensland Press, St Lucia

Kamenka, E. and Tay, A. E-S. 1975, 'Beyond bourgeois industrialism: the contemporary crisis in law and legal ideology', in *Feudalism, capitalism and beyond*, E. Kamenka and R Neale (eds), Edward Arnold, London.

—— 1986 'The traditions of justice', in *Law and philosophy*, 5, 281

Keeves, J.P. 1990, 'The expansion and rationale of Australian education: to the 1990s and beyond?', in *Schooling and society in Australia: sociological perspectives*, L.J. Saha and J.P. Keeves (eds), Australian National University Press, New South Wales

Ketcham, O. W. 1977, 'Why jurisdiction over status offenders should be eliminated from juvenile courts', in *Boston University Law Review*, 57, 2, pp. 645–662

Klein, M. W. 1979, 'Deinstitutionalization and diversion of juvenile offenders: a litany of impediments', in *Crime and justice: an annual review of research*, Vol.1, N. Morris and M. Tonry (eds), University of Chicago Press, Chicago

Knight, T. 1985, 'Schools and delinquency', in *Juvenile delinquency in Australia*, A. Borowski and J.M. Murray (eds), Methuen, Sydney

Laster, K. 1989, 'Infanticide: a litmus test for feminist criminological theory', in *The Australian and New Zealand Journal of Criminology*, 22, Sept, pp. 151–166

Leaper, P. 1974, *Children in need of care and protection: a study of children brought before Victoria's childrens' courts*, Criminology Department, University of Melbourne

Legislative Review, 1991, *Laws for people: the report of the legislative review*, Perth, Western Australia

Lipscombe, P. 1989, *Walking the tightrope: rights and responsibilities in the welfare system*, Department for Community Services, Western Australia

Luke, G. 1990, 'Keeping alternatives as alternatives', in *Keeping people out of prison*, paper presented at the Australian Institute of Criminology Conference, Hobart, 27–29 March, 1990

MacIntyre, A. 1981, *After virtue*, Duckworth, London

McBarnet, D. 1981, *Conviction: law, the state and the construction of justice*, MacMillan, London

McCorkle, L. W., Elias, A. and Bixby, F. L. 1958, *The Highfields story*, Holt, New York

McGregor, S. 1986, 'The South Australian Children's Interest Bureau–seeking justice for children', in *Australian Law Journal*, Vol. 60, pp. 320–321

Martin, F., Fox, S. and Murray, K. 1981, *Children out of court*, Scottish Academic Press, Edinburgh

Matthews, R. 1987, 'Decarceration and social control: fantasies and realities', in *Transcarceration: essays in the sociology of social control*, J. Lowman, R. J. Menzies and T. S. Palyes (eds), Gower, Aldershot

Mead, M. 1967, *Male and female: a study of the sexes in a changing world*, William Morrow, New York

Mohr Report 1977, *Report of the Royal Commission into the Administration of the Juvenile Courts Act and associated matters*, Adelaide

Morgan, P. 1978, *Delinquent fantasies*, Temple Smith, London

Morris, A. 1978, 'Revolution in the juvenile court', in *Criminal Law Review*, pp. 529–539

Morris, A., Giller, H., Szwed, E. and Geach, H. 1980, *Justice for children*, Macmillan, London

Morris, A. and Giller, H. 1987, *Understanding juvenile justice*, Croom Helm, London

Morris, A. and McIsaac, M. 1978, *Juvenile justice? the practice of social welfare*, Heinemann, London

Murray, J. 1981, *Innovations in Juvenile Justice, Victoria 1970–1980*, Unpublished Masters in Social Work Thesis, Bundoora, Melbourne: Department of Social Work, La Trobe University

Murray, J. M. 1985, 'The development of contemporary juvenile justice and correctional policy', in *Juvenile delinquency in Australia*, A. Borowski and J.M. Murray (eds), Methuen, Sydney

NACRO, 1986, 'The future of the juvenile court in England and Wales', in *Juvenile crime briefing*, NACRO, London

Naffine, N. 1990, *Law and the sexes: explorations in feminist jurisprudence*, Allen and Unwin, Sydney

Naffine, N. and Wundersitz, J. 1991, 'Lawyers in the Children's Courts: an Australian perspective', in *Crime and Delinquency*, 37, 3, pp. 374–392

Naffine, N., Gale, F., and Wundersitz, J. 1991, 'Back to justice for juveniles: the rhetoric and reality of law reform', in *The Australian and New Zealand Journal of Criminology*, 23, pp. 192–205

National Committee on Violence 1990, *Violence: directions for Australia*, Australian Institute of Criminology, Canberra

Nichols, H. 1985, 'Children's aid panels in South Australia', in *Juvenile delinquency in Australia*, A. Borowski and J.M. Murray (eds), Methuen, Sydney

Nino, C. S., 1989, 'The communitarian challenge to Liberal Rights', in *Law and Philosophy*, 8, 1, pp. 37–52

Northampton Juvenile Liaison Bureau 1982, *Information handout*, Northamptonshire Social Services, Northampton

—— 1985, *First Annual Report*, Northamptonshire Social Services, Northampton

O'Connor, I. and Callahan, M. 1989, 'Social crisis and social policy in Queensland: patterns of control', in *Australia & New Zealand Journal of Criminology*, 22, June, pp. 109—123

O'Connor, I. and Sweetapple, P. 1988, *Children in justice*, Longman Cheshire, Melbourne

O'Connor, I. and Tilbury, C. 1986, *Legal aid needs of youth*, Australian Government Publishing Service, Canberra

O'Hagan, T. 1984, *The end of law?*, Basil Blackwell, Oxford

Opotow, S. 1990, 'Moral exclusion and injustice: an introduction', in *Journal of Social Issues*, 46, 1, pp. 1–20

Pace, D. 1983, *Claude Levi-Strauss: the bearer of ashes*, Routledge and Kegan Paul, Boston

Packer, H. 1964, 'Two models of criminal justice', in *University of Pennsylvania Law Review*, 113, pp. 1–68

Parker, H., Casburn, M. and Turnbull, D. 1981, *Receiving juvenile justice*, Basil Blackwell, Oxford

Parsloe, P. 1978, *Juvenile justice in Britain and the United States: the balance of needs and rights*, Routledge and Kegan Paul, London

Parton, N. 1985, *The politics of child abuse*, Macmillan, Basingstoke

Pilavian, I. and Briar S. 1964, 'Police encounters with juveniles', in *American Journal of Sociology*, 70: pp. 206–214

Platt, A. M. 1969, *The child savers: the invention of delinquency*, University of Chicago Press, Chicago

—— 1977, *The child savers: the invention of delinquency*, 2nd ed., University of Chicago Press, Chicago

Polk, K. 1984a, 'Juvenile diversion: a look at the record', in *Crime and Delinquency*, 30, pp. 648–659

—— 1984b, 'The New Marginal Youth', in *Crime and Delinquency*, 30, pp. 462–480

—— 1987, 'When Less Means More: an analysis of destructuring in criminal justice', in *Crime and Delinquency*, 33, pp. 358–378

—— 1989, 'School of delinquency prevention as management of rabble', in *Crime prevention and intervention*, P. Albrecht and O. Backes (eds), Walter de Gruyter, New York

Postman, N. 1982, *The disappearance of childhood*, Delacorte, New York

Pratt, J. 1983, 'Reflections on the approach of 1984: recent developments in social control in the UK', in *International Journal of the Sociology of Law*, 11, 4, pp. 339–360

—— 1984, 'Delinquency as a scarce resource', in *Howard Journal of Criminal Justice*, 24, pp. 93–107

—— 1985, 'A Comparative Analysis of Two Different Systems of Juvenile Justice', in *Howard Journal of Criminal Justice*, 25, pp. 35–51

—— 1987, 'A revisionist history of intermediate treatment', in *British Journal of Social Work*, 17, pp. 417–436

—— 1989, 'Corporatism: the third model of juvenile justice', in *British Journal of Criminology*, vol. 29, no.3, pp. 236–254

Pryke, R. et al. 1983, *Report to the Minister of YACS on restructuring services for young offenders*, Department of Youth and Community Services, Sydney

Quinlan, M. 1979, 'Australian trade unions and postwar immigration: attitudes and responses', in *Journal of Industrial Relations*, 21, 3, pp. 265–280

Raynar, M. 1988, *Fending for yourself*, Report to the Human Rights and Equal Opportunity Commission's Inquiry into Homeless Children, Perth

Reiss, A. J. 1971, *The Police and the Public*, Yale University Press, New Haven

Rothenberger, D. and Shepherd, J. 1978, 'Police juvenile diversion: a summary of findings', in *The Police Chief*, 45, pp. 74–77

Rousseau, J. 1984, *A discourse on inequality*, Penguin, Middlesex

Saha, L. J. and Keeves, J. P. (eds) 1990, *Schooling and society in Australia: sociological perspectives*, Australian National University Press, New South Wales

Salvation Army. 1989, *Forced exit*, The Salvation Army, Melbourne

Sandel, M. 1982, *Liberalism and the limits of justice*, Cambridge University Press, Cambridge

Sarri, R. 1983, 'Paradigms and pitfalls in juvenile justice diversion', in *Providing criminal justice for children*, A. Morris and H. Giller (eds), Edward Arnold, London

Sarri, R. and Bradley, P.W. 1980, 'Juvenile aid panels: an alternative to juvenile court processing in South Australia', in *Crime and Delinquency*, 20, pp. 42–62

Searle, G. 1971, *The quest for national efficiency: a study in British politics and political thought, 1899–1914*, Blackwell, Oxford

Second and Final Report of Commission Appointed to Report on the Destitute Act, 1881, South Australian Parliamentary Papers, 1885, 4, p. 228

Seymour, J. A. 1982, 'Dealing with young offenders: the report of the Australian Law Reform Commission' 15, in *Australian and New Zealand Journal of Criminology*, 15, Dec., pp. 245–254

—— 1985, 'Children's courts in Australia', in *Juvenile delinquency in Australia*, A. Borowski and J. M. Murray (eds), Methuen, Australia

—— 1988, *Dealing with young offenders*, Law Book Co., Sydney

Sinclair, A. 1977, *The savage: a history of misunderstanding*, Weidenfeld and Nicolson, London

Smith, G. 1975, 'Kids and Coppers', in *Australia and New Zealand Journal of Criminology*, 8, Sept/Dec., pp. 221–230

Sommerville, J. 1982, *The rise and fall of childhood*, Sage, Beverly Hills, Calif.

Stafford, M. C. and Galle, O. R. 1984, 'Victimisation rates, exposure to risk and fear of crime', in *Criminology*, 222, pp. 173–185

Stewart, G. and Tutt, N. 1987, *Children in custody*, Gower, Aldershot

Sykes, R. E., Fox, J. C. and Clark, J. P. 1985, 'A socio—legal theory of police discretion', in *The ambivalent force*, Abraham S. Blumberg and Elaine Niederhoffer (eds), Holt, Rinehart and Winston, New York

Taylor, L., Lacey, R. and Bracken, D. 1980, *In whose best interests? The unjust treatment of children in courts and institutions*, Cobden Trust/NCCL, London

Terry, R. M. 1967, 'The screening of juvenile offenders', in *Journal of Criminal Law, Criminology and Police Science*, 58, 2, pp. 173–181

Thornton, C. 1988, 'The Children and Young Persons Bill, 1987', in *Law Institute Journal*, 62, March, pp. 160–163

Thornton, W. E. Jr., James, J. and Doerner, W.G. 1982, *Delinquency and justice*, Scott, Foresman & Co., Illinois

Thorpe, A. 1983, *Linking: one year review*, National Youth Bureau, Leicester

Thorpe, D. H., Smith, B., Green, C. J. and Paley, J. H. 1980, *Out of care: the community support of juvenile offenders*, Allen & Unwin, London

Tilly, L. A. and Scott, J. W. 1978, *Women, work and family*, Holt, Rinehart and Winston, New York

US Commission on Law Enforcement and the Administration of Justice, 1975, 'Police practices', in *Issues in Law Enforcement*, George G. Killinger and Paul F. Cromwell Jr. (eds), Holbrook Press Inc., Boston

Victorian Child Welfare Practice and Legislation Review Committee. 1984, T. Carney Chair, Report: *Equity and social justice for children, families and communities*, Victorian Government Printer, Melbourne

von Hirsch, A. 1976, *Doing justice: the choice of punishments: report of the Committee for the Study of Incarceration*, Hill and Wang, New York

Walvin, J. 1982, *A child's world: a social history of English childhood 1800–1914*, Penguin, Harmondsworth

Warren, I. 1991, Masculinity culture and juvenile gang violence: a cross cultural examination of current trends in Australia and Japan, Honours Thesis, University of Melbourne

Warren, M. Q. 1976, 'Intervention with juvenile delinquents', in *Pursuing justice for the child*, M.K. Rosenheim (ed), University of Chicago Press, Chicago

→Weber, M. 1971, 'The ideal type', in *Sociological perspectives*, K. Thompson and J. Tunstall (eds), Penguin, Harmondsworth

Welstat 1983, *Children under detention collection*, Australian Institute of Criminology, Canberra

Wesley, J. 1986, 'Sermon 96: on obedience to parents', in *The works of John Wesley, volume 3, Sermons III 71–114*, A.C. Outler (ed), Abingdon Press, Nashville

Western Australia Department for Community Services, 1986, *Report on the Review of Departmental Juvenile Justice Systems*, Perth, Western Australia

Western Australia Department for Community Welfare, n.d. (probably 1976), *Report of the Committee on the Future Development of the Juvenile Judicial System in Western Australia*, Perth, Western Australia

White, R. 1990, *No space of their own*, Cambridge University Press, Cambridge

White, R., Underwood, R. and Omelczuk, S. 1991, 'Victims of violence: the view from youth services', in *The Australian and New Zealand Journal of Criminology*, 24, March, pp. 25–39

Wilson, E. 1979, *Women and the welfare state*, Tavistock, London

Wilson, P. and Arnold, J. 1986, *Street kids*, Collins Dove, Melbourne

Winzer, S. and Keller, M. F. 1977, 'The penal model of juvenile justice: is the juvenile court delinquency jurisdiction obsolete?', in *New York University Law Review*, 52, Nov., pp.1120–1135

Wolff, R. 1976, 'There's nobody here but us persons', in *Women and philosophy: toward a theory of liberation*, C.C. Gould (ed), Perigree, New York

Women's Co-Ordination Unit. 1986, *Girls at risk*, Report of the Girls in Care Project, Premier's Department, New South Wales Government

Wundersitz, J., 1989, *The net-widening effect of aid panels and screening panels in the South Australian juvenile justice system*. Report prepared for the Department for Community Welfare, Adelaide

Wundersitz, J., Bailey-Harris, R. and Gale, F. 1990, 'Aboriginal youth and juvenile justice in South Australia', in *Aboriginal Law Bulletin*, 2, 44, pp. 12–14

Wundersitz, J. and Naffine, N. 1990, 'Pre-trial negotiations in the children's court', in *Australian and New Zealand Journal of Sociology*, 26, 3, pp. 329–350

Wundersitz, J., Naffine, N. and Gale, F. 1988, 'Chivalry, justice or paternalism?: The female offender in the juvenile justice system, in *Australian and New Zealand Journal of Sociology* , 24, 3, pp.359–376

—— 1991, 'The production of guilt in the juvenile justice system: the pressures to plead', in *Howard Journal of Criminal Justice*, 30, 3, pp. 192–206

Yablonsky, L. 1976, *The violent gang*, Pelican, London

Youth Justice Coalition (NSW), 1990, *Kids in justice: a blueprint for the '90s: full report of the Youth Justice Project*, Youth Justice Coalition, Sydney, New South Wales

Statutes

Child Welfare Act 1939 (NSW)
Child Welfare Act 1984 (WA)
Child Welfare Amendment Act No. 2, 1990 (WA)
Children Act 1908 (UK)
Children and Young Persons Act 1933 (UK)
Children and Young Persons Act 1969 (UK)
Children and Young Persons Act 1989 (Vic)
Children (Criminal Proceedings) Act 1987 (NSW)
Children, Young Persons and their Families Act 1989 (NZ)
Children's Court of Western Australia Act 1988

Children's Protection and Young Offenders Act 1979 (SA)
Children's Services Ordinance 1986 (ACT)
Community Welfare Act 1982 (NSW)
Crime (Serious and Repeat Offenders) Sentencing Act 1992 (WA)
Crimes Act 1990 (NSW)
Criminal Justice Act 1982 (UK)
Infant Life Protection Act 1890 (Vic)
Model Juvenile Delinquency Act 1987 (USA)
Sentencing Act 1989 (NSW)
Social Work (Scotland) Act 1968 (UK)
Summary Offences Act 1988 (NSW)

Index